My LIFE

Not Mine To Control

Colette Keefe

Suite 300 - 990 Fort St
Victoria, BC, Canada, V8V 3K2
www.friesenpress.com

Copyright © 2015 by Colette Keefe
First Edition — 2015
All rights reserved.

Edited by Susan Huebert.

No part of this publication may be reproduced in any form, or by any means, electronic or mechanical, including photocopying, recording, or any information browsing, storage, or retrieval system, without permission in writing from the publisher.

ISBN
978-1-4602-6331-0 (Hardcover)
978-1-4602-6332-7 (Paperback)
978-1-4602-6333-4 (eBook)

1. *Self-Help, Abuse*

Distributed to the trade by The Ingram Book Company

This book is dedicated to my wonderful husband Eugene who has stood by me through all the years. His dedication and devotion to me has been absolutely outstanding. To the greatest psychiatrist, Dr. Brent Joseph Armstrong; his secretary Wendy Malko; my therapist, Linda Fadden at the Laurel Centre for Sexually Abused Women, and to all the therapists I encountered there. They are truly remarkable. I would also like to thank Dr. Theresa DeCloedt for caring and being absolutely sincere in her profession. Also, Cathy Motriuk, Social Worker at Grace Hospital. Without all of you, most of my recovery could never have been possible, and my healing journey continues.

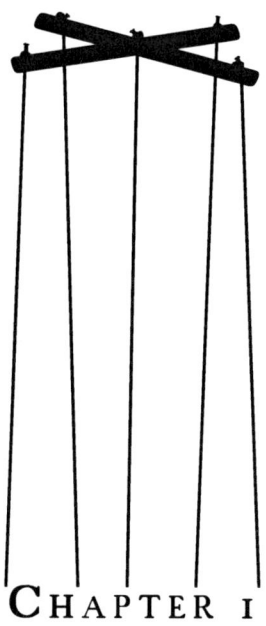

Chapter 1

My life has not been easy. I'm not sure how I have survived so long. I feel like I've been to hell and back several times. This book is dedicated to those who have mental illness, or have been physically, emotionally, and/or sexually abused. Also, this is for those with addictions and those who are homeless. My heart is truly out there for you. My story may be different from yours, but I'm sure many of you can relate to some of it.

I have two brothers, two sisters, and a brother who died at birth. I'm the youngest of six children. My siblings were much older than me and took good care of me. I remember hearing stories of my eldest brother biting my ear when I was a baby because he loved me so much.

I was born on September 3, 1958, and I am now 55. Many things I experienced in my childhood were not good, and I lived in a violent environment.

My mother moved at a very young age to the city of Winnipeg. She then met my father and they were married shortly afterwards. My mother and father were married for life, since both were French Roman Catholics;

because of this, my father would never have left my mother. He took care of her until he died, and he asked us to continue taking care of our mother after that. These were his dying wishes—wishes that were very hard to fulfill.

Having such a large family was hard on my parents. When my mother found out that she was pregnant with me she cried, horrified about having another child. My brother, who is three years older than me, was also an unplanned child. I remember stories being told about how much he touched things as a toddler. I guess he was just a busy little boy who liked investigating. I'm sure this drove my mother crazy. My brother was born with something wrong with one of his kidneys, and had to have it removed as a baby. Throughout his childhood, my mother would not let him play sports for fear of hurting the other kidney.

When my mother was pregnant with me, her sister tried to comfort her and would tell her that I would be born as a special baby, and that God intended the pregnancy to happen. This particular aunt ended up being my godmother, and was a very loving, caring, nurturing person. The only problem was that she and her family lived in the country, on a farm in Manitoba. We did not get to see them very much because of the distance. One of the memories I have was that when we did see them, I was afraid to go to the outhouse and did everything I could not to enter it. Bugs and spiders, things I was afraid of, lived there. Another memory is that my brother and I loved playing with their indoor water pump because we had never seen one of them before. We thought this was so neat.

As my aunt and uncle grew a lot older, they eventually moved to Winnipeg and bought a house near my parents' place. I got to see my aunt much more often than before and saw that she was a very energetic person, cutting the grass, shovelling snow, and grocery shopping. She also looked after her husband, who was diagnosed with Alzheimer's disease. She took very good care of him. She would meet us for coffee at least once a week. I loved her, and so did my own children. Although they were very young at the time of her death, they still do remember her. She was terrific.

I remember celebrating her birthday on the day she turned seventy, together with my husband, children, parents, my aunt, and her husband. I had made an angel food cake and decorated it just for her. Unfortunately, she was unable to eat any of it because she was waiting for gallbladder surgery and did not want another attack. The surgery happened shortly after, but when she didn't seem to be recovering, we found out that the doctors had discovered she had liver cancer. She did not live long after that, dying a few weeks after her diagnosis. I remember going to see her a few days before her death and will never forget what she said to me. She was telling me that it was not fun being sick. I also noticed that her ankles were extremely swollen. She died at seventy. May God bless her.

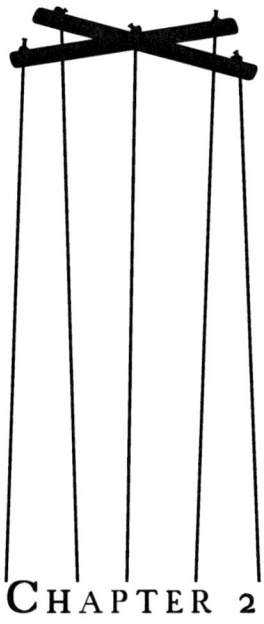

Chapter 2

After my birth, my very first memory of my mother was probably when I was just under two years old. Potty training with her was done far more severely than it was with others. I remember her tying me up and leaving me for hours, making me sit until I would actually urinate or defecate. Only then was I allowed to get out of the bathroom, but not for long because she was always worried that we children would end up dirtying the floor. Because of that, I was placed back on the toilet, pretty much for the day. No one knew it, especially back then, but my mother suffered from mental illness and Obsessive-Compulsive Disorder.

We were not allowed to get dirty or to dirty anything else. My sister was so scared of getting dirty that one time when she went down a slide at school, she decided to slide down on her feet so as not to dirty her clothes. She landed on her head and ended up unconscious with a concussion. She spent a whole week in the hospital.

At the back entrance of our home, my mother would place newspaper all through a big area so that no one who came in would dirty the washable carpet. She would freak out if you were to step off the newspaper. No one was allowed to come in through the front door. If anyone put keys on the table, she would scream and say to take them off because they were dirty. Everyone cringed around her.

No one was able to sit on the couch unless she first put white sheets over the whole thing; in that way, you wouldn't dirty it. Jeans were inappropriate for all of us, whether girls or boys. When my brothers got older, they then got to buy jeans on their own; but she would still tell them not to sit on the couch because of the dye. She said that it would stain the sheets. She also would not let you sit on the couch when you came home from work, because you were dirty.

I remember all of the screaming that this woman would do in my earlier years. She had no normal voice; it was all screaming, yelling, swearing in French and English, and saying things that no one else would ever say. She was always in a rage. Why? I never knew, but I tried to keep quiet and to stay away from her as much as possible. Bringing a friend home was something that none of us ever did. We were far too embarrassed to have anyone over.

My mother was very unmanageable, but my father didn't hear or see all of the things that she would do because he worked at two jobs to make ends meet. Still, I'm very sure that he knew what kind of woman he had married. She would hit my sister on the head with pots and pans. She once threw an iron at my sister, and would throw anything at hand. We were all brought up by her to be her servants. Household work was something that took hours to complete for each and every one of us. There was no slacking off.

I don't actually recall having any play times or good times during my years in that house. There was a lot of screaming, and all of the neighbours hated my mother. I was terrified of her, and I always kept to myself, being very quiet. Reading books, listening to nursery rhymes, playing together, or even hearing her say "I love you" never occurred once in my childhood.

However, I do have a memory of staying in a cabin near Kenora for one night. I still remember how exciting this was. The only bad thing was that we had to come back home and be brutalized with brooms, straps, walking sticks, hair pulling, punching, and having our arms grabbed so hard that it would leave bruising. We were not allowed to cry or our mother would make it worse. I remember kneeling down in corners for hours on end and not being allowed to move my head or sit on my legs. This was very painful, and if she saw you moving she would hit you in the head and grab it so that your face was touching the wall. This way, we were being penalized even longer for moving.

There were times I remember being strapped to a chair, and then she would laugh. It was an evil laugh, one that I will never forget. She would tie my hands and feet so that I couldn't move, and she seemed to enjoy every minute of it. This happened on many occasions when no one else was around. My siblings were probably in school at the time, and she didn't want me to dirty the house. It didn't occur to me to tell anyone else what was happening. I thought that this was normal in everyone's home because I didn't know any better.

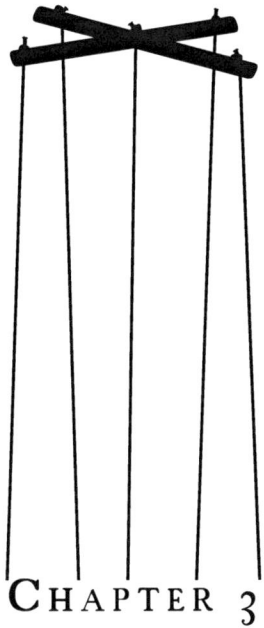

Chapter 3

My father's family and my mother's own family despised her for her rudeness and unsympathetic feelings. She showed no emotion and truly hated everyone, and she would say so to my dad. My dad's family was always important to him, but she turned into such a monster that she would not allow him to see his side of the family. Therefore, they started to reject my father and wanted nothing to do with any of us. We knew only very few cousins, but were ostracized from them eventually, too. In the first years after they got married, my brother and sister were introduced to these cousins and got to know them very well.

All I can remember of my grandma is that she was nasty and didn't like us. She was argumentative, and she smoked, drank, and played cards all the time. I don't remember anything nice about her. Two of my aunts owned the florist shop across from the St. Boniface Hospital. They did very well financially. I was never close to them, but my sister Monique and her husband Pierre were always there, visiting them. My aunts loved Pierre's personality, but my mother was furious. She felt that she was being betrayed by her own daughter. She was very angry towards Monique and Pierre, and would say so to my father and my other siblings.

My mother also disliked animals. There were times that cats would end up in our yard, and she would get my brother to catch them and put them into potato sacks and drown them in the Seine River. At that time, I saw nothing wrong with this because it happened so often. It was only maybe 50 years later during all the therapy that I have gone through that therapists have told me that if my mother was cruel to animals, she definitely would be cruel to human beings.

As I grew older, all I could remember when I looked back was how intimidating my mother was. We were all scared and never talked back to her because we knew better. I don't have much of a memory of the time I was two or three years old, but perhaps it was better to forget than to remember. It was a hell that I will never forget; especially considering that I was extremely timid and shy and did whatever it took to make my mother happy.

One time, she told me to bring her eye shadow to her bedroom. It was from Avon, and there were all different colours attached together. My mother had seen some of the eye shadow on her floor because I had dropped it, and she accused me of drawing a face with it. I was severely punished, even though I had done nothing wrong. She hit me in the head, pulled my hair, and grabbed me by the arms hard enough to cause bruising. I was then punished in the corner, which she really seemed to enjoy. Evil? Yes she was. What a horrible mother!

When I was four, my father was working at Taché Nursing Centre, working for the nuns. He started as a baker and ended up being a dietician as he grew older. There were times when he would take me to work with him. I was always so excited. At the old hospital, they had very old elevators. I always thought this was really neat. My brothers and sisters would all sneak the goodies from the box that my dad brought home every day. The nuns always permitted my father to bring home his homemade bread and cinnamon buns and other types of baking. We could eat what we wanted, and food was not kept from us until I was a teenager. We were fed properly, and my father enjoyed making huge meals that could feed a dozen. His skills in cooking and baking were unbelievable, and amazing. He was very artistic. He loved his work.

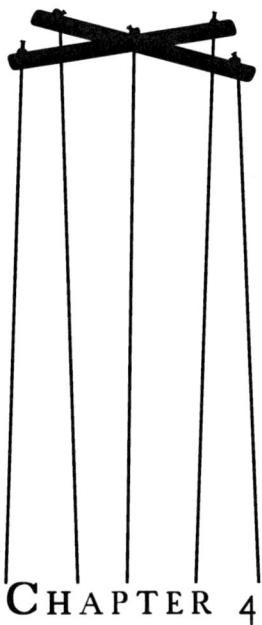

CHAPTER 4

My dad was very eager to introduce Pierre from Montreal to my sister. Pierre was working at the nursing home.

At the time, he charmed my sister and everyone else in my family. Everybody loved him and thought he was the nicest guy—joking, with a great personality, and always charming towards everyone. He also spoke only in French.

While my sister was going out with him, nobody knew that Pierre was actually a pedophile. My memories of him are of Sunday nights after supper, sitting on his lap while we were watching a Disney movie at 6:00 p.m. after we had eaten a big meal and finished the dishes. My entire family was in the living room, but no one noticed how he placed his hand underneath my dress and into my panties. I was unsure and confused, but I said nothing. I knew it was wrong, but he always asked me to sit on his lap and I couldn't say no in front of my family.

This would happen only on Sundays at first because I always wore a dress to church. I never told anyone about it because I was scared and afraid to approach anyone. Pierre got progressively worse as time went on. My father found out that Pierre was having an affair with another woman before Monique and Pierre got married. He was very angry with Pierre, but Pierre promised my dad that this would never happen again. My dad was satisfied with that promise, and Pierre and Monique were married on June 11, 1966.

I remember how much I cried on their wedding day because they were going to Montreal for their honeymoon for two weeks. I was seven, and I really didn't have any concept of how long two weeks were. I remember sitting at the end of the table at their wedding and crying for a long time. I thought that they would be gone forever. They did say that they would send me postcards, and on the following day before leaving Winnipeg, they put one in the mailbox for me. I was thrilled.

On their return from Montreal, I was extremely happy to see Monique. Every day after school, I would go to her workplace next to my school. She worked then on Provencher Boulevard for the Provincial Government at the Health Unit. She also worked a block away from her apartment. I would go see her, and always hoped that she would keep me for supper. There were times when she would just drive me home. We lived about one mile away, if that. But nonetheless, I would go see her every day after school. She was always kind and paid a lot of attention to me. She did not scream, and things in that environment were much more controlled than at home.

Pierre was an electrician, and he was also very charming. He definitely had many affairs that Monique never knew about. If he got home late for supper, he would always say that it was because he got delayed at work. Because of what he had done to me, I wasn't sure if I should trust him, but I thought that he had changed since he was married. Still, I was always on the alert. Monique and Pierre would take me out for supper and buy me things. Every Friday night, we would go ten-pin midnight bowling from 10:00 p.m. to 3:00 a.m. My eldest brother George, his fiancée France, my sister Angel, and my other brother Emile would all attend. Pierre would bring us treats and we would get so excited.

My sister Angel had become very jealous about how I was treated by Monique and Pierre. She had come to despise me because she thought that I was the princess. Later when I was in my teens, she stopped interacting with my mom, dad, and me for decades. I only found out many, many years later when we started speaking together again how twisted our stories really were. I'd had no idea that she was jealous because my sister Monique was paying so much attention to me. I was drawn to my sister's place because of my mother, but with a very big price to pay.

My home was so violent, with never-ending screaming, punishments, swearing, and being brutally victimized. I guess I must have come to the conclusion that it would be better to be sexually abused than to live in the house of horrors.

Still, I found it difficult to endure what was happening to me. There was a time when I had to sleep over at Pierre and Monique's place for a few weeks. They had put a cot in the living room of my sister's apartment, and I remember looking from my bed in the living room to the bathroom and seeing Monique getting ready. It was late at night, and she thought that I was sleeping. I had been told to stay with Monique and Pierre because my mother was chaperoning George and France on a trip to Montreal for Expo, and she would not let them go together on their own for fear of them having sex. She was in charge and would take control of that situation. My father was to look after Angel and Emile.

Pierre was very deceptive and a very sneaky person who got away with sexual abuse each and every time he touched me. One evening he pulled my pajama bottoms off as my heart was beating very fast, and he fondled me and then kissed me on the bottom before he went to bed. I was horrified when that happened and did not know what to do. I kept very still and quiet and that pleased him. I was in a frozen state and nothing would come out of my mouth. It was terrifying, and this is how I reacted to the situation. Now he was on the road to sexually abusing me even further. On the following day, I was so distraught by this that I actually took a razor and cut myself quite deeply on the thumb. This was just the beginning of my many years of self-harm, in which I never could understand or know what it was all about. I was eight years old.

Many years later when my sister Angel was a little older, she went with Pierre to a job site where he had employees working for him. He wanted to introduce her to Sam, who was one of Pierre's employees. Sam was a very hardworking man. He had such a deep attraction to Angel that he started calling her every day to speak to her. He wanted to sweep her off her feet and take care of her. However, my sister was going out with someone else at the time, although she wasn't really sure about their relationship. She would get me to answer the phone and give Sam excuses, like she was washing her hair or showering.

Sam knew that Angel was not sure if she would ever go out with him. He definitely was a very persistent person, but he was not sure whether she was deliberately avoiding him, or if she was just a very clean person. Of course, it seemed like I was always the one who answered the phone and had to try to make excuses for her not to talk to him.

My parents were not impressed with Sam and did not want Angel to date him. My mother and father wanted her to go out with a French Roman Catholic. My mother never trusted anyone and was very paranoid about people. There was something about Sam that she did not like, but she never expressed it to Angel. The air was thick with tension when Angel started dating him.

In the meantime, Sam noticed how terrible my mother was. She was not trusting of anyone. If anything was misplaced in our home, she was quick to conclude that someone had stolen it. She then would find whatever was missing. She was always strange in that way and would blame people if anything went missing. Meanwhile, she was usually the person who had actually misplaced things, but she never apologized to anyone. She was very hard to deal with and had mental issues that no one knew about back then.

Her reactions to events often seemed odd. There came a time when I was out with my parents and my father's car stalled on the train tracks. He tried and tried to start the engine but was unable to do it. The train was coming, and I remember screaming for him to get out of the way. My father was so desperate to get his car off the tracks that he didn't walk away until just before the train hit his car. His car was totally wrecked and he was in such despair. I remember feeling so bad for him, and I was worried that he would not get out of the way in time. My mother, of course, did not seem concerned. She was more worried about the car being damaged than about my own father.

My sister Angel eventually started going out with Sam, and they decided to get married quite quickly. Sam's mother was dying of cancer at that time. My parents wouldn't allow Angel to marry someone who was not a Roman Catholic. Sam was forbidden to marry her until he changed his religion, which he did. They married shortly afterwards and moved up north to Gillam. I missed Angel very much. After a few months, she came back unannounced, and I was thrilled to have her back. However, because of trust and abuse issues, Sam and Angel could not tolerate my mother and father anymore and decided to shut us out of their lives forever. I never really knew why.

Now that I'm in my fifties, Angel is the sister who is closest to me, and she has always been there for me later in life when I have had troubles. We speak at the same time, saying the same things. It's been just like we were twins. I love her and her family more than anyone could ever know. She is so sincere and forgiving, and she is a wonderful person to talk to when you are down. She always has a positive outlook for me. How sweet! After some time of not communicating, we started talking again, and I found out why she hadn't been talking to me. She was jealous because I thought the world of Monique. She couldn't understand why I was so attached to her. We did not speak for decades, and she did not speak to my parents either because they did not like her husband, Sam.

Angel had a great hatred towards my parents. I was the lucky one, because in my fifties we reconciled, and we have been together for several years. We know the whole situation of what happened in the past. I love her very much and would help her through anything. In fact, I love spending time at her cottage because I don't think that anyone could treat me better. She has always given me hope in the times when I needed it and has listened to whatever was wrong at the time. Sam, my brother-in-law, would speak to me very calmly and never make decisions for me. They have a girl and two boys. Their daughter has two children who are very well brought up. The younger child talks a lot and is so lovable. She is so sweet, and her brother is the shy one who likes to help out on the farm. He can drive a combine on his own, with his uncle sitting next to him. He stays up late in the evening and loves it. He could fix mechanical things before he even turned ten years old.

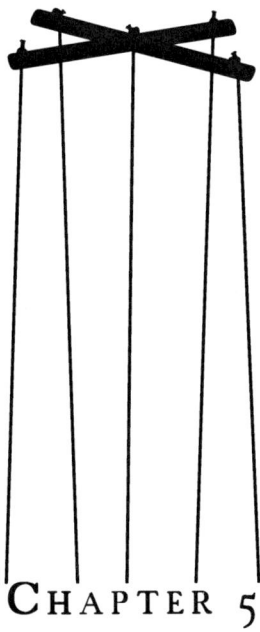

Chapter 5

I have been more open in recent years about the sexual abuse I experienced, because of all my therapy. I have told my story to many other people, but I still feel shame and guilt towards my husband and children. However, I know that it was not my fault. It's taken many years for me to allow others to learn what I went through, but I still haven't told all of it. I do know of other children who were victimized by the same monster. Some of them were related to me. I was unable to help any of them.

I have travelled a long, hard, painful journey that no child should ever have to live through. Shortly after my brother-in-law first touched me, he was driving me home from their home and was stopped at a red light at Des Meurons and Marion. He took his penis out and told me to touch it. He told me to stroke it and I would see something magical happen. I was scared, and I was wondering why he was doing this. He told me it would grow like a plant, and I panicked and kept my hands very tight around my body. Nevertheless, he was much stronger than me and made me touch it. I remember it having a soft touch, but I kept my eyes closed the entire time because I did not want to see it. In my mind, I was thinking how my mother and father would react if they had known about this. I felt safer not looking even though Pierre insisted on it. I would definitely have been blamed if I had looked, and I would have been severely punished for doing so. My parents would have thought that I instigated it.

I would go home and never talk about it for fear of getting beaten even more. In my heart, I felt that no one would have believed me, and I had nowhere to go. This was kept as a deep, dark secret. In those days, sexual abuse was not really mentioned very much, but if I had mentioned it now, Child and Family Services would have taken us all out of our home because of the beatings. I would have been saved from sexual abuse, and I would also not have had to sleep in a crib until I was eight.

Eventually, when Pierre would bring me home, he would hide his car behind two apartment blocks facing my home. In his own sick and twisted mind, he thought that I had become old enough to start to touch his penis and stroke it. He would keep on telling me, "Faster" in French. He would kiss me as I struggled to get away, but he told me to keep quiet and threatened me. I recall how awful he smelled, mostly from alcohol and cigarettes. He breathed heavily, and eventually this sticky white liquid would come out onto my hands. I had no idea what this was, but I was scared of him.

A few weeks later, he pushed my head into his groin and held it down and told me to suck his disgusting, stinky penis while he probed me in all areas and put his fingers in my vagina. I was distraught and felt so hopeless. I remember choking on his penis because I wasn't very old and did not know that people actually did this. As he put it in my mouth, I felt that I would rather die than to have to go through this. It was absolutely disgusting and inhumane. He kept on telling me not to bite it because it would hurt, even though I didn't realize that I was doing so. It sometimes took him a while because I wasn't sure what he meant about sucking it. He would always say that the more I practiced, the better I would get. My heart would sink, thinking that I would have to do this again.

When sperm entered my mouth, I was not expecting this and simply gagged on it. He would tell me to swallow it. It was the most horrible taste ever. His smell of sperm made me feel like throwing up. I was so ashamed and I hated myself. He would then drive me home and I would wash my face and brush my teeth over and over again to get that disgusting taste out of my mouth. I felt so dirty, like the worst person on the planet. At times, he drove me home quite late, and I would get into trouble. My mother would scream and yell at me, and of course hit me. It wasn't my fault, because my abuser had spent so much time doing these horrible, sadistic things. They happened on a very regular basis.

He would chase me around my home, and I would be terrified. Several times, he would show up at our house when he knew I was alone. He would ask to come in and I wouldn't let him in, but he always had the upper hand and would threaten to tell my parents if I didn't let him in. I was so scared of him, and I knew that no one was there to help me. He would chase me around the house until I was cornered and I could never get away. I wasn't able to get out of the house because he was always so close and I knew I had nowhere to go. I was like a caged animal, taken advantage of whenever he wanted, and not one person knew.

When he did things to me, I would depersonalize from the situation each and every time. I felt disengaged from my surroundings and wondered if was in my body or not. I felt like my body was floating around some kind of spirit world. It was my way to cope. I could see myself on the floor with him but felt dead. I had feelings of being disconnected or detached from my body. These feelings were a protection for me, and I felt like I was observing myself from outside my body, or I felt like I was dreaming. I would have to say that I'm really happy that I felt this way because I don't know how long I could have survived this type of torture. However, I would still visit my sister because it was better than being in my own home with my mother. How sick is that!

I would sometimes have to push my breasts together and my attacker would stick his penis between them. This was another form of enjoyment for him. However, this wasn't as bad as the other things he did. He would assault me in every possible position. Sometimes I wasn't even able to comprehend it, but it was what he liked. He was the most disgusting person anybody would ever know. The first time we had sex, I felt like he was actually splitting me apart and cutting me with a knife. I bled for a while and did so several times after that. I felt like I had been ripped apart. I was indeed so scared that I didn't know what to do; the only problem was that he was liked by everyone, even me. I know that this might sound strange, but when he wasn't touching me, he would do anything to make me happy.

There were times when my sister would be in the house and I had to keep extremely quiet. She never knew through all of those years. I was very quiet and scared of her husband, and I never said a word; mostly because if my mother had found out, she would have blamed me and I would have received the punishment of my life. He most definitely threatened me all the time, even to the point of yelling at me that no one would believe me because I was a child and he was an adult. I truly believed this was true.

I knew that my dad, who was so sympathetic, compassionate, kind, and wonderful, would never have helped me because of his devotion to God. He would have told me to keep quiet in order not to ruin anyone's marriage. He likely would have got mad at me if I had told him these deep, dark secrets. To this day, I understand that completely. He had given his life to God and would not retaliate even if my mother would hit him and be very abusive to him. He was married for life. My sisters and brothers were also to follow in his footsteps. Monique and Pierre were already Catholic.

My eldest brother, George, was engaged to France, but my parents would not allow them to marry unless she changed her religion. She loved George and would do anything to be with him. There was one big problem—her father did not want her to do this. He threatened to disown her if she changed religions. She had to decide whether she should change and be disowned or stay and give up George. She did change religions and was probably still hopeful that her dad would come around. She went to see him when he was dying, but he never forgave her. She did get along with her mother by that time. They were close, but her mother ended up getting sick and also dying.

My parents were finally getting desensitized to non-Catholics when Emile and Brittany got engaged. She did not have to change religions, but they were to be married in a Catholic church. She had wonderful parents. I was included in the bridal party, and her mother made all of the dresses. My mother would tell Brittany that she would not be able to make a dress for me because I was so fat. Brittany's mother always told me that I looked good, and she never put me down. To this day, when I see her she is still the same. They were from Germany, and he had his own band.

I was the next one to marry. Rite was Protestant, but they did allow us to get married in a French Catholic church. We got married at Precieux Sang in St. Boniface. We were lucky that due to my mother and father's attendance at the church, they changed the rules for us and we were able to say our vows in English. We were to go to church every Sunday or we would get a call from my parents. We also had no choice but to baptize our children Catholic. Angel disagreed with this and never had her children baptized, because she thought that they should make that decision when they were older. My parents were very angry, but eventually it didn't matter because Angel and Sam had stopped talking to them.

Meanwhile, my sexual abuse went on for eleven extremely long years. I'm not sure how I have survived this in such a quiet way. Depersonalization was something I would do when things got too hard. I felt like I was living in two different bodies. I had my ways of not thinking about it, but my scars have lasted a whole lifetime. However, I daydreamed many times that something would happen to my abuser's penis and that all of this would stop. It never did.

On the day I started menstruating, my mother announced it to the entire family. I was so embarrassed. This was not something to be announced to everyone. Pierre was happy and told me that I was finally a woman now. I felt so devastated since I knew how much more sexual abuse I was in for. I felt that I wanted to die so that I could be left alone. However, since I was very healthy and rarely got sick, this was not a possibility.

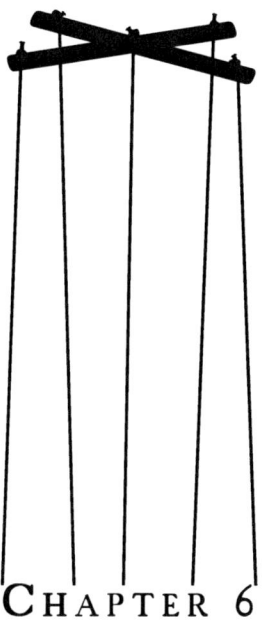

Chapter 6

I went to a French Catholic school taught by nuns and priests, the Fathers. Some were nice, but others were very strict and believed in the old ways. Spanking was still tolerated in those days, and the principal was allowed to use the strap to hit your hand if you were out of line. This is how they punished unruly children. I was very frightened of the teacher.

One time in grade 8, I brought a sheet of paper with dirty jokes on it to my classroom. I showed it to a couple of people, but my teacher, who was a Father, wanted to see what I had. I immediately went to the washroom and ripped the paper into pieces. My teacher then told me that they had pieced the paper back together and that I was to see the counsellor, who was a nun. I knew that what he had said was impossible, considering how small I had ripped up the paper, but eventually I did tell the nun what the joke was about. I remember telling her that it was a joke about how men would pee in different ways. She asked me who had given me the joke, and I told her Pierre. She told me to stay away from him. She obviously felt that this was a sign of something wrong. The upsetting thing was that she let me leave, and I knew that I would still be encountering Pierre all the time.

I had no friends because I didn't want to get close to anyone; I felt so dirty. I did not want anyone to know about the physical and sexual abuse that I suffered at the hands of my mother and brother-in-law. I was caught up in my own little world of lies and deep, dark secrets. It took me years to talk about it, but perhaps my life was ruined already. I had no self-esteem and constantly felt like a very stupid person, not good enough for anything or anyone. Believe me, my mother assured me of this throughout my life. I definitely believed it because I was told this throughout the years. I am now 55, and I still think the same way as my brothers and sisters do. Nothing but brain dead, extremely stupid, and fat. I wanted to hurt myself.

It is somewhat difficult to describe what self-harm is all about. I never knew that all the horrible things I had been doing my entire life would be considered that. I harmed myself but didn't even know it. It was a natural feeling that seemed good at the time, even though it hurt afterwards. I had a need to punish myself for being so bad. I felt the need to suffer at all times; otherwise, I didn't feel normal. I wanted to suffer because I really didn't know any other way. I couldn't seem to stop, but I couldn't understand the reason behind it.

In my case, I craved skin and would peel all my burnt skin and scabs off to chew and spit out. I know that it sounds disgusting, but never knew that there was a name for this extremely bizarre disorder. I was very close with my therapist and discussed it with her. She knew the name of this disorder and it was called Pica. I'm not sure if this is hereditary because when my youngest daughter is pregnant she craves rocks and small stones. She loved vacuuming because of the sound that the vacuum cleaner would make when things would go through it. She would tell me that she actually salivated over this. Washing her SUV was another great delight. I know this sounds strange, but it really does happen to people.

I have burned myself with chemicals for many years over my entire body, except my face. This was seriously painful, but I would do it twice a day to make sure that I would suffer even more. Where my skin was burned, with open sores weeping, I could barely move; but I would still make sure to put the chemicals on the sores twice a day. I looked disgusting, and I fooled all the doctors. They suspected that it was cancer, but then they concluded that it was something else. I was very conniving. I wasn't able to tell anyone what was going on because I didn't even know myself. It was so strange, and I had never heard of people hurting themselves before. I would never have gone to see a doctor, but Rite was worried and made me make an appointment with my family physician. Then I was referred to two specialists. They did several biopsies, but it was not cancer, as they had thought.

My self-harm is a result of the pain that I have gone through. As a teenager, I felt very alone. I was never allowed to wear jeans or to have my hair grow long. My mother would do these really ugly perms called Tony's in my hair. I had no voice or choice. I was to listen and obey. It was devastating when people in my school would laugh and make fun of me. I took it all in and never reported them to anyone. Sometimes when I was walking home, they would whip me with a wet towel. I did not cry when they got their kicks out of this. I would come home with welts on my body, but I always tried to hide them. No one seemed to care what kind of marks I had on me, and I would just say that I was clumsy.

One time, my mother was punishing me for something I did, and put my forearm on the element of a stove that was on high. I had burn rings on my arm for a very long time. They got somewhat infected but eventually healed, and disappeared after several years. I do remember my father being in the house at that time. He never had the nerve to confront my mother.

In my early school years, I would go home for lunch. One day, it had been very stormy outside, and the snow was very deep and hard to walk through. It took me longer than usual to get home, and I was covered with snow. When I got home, my mother went into a rage when she saw me covered in snow, and she took the broom and swept me out the door in order for me not to wet anything. She took that broom and hit me with it so much that I was bruised for days.

As I got a little older, my weight seemed to be a big concern of my mother's. She thought I was too fat so she put me on Weight Watcher's. She would monitor everything I ate. Every day, lunch was boiled codfish. I hated it. She would weigh me every day, and pinch me and stick her nails into my upper arms if the scale would fluctuate. She would go into a rage and beat me. Her hands would go flying in every direction in order to hurt me.

If you ever gained weight at Weight Watcher's, you would get a foam pig pin to attach to your clothes. One day when I got home from a meeting, I knew that I would be in trouble. At the time, I had started eating junk food behind my mother's back, and I had gained quite a bit of weight. My mother always said that I would never have a boyfriend or get a job in the future because I was too fat to look at. She told me that I was disgusting and looked like a large cow; but she said so in French, which was more demeaning.

When my parents went to Florida one year, I retaliated and went to buy my first pair of Lee jeans. When I wore them to school for the first time, a classmate (who was a boy) asked me where I had them tailored. I was so embarrassed. When my parents got back from their trip, they were appalled by the fact that I had gone out to buy jeans behind their back. If I were capable of buying jeans, then what else would I do?

My mother would give me her Valium to calm me down if I got upset. She popped those pills into me like there was no tomorrow. My mother was prescribed this to treat her anxiety. Not that I could say it ever helped her. She stilled seemed like the same person with or without them. Valium was my mother's prescription. It caused me to be dizzy and drowsy, and to have blurred vision. I was tired and uncoordinated, and these pills were highly addictive.

Shortly after this an eating disorder began for me, which I still live with. I am unable to eat in front of anyone because I feel so self-conscious. I feel like everyone is staring at me and thinks that I look like a pig. Even when I was size 0, I was still too fat. I used laxatives for many, many years in hopes that I could empty my stomach of any food I would eat. There were times when I could not control my bowels because of the Ex-lax, and I would go in my pants.

One time when I was in the hospital, I woke up feeling like I needed to go, but the hospital pajamas could not hold it in. When I let go of my bowels, everything ran down my leg onto the floor. I tried to wipe it up; but the longer it took to go to the washroom, the more ran down my legs. There was a trail from my room to the washroom. I felt so embarrassed and so ashamed. When I finally walked out of the washroom after cleaning myself up, I returned to my room and saw the trail I had left behind was all cleaned up. How humiliating.

My nurse did talk to me about it, and I had to be honest, but I felt such horrible guilt. I had OCD, and I was doing such terrible things to myself. I was embarrassed even to drink a diet soda or coffee in public. Water had no calories, but I knew that it could make you bloated if you drank any of it. My weight fluctuated. I needed to discipline myself most of the time. I tried to throw up several times, but it just never worked for me. I would stick things down my throat, but all I could do was gag. I knew I wouldn't be able to perfect this method, and so my only choice was not to eat at all and to exercise excessively. No one knew.

The shame I've felt with food is something I still live with. I've weighed myself every day, and even several times a day. When we would go on holidays, I would always have to pack a scale. I needed to make sure I wouldn't gain weight. I was especially afraid to gain weight when we were away because I wasn't eating the same foods I ate at home. It sometimes ruined my holidays. Later, while I was in the hospital, I refused to eat anything there. The nurses would get upset and sit with me and make sure I shoved in some mouthfuls. My doctor at the time did not eat breakfast or lunch, either, and the nurses were told to leave me alone. I haven't eaten a crumb from the hospital.

I sometimes got to go out with my husband for supper, but even then, I had to be very careful about what I ate. There were times that I would arrange my food on my plate to make it look like I had left a larger amount. I literally would cut the bottom of a boneless chicken breast so no one would notice. I ate very few calories and I counted everything I put in my mouth. My sister kept on calling me anorexic.

Sometimes, it seemed like my thinness influenced everything else. One day, my husband and I went to buy a smaller tree than the one we had because we had so many children in the house. I had my daycare and my own three children, and they took a lot of room. The tree was a "thin pine", and did I ever get bugged about this! The tree and I were both anorexic. Ridiculous!

There were times when my husband would take me out, and I would feel such pressure to eat. I would order whatever had the fewest calories. I would check around the room to see if anyone was looking and then tell my husband that someone was staring at me. I didn't want to live in my own skin. Dessert I would say "no" to, unless we went out for ice cream.

We did not eat it in the restaurant, but only in the car. As other cars would drive by, I would lower the cone so that no one knew I was eating. Later in life, Monique and her daughter were both overweight, and they would talk about desserts they had eaten in Las Vegas. They would rant and rave about this, but I couldn't understand how they could live this way. I certainly would not want to be present with them when they ate. Food was always so glamorous to them. I did not think so, and I thought that everyone must be staring at them and thinking that they were such pigs.

I gained weight on a prescription that the doctor had me on. I was disgusted with myself and wanted to die. He would tell me to tape my mouth. I don't even recall eating more, but I did gain weight. I guess that I should have Super-glued my lips for nothing to get through. I wonder if this would have helped. To me, it was just another indication of how fat and disgusting I had become, and I worried about how much someone from outside would notice.

The doctor would ask me how much I weighed, and I would literally cringe in the chair, feeling such shame. In my mind, he was also thinking that I was extremely fat. I could not speak. The first time I had seen him, I was a size 0 and now I had gained 60 lbs. This was so devastating, and then being told to stop eating was humiliating. I have felt humiliated about my weight my whole entire life and things never seemed to change. I hate myself and want nothing but to end my life because I am so ashamed of myself. I call myself a pig, hippo, elephant, whale, cow, and anything that is big. I even went to the extent of buying an elephant shirt to prove what I looked like. My mother always called me a fat cow in French. To this day, I feel nothing but shame when I talk to my doctor about weight. He may as well shoot me in the head. I dare not even drink water in front of him because of my shame. I eat minimally, but I have ended up with thyroid problems. This was a curse. I now know that I will never be thin until my dying days. This will be when I have cancer and will just fade away. Great time!

My weight was only one of the problems I faced. As I was beginning my teenage years, I felt very lonely and without friends. There was one time when I went camping with a few people from school. Although they were not my friends, they had asked me to join them. It was a night of alcohol and weed and sex for most of them. If I had known that I would have such a horrible time, I certainly would not have joined them at Birds Hill Park. I did marijuana on occasion, but it was always given to me. I never went out and bought some on my own. Of course, I really never felt anything from it because back in the seventies, it wasn't as potent as it is nowadays. However, I rarely got invitations to go anywhere or do anything. I was a totally fat geek that no one wanted around, not even my family.

Around age 13, I became friends with Giselle, and we became very close. She was actually the school bully, but she started hanging out with me even though I was scared of her. As time passed, we got closer and closer. She was skinny and I fat, but she treated me pretty well. We became best of friends. I was able to escape my home prison by sleeping over at her house on the weekends. We would go grocery shopping every Friday night with her dad. When we would get back, we would always make a Chef Boyardee pizza and eat it with whoever wanted some.

I recall that Giselle's three-year-old brother was totally out of control and used to spit on people and swear in a very bad way. He was obviously not brought up right. Although Giselle's father was nice, her mother was a little odd. Not like mine, though. Giselle's bedroom was on the second floor of the house, which was a house for boarders, except that the family used it all up. She had a lock on her door, and we always had privacy. This is when I experimented with smoking. I remember buying a pack of Export A cigarettes, which were probably the strongest. I did not like smoking because it made me dizzy. That was the end of my smoking career.

It was also the beginning of a short friendship that I thought would last forever. Giselle and I were together all the time and did many activities with each other. I usually spent my weekends at her place and away from the devil herself. Marie, my mother, would sometimes complain that I was over at Giselle's place too often and would wonder why my friend never came over to our place. My friend despised my mother, just like everyone else we knew.

One summer, my parents did not want me to stay alone while they went on holidays. They both agreed that I should bring Giselle with me. They paid for everything except her food. We went to Colorado for ten days, and I had a lot of fun. Some evenings when we went out together, she would really try to attract the boys, whereas I felt foolish because I was so fat. I had no self-confidence. She would purposely talk to guys. I was too shy. After ten days of a holiday when we'd had so much fun, we got home. She hugged me goodbye and thanked everyone and then walked to her house.

The following day, she wanted nothing to do with me. She never talked to me again, and I never knew why. She would make fun of me at school and would deliberately hit me in the back. To this day, I don't know what happened. I was extremely distraught by this. At times in class, we would have to pass our tests to the person behind us for marking. She would make sure that she would make my test a mess. If anything was wrong, she would put a big red X on the paper. It was really humiliating and heart-wrenching.

Shortly after that time, I had gallbladder attacks that were excruciating. I had to go for surgery, and the doctors told me that I was their youngest patient to have surgery on this. Another friend who was not really a friend phoned my hospital room and wanted me to keep any drugs I could get to give to her. I never did. She was only using me.

There was no one to be friends with, and I was devastated. It was a very lonely time in my life, especially since Pierre sexually abused me even more because I was more available than before. I was asked to look after his daughter, Melanie, about five times a week. He and Monique were always so busy socializing. He was the Grand Knight of a Catholic church. How deceptive he was! When he drove me home, sometimes nothing would happen, but at other times it would. I could never be sure. Why was I such a sucker for punishment? It was probably because I loved my sister and my niece so much. I would never see my niece unless I babysat.

There were times when I would sleep over because Monique and Pierre were coming home so late. One morning Pierre had to get up early while my sister was asleep because he was going fishing with my cousin. I felt him standing by my bed as I lay paralyzed with fear. I knew that he was naked, and my breathing became heavy and my heart seemed to drop to the floor. That morning, all he did was to touch my back and then he left.

To this day, I have recurring nightmares when my husband leaves for work. I am paralyzed in bed, and I can't move or open my eyes. I feel a presence in my room. I try very hard to open my eyes, but they won't open. There is such a fear in me that that I feel there is someone who's looking at me and is going to touch me. As hard as I try to open my eyes to see who it is, I'm unable to do so. It's the most horrible and disturbing feeling I've ever experienced. When I finally open my eyes, I soon fall back to sleep and the nightmare continues on. I was always afraid of someone breaking into our house, and now our condo. I wish that this feeling would go away. I do not know why I still experience this kind of thing at my age.

I always feel presences in my home; even other people, like my neighbours. It's like having my fingers caught between the doors. I am frightened and can't move. There is always something creeping up on me. You would think I would become desensitized by this time, but it is not an everyday occurrence. Sometimes it doesn't happen for months, and then it can start again once or twice. I do not watch television or listen to the radio on those days because I need to listen to everything that is going on around me. In bed, at times I feel as if someone is breaking in, and I even hear it. I'm terrified. I am so paralyzed with fear that I can't move in bed or try to wake up my husband.

My life has spiralled into very uncontrollable directions. As I got into my late teens, my friend wanted me to date one of her cousins out in the country. Her cousin was interested in only one thing, and that was having sex. He said that he would love me if I did it. I hated having my breasts touched by anyone because it reminded me of Pierre. It is now 34 years later, and I still do not want my husband touching me. I seem to move and wriggle around, showing him how much I dislike it. He still does try now and then, and I become so anxious that I want to push him off.

On November 20, 1975, my brother-in-law's second child was born. It was a boy. That day, Pierre and Monique were waiting for me to come home from shopping. I needed to look after their daughter while Monique delivered the baby. At that time, Pierre was having an affair with a school teacher while he was on the *Lord Selkirk*. He was working for the CBC and had met her through work. My sister Monique found letters in the garage written to Pierre by his girlfriend. When Monique's son was born, this girlfriend sent a lot of clothes for the baby. Monique threw them all out.

After the birth, Pierre got home and tried to rape me again since I was completely alone with him, while my sister was in the hospital. However, this time I scared him by telling him that I was going to report him. I told him that I was not going to be quiet any more as he lay on top of me. He had always had me pinned down where I couldn't move. I do not like to be tickled or touched in any way. I went absolutely crazy that time. Why then? I don't know why. He had just witnessed the birth of his son and he wanted sex. I was sickened. I yelled and screamed like I never had before. I threatened him and said that I would tell, and that he would get into trouble; perhaps go to jail. He snickered, but he left me alone. This was the final time he ever touched me. I will never forget the date when I finally stopped all the years of sexual abuse. I must have scared him seriously that time. I did still think that he would prey on me, but I think that I got him extremely scared this time. This hell was finally over for a while.

Chapter 7

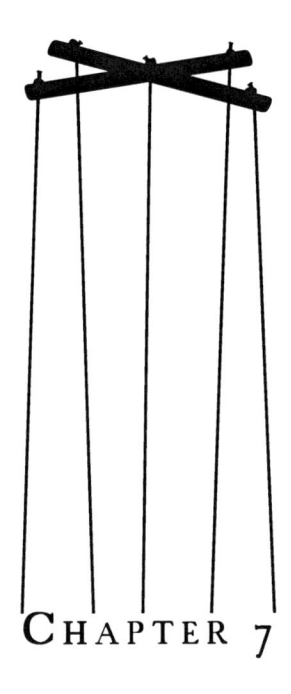

I ended up graduating from College Louis Riel. I did not go to my graduation celebrations because I was an outcast. All of the others were planning what they were going to wear and which date they would be with. I of course had none, and stayed home. My mother had already decided all of the girls' careers for them, after graduation. We were all to be secretaries fresh out of school and were told to pay rent. I also had the option of becoming a nun. Yeah! We all became secretaries, and I worked for the Provincial Park Branch of Manitoba. I wanted to work in the medical field, but money was more important to my mother than a career.

I made friends with four other girls. We got along very well. Two of them were sisters, and we would do everything together. All of us were somewhat overweight except one sister. We travelled to Detroit Lakes several times and always met guys. It was thrilling. We were really good friends, and we went out to bars, looking for guys and making conversation with many of them. The two sisters came from a family of fourteen. Their mother was pregnant at the same time as the eldest daughter. That was bizarre. Pierre liked it when I would bring them around to his place because they were all big-breasted, and he always joked about it and would pretend to accidentally brush up against their breasts so he could touch them. I can never be sure if anything else ever happened with any of them because we have never discussed it, and he was so conniving.

My best friend Ellen and I liked the same guy. How awkward! He did ask me first to go out with him. Whenever we hugged, I felt like I was hugging a big teddy bear. He had a motorcycle, and we would go out riding. Eventually, we split up for unknown reasons. He then went out with Ellen, and they were together for a short while. Finally, he pressured her into having sex even though she wasn't ready, and there the relationship ended. Ellen ended up going out with one of my cousins and got married shortly after that. Her sister Sheila, who was younger than her, got pregnant and had an abortion. She was just in her teens. Ellen had a brother named Todd, who was good friends with her husband, Homer.

Every year on Christmas Eve, we all attended midnight mass and then separated to go to our homes. Christmas was usually a little calmer than normal as long as you behaved and stayed out of my mother's way, and helped with the work. My father would make a huge feast at 2:00 a.m. after the presents were opened. He would cook and stuff a turkey and make potatoes, gravy, meat pies, salad, several vegetables, buns and pickles, with alcohol and wine for everyone. We then would have dainties with coffee and tea. I remember being so tired, and not hungry at that time of day, but we all had to stay up to clean after we finished our meal.

On the following day, Christmas Day, my father would make another turkey and all the trimmings, and we would eat it all over again. We definitely had lots of leftovers. My father had been a baker for years, and was very artistic. He made desserts in the shape of swans, a cake that you would light on fire, and of course everybody's favourite homemade fudge. Before my father passed away, he showed a few of my siblings how to make it, and gave them his secret recipe.

On Boxing Day one year, Sheila and Homer had gone out on their Ski-Doos with her brother in the country. It was -40 ° Celsius and windy, when Homer had an accident. He had lost his shoe and was severely injured. Sheila's brother put a sock on the exposed foot. By the time help came, Homer had frozen his hands and feet, as well as having a fractured leg. He was in the hospital for months, not knowing if gangrene would set into his foot. He had several operations on his leg. I'm not sure if he lost some toes, but he limped because of the injuries to his leg.

My father made his own red wine, which was absolutely potent. All you needed was one glass, and you would be drunk. He liked making people feel welcome and would pour glasses of wine, one after the other. There were lots of people who stumbled out of our house. My father was the kind of man who wanted to give, and make people happy. In those days, drinking and driving was not such a big deal. Every day, my father would go into the basement and drink some wine before supper. Not that I blame him, because he was living with such an abusive woman who would go crazy when he would invite people over. She would be extremely rude and obnoxious to everyone, but the guests loved my father. He was a very giving, loving man, even though I never heard him say the words, "I love you." He was a very sympathetic, generous, caring, and wonderful person. I would never be able to express how lucky I was to have such a wonderful father. The only hard thing to take is that he never protected me.

Somewhat of a funny experience which turned me off of alcohol, was when I was younger and I had siphoned some of his red wine off to take to a dance. I regretted doing that after being very sick all night long. I remember sitting on the floor near the toilet and throwing up all evening. Did I ever regret that! That was one lousy school dance, even though no one would have asked me to dance anyway.

I met a boy at a social I went to with my friends, and I ended up ignoring my friends after that. I was involved with Aaron, and we went out for a year and a half, although I did not know at the time that he was bipolar and out of control. We spent so much money together. He did not drive, and so I would take a taxi to his house and back. I spent a lot of my savings on this.

I always felt that there was something strange about Aaron, but I didn't know what it was. He would smoke a third of a cigarette and then butt it out. He lived a strange life with his sister and dog. He was a very strange individual, and no one in my family liked him. They wanted me to stay away from him. I would not listen because he was so handsome and he liked me. Through the years of having sex with him, not one sperm came out of him. I was so naïve that I didn't know why. It was probably his medication that caused this problem. I did not know about the suicidal feelings he was having until much later in our relationship.

There was a time when he wanted to commit suicide and called the police, and they came and apprehended his gun. I did not know that he was that sick. I could never get in touch with him because he would never answer the phone. He would sleep in until late in the afternoon sometimes before I could reach him. I felt unwanted, but I was a fat girl with an attractive man. He would do anything for me. He took me to the finest restaurants and made me happy. I never thought about his sexuality until later on in life. He seemed all right to me, but there was always something peculiar about him.

We were out shopping one day downtown at The Bay when suddenly he broke down and told me how much he had wanted to stay in the Armed Forces but was unable to. He showed me memorabilia with his last name printed on his army outfits when we got back to his place. I was pretty naïve, and I did not know at the time that these were his father's things. I did not know any better. I was never in love with him, but I found it to be a convenience to be with him. He obviously didn't love me either, because he was too sick to be involved in a relationship. Soon, the relationship became a financial burden for me. I used up a lot of my savings on taking taxis to go see him. Also, when we went out, I would pay for quite a bit of the bill.

His mother was an alcoholic and his dad very controlling. One time when we were watching television at his home, his dad kept on going, "Shhh," so that I was afraid to breathe or clear my throat. I sat there in such discomfort that I couldn't wait to leave. This was the only time that I was ever invited to his home in eighteen months together, though I spent one night at their cottage near Gimli. I just remember his mother being extremely drunk and going to the outhouse, calling me. I was very appalled by this.

The strangest thing ever was at the Red River Exhibition by Polo Park. We were with one of his cousins, and Aaron simply snapped. He was spending money foolishly to win a prize. When I asked him if I could play, he refused me, which was the oddest thing ever. At one point, he offered his gold chain to a stranger. I had bought him that as a gift, but of course this person definitely wanted it. Rather than letting him give it to a stranger, I literally pulled it and broke it off his neck.

At this point, his cousin and I had a hard time getting him out of there and to the hospital. We ended up taking him to the Misericordia Hospital, where he worked in Emergency. Whoa, was that ever the end of my relationship with his mother. She was so mad that we had taken him to his place of employment that she tried everything possible to prevent me from seeing him. He was then transferred to the Victoria Hospital under his family doctor's care. He never saw a psychiatrist because his mother did not want him to. He spent three months there, and my family was adamant that I leave him after that. I would not do so, and our crazy relationship continued.

When he got out of hospital, we decided to get engaged. That was one of the worst mistakes I ever made, considering that I really didn't love him or he love me. My family was in disbelief, and this was the first time I ever saw my father crying. My fiancé's mother was so angry that she did everything in her power to separate us. Shortly after our engagement, he got sick with pneumonia and he ended up having his mother take care of him. Every time I called, his mother would not allow me to talk to him or see him. This went on for several weeks. Her plans were to destroy our relationship.

Once he got better, he moved back in with his sister, but our relationship was on shaky ground. He then decided to move into an apartment on his own. There were many times when I would take a taxi there, but he simply would not answer the door. This was happening on a regular basis. He would not answer the phone, and so I would panic and go to see if he was at home. Sometimes he talked to me through the door but would not let me in. I was already a very insecure person, and I did not love him, but this was definitely not good for my self-esteem, considering that I didn't have any, anyway.

Once we started talking more, I suggested that he see a psychiatrist instead of a family doctor. If he was supposed to be bipolar, then I thought that he was clearly seeing the wrong doctor and needed to see a professional. He endured many electroconvulsive therapy treatments, but they did not seem to work. I don't think they put you to sleep in those days. I simply remember him telling me about convulsing, and he had red marks on his temples.

He finally agreed to see a psychiatrist who my friend had recommended. We went to see the doctor, who had a long talk with Aaron and then I was called into the office. The doctor then explained to me that I would have to end the relationship because Aaron was too sick to be in one. I was devastated, but I knew that he was right. I just needed to hear it from a professional viewpoint. We stopped seeing each other, and I remember coming home from work on the bus and watching couples walking hand in hand. Because of all the things that my mother had told me, I knew that I would never have all of that. No one would ever love me, and I was a disgrace.

Aaron and I did not talk for three weeks until one day he called me and asked if I was going out with anyone. I told him yes, that I was dating someone, to make him jealous.

Well, it turned out that I went out with an old friend of mine to the bar that night, and we asked the bouncer to seat us with nice guys. We sat and drank with two Armed Forces guys, but we did not speak to them at all. When they noticed that we were leaving, they tried to leave before us so they wouldn't feel as uncomfortable.

We all left the bar and at a red light, they decided to ask us out for a drink. Since we had nothing to lose, we ended up at a gay bar downtown, Apparently, the guy named Rite had already claimed me to go out with him or he was not going to go out at all. We had a drink and switched cars, and we did a lot of talking.

I could not understand anything he was saying to me because of his strong accent. I made him repeat everything over and over again. He came from a tiny little island in Newfoundland named Twillingate. You could get across only by ferry, but it was connected to the island once they built a causeway to attach it. Rite would go to work with his dad at night. My future father-in-law was employed as a fisherman, built boats, and worked on the ferry before the causeway was finished.

The reason that Rite had joined the Armed Forces was that there was no employment out in Newfoundland. He had gone through basic training and had been to several places in Canada. He had left home and was on the road to a new future and did not care about the people he had left behind. He was too busy having fun.

He was now stationed at the Kapyong Barracks on Kenaston and Grant. He was quite wild at the time but just needed someone to straighten him out. Before that time, he had never seen a store open late in the evening, but he came to love McDonald's and spent a lot of time there. He was free to do what he wanted. His mother missed him a lot during that time. This was her youngest child, and now he was gone for life.

On the night we met, I was amazed at how honest Rite was. My ex-fiancé was the biggest liar I had ever known, but Rite was different. On the first night, he had said that he would call me the next evening. My friend and I did not believe that he would actually call the next day. We both told him, "Yeah, right." To make me believe him, he gave me a ring that his parents had given him. This was to ensure that he would call. He was the most honest person I had ever met in my life. To this day, he is still the most honest person I know. Meeting him was unbelievable, especially considering that my ex called me that same afternoon and asked me if I was going out with anyone, and that same night I met Rite.

The Administrative Secretary at Parks Branch was extremely excited for me. She looked at the ring and said, "He is a keeper." Meanwhile, as I was getting to know him more and more I finally came to the realization that my ex was one of the biggest liars I ever knew. He lied about being in the Armed Forces; I had found out that everything he showed me from the Armed Forces was his dad's. He had never been in the Forces. His late nights awake were spent at gay bars in which he was confused about whether he should be with a man or a woman. He was horribly confused and led two lives, one of which I didn't know existed.

Chapter 8

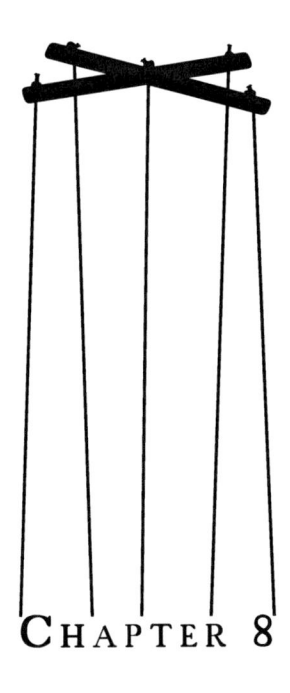

I was now beginning a new life with Rite but had mixed feelings about him. I had only been separated for three weeks and I was already in another relationship. I wasn't sure what to think, and I was confused. I knew that Rite came from a humble background. He was never as surprised as he was one day in July 1978 when I showed him tickets I had purchased for the Eagles concert that summer. Most of his friends were also going and I now had a different class of friends. They were very much into marijuana and alcohol. I didn't want anything to do with this, and I wanted Rite to stop. It didn't take very much time for him to stop because he was coming to pick me up every day. He was definitely interested in a relationship with me. We would go out every night. Sometimes we would go to the Air Force base and go drinking and dancing. Other times, we went to the base to watch movies, which were cheaper there.

    I had fallen in love with a super great man. He was everything I wanted and I know he felt the same way. No one could ever separate us. He was wonderful, kind, gentle, and quiet in his own way. He was hard-working and I could please him easily. He was supposed to go to Cyprus for six months. I did not want him to go because I felt that it was too long for him to be gone at that stage in our relationship. After getting back, he was to live in Germany for four years. I thought that this was not where I wanted to live or have a baby if we got married. I didn't know enough about these kinds of changes. Instead of following this plan, Rite eventually got out of the Armed Forces and became a self-operator at a delivery company. He had to buy his own truck, and he worked the hardest in the company.

Rite moved into a boarding house and bought a budgie to keep himself entertained. Meanwhile, while he was working, he was asked to go to two interviews, but he was always too busy to go. One was for him to join the RCMP, which he had wanted to do all of his life, and the other was to become a fireman. He never took the chance with these opportunities because he didn't want to disappoint the owners of the company where he worked. He would even take the small deliveries that didn't pay much, and he was an expert on prioritizing them so that he didn't spend much money on gas. He also got to know a mechanic who would fix his truck immediately if it broke down. He was always back on the road in no time. He always paid his bills on time and was extremely honest. Eventually, when we were married, he had a second job in the evenings so we could get by and pay our mortgage and all our bills. Never once did he not make a payment. He has always had great credit.

One time, I invited a school friend to come with us to the bar. She went after Rite, which made me extremely mad. She thought that because she was skinnier than me, she could steal him away from me. Even though this never happened, I've never really talked to her since then. I then realized that she was never really my friend, and I began to think of her as a geek. How dare she?

After Rite and I had been together for a few weeks, my parents went on holidays. I obviously had been on birth control pills for years, and I had Rite sleep over for a couple of weeks. I had a great time, but I knew that my mother would have beaten me if she had ever found out. This was the beginning of a lifelong relationship with Rite. I fell in love with him and began to realize how much of a loser my ex was. The realization of how often he had lied to me finally kicked in. How naïve I had been! How stupid! I just hadn't known any better, but now I was finally finding out what kind of person Aaron had been.

Not everything was perfect with Rite, either. There was a day when he wanted me to post a letter to an ex-girlfriend for him. I was wondering why he was writing to someone in Newfoundland if he was going out with me. He never heard from her again. This was a relief to me.

Meanwhile, my more abusive days were beginning to end. At one point, I told my mother what Pierre had done, but without details. Her response was, "Did you like it?" How cruel, but I have never been surprised by this.

The very first time that Rite came to pick me up, my father was painting the fence with my uncle. I introduced Rite to them, and then to my mother. This was a very scary situation. I was hoping that she wasn't going to go into a rage of some sort for whatever reason. Alone in the kitchen, the first nice words she ever said to me were that Rite looked like a very nice man and that she could tell that he was better than my ex. This was the first time that she had met him. I was impressed.

Rite and I went to the park, hung out with his friends, went to the States with my friends and went to the famous bar in Detroit Lakes. I no longer needed to take taxis, and he was always there at the right time to pick me up. He was so honest, just hard to understand. He came over for supper just about every night and my dad would offer him a drink. My father called Rite by the title of Captain until the day he died. He treated him so great. This was the beginning of Rite's long relationship with my dad. They became best friends and Rite would do anything for my parents. My mom was beginning to calm down ever so slightly, but Rite would still jump to every command until the day she died. He does know how horrible she was, but he always helped her whenever she would call him for anything. He still felt annoyed by this, but he believed in respect.

While Rite and I were dating, there were times when my father would come to check and see what we were doing while he and my mother were out. One time, he said that he needed to change his tie. We got out of bed so fast and I got dressed and made my bed before he got upstairs. Rite was in the washroom, and I know that my dad thought this was suspicious. He even commented on why Rite was upstairs at the time. I told my father that Rite only had to go to the washroom.

Rite and I dated until 1979, until one day he asked me to marry him. I was thrilled, and my parents were also happy. My father had developed a very deep bond with Rite and said that this was his best friend ever. Their bond made me feel like my dad did not like me, but only Rite. As wonderful as my dad was, I had never heard him say, "I love you" in all my years. I felt slightly distant from Rite and was actually jealous of him because I felt that my father liked Rite more than he liked me.

We got married on November 17, 1979 in a Catholic church, even though Rite was Protestant. We exchanged our wedding vows at Precieux Sang in St. Boniface. Half of the service was in French and the other half in English. My parents paid for the hall and dinners at what is now the Holiday Inn on Portage Avenue. About one hundred people attended the wedding. Most were family from my side, and there were a few of Rite's army buddies.

On the day of the wedding, Rite went to pick up the best man, who had forgotten that the wedding was that day. The best man was very drunk and on duty at the military base. He did make it to the church ceremony but had to leave directly afterwards. These were the kinds of friends Rite hung out with—party animals. None of his family attended because they could not afford to fly to Winnipeg. We got telegrams from them and one from his aunt and uncle. Things have sure changed since those days. We now have cellular phones, texting, Skype, and other ways of reaching people.

I was sad when my special day was over. I wanted it to go on forever. The following day, my father wanted to take my entire family out for supper, but Rite wanted to be alone with me. I found this to be very depressing since I liked to be with people. This was the start of pulling away from my family at times. Rite loved being with me and me only. I felt trapped, but I smiled and pretended for decades that everything was all right. We had a great time in those first weeks and went to Newfoundland a month later for our honeymoon.

We had a few laughs with my parents. One example was when Rite would take them to the airport and pick them up after their holiday in Hawaii every year. Rite was very active and one year he grabbed everything at the back door and put it into his trunk. As they were putting their suitcases on the belt at the airport, my dad asked Rite what was in one of the bags. They looked and discovered that Rite had actually brought the

My LIFE Not Mine to Control

garbage with him. He was always so eager that he took everything. My dad laughed so much that he was literally crying.

Rite and I lived in an apartment, and we often had Pierre and Monique over or went to visit them. I was still friends with Pierre. It was like nothing had ever happened. My sister was so close to me, and I loved her so much. One time, we were going to Newfoundland to visit Rite's family and leaving to go to the airport at around 4:00 a.m. Pierre was still over late that evening and was drunk and pulled the fire alarm in our building. We could hear the fire engines coming when we went to bed. We got away with this, and we thought it was really funny. Yes, this man who had sexually abused me did not seem to bother me anymore. Why? I can't tell you. I simply blocked everything from my mind and everything felt all right.

The very first time Rite and I went to Newfoundland, we landed in Gander. All of Rite's family that lived there came to greet us. I was really nervous, and I remember the look on his mother's face as she stared at me from head to toe. This was her baby, and she wanted nothing but the best for him. She seemed disappointed in me. At the time, I didn't know that she had an obsession about fat girls. She was somewhat like my mother and would put people down if they were overweight.

As we got into the car, it was clear that Rite's dad was so excited to see us. His sister and brother all greeted me very nicely. His father began teasing me and telling me Newfie sayings that I didn't understand. Rite's sister was telling me how big a baby he was when he was born, apparently over 12 lbs., even though now he was so slender and lean. We still had a 90-minute drive before we would get to the island of Twillingate. We chatted, and Rite's sister Mary would not stop hugging him. He had lived with her and had slept over many times when he was younger. She definitely spoiled him and gave him anything he wanted.

From the first moment I met Rite's father, I felt loved for the very first time. He hugged me so tight and made me feel so welcome it was overwhelming. His sister was telling him about all of the favourite cookies and baking she had stored at home for him. She was very much like my sister, looking after me; maybe because we were both the youngest in our families. Rite's sister had one child named Chris, who Rite was very close to.

Rite's father was a real joker, with a great memory and fun to be around. He had so many stories to tell me. He talked about their well and outhouses and about living with no electricity. This seemed so foreign to me because I'd had all of those necessities my entire life. Rite talked about them sharing a can of corn for supper because they were so poor. One time, he had holes in the bottom of both his shoes but was afraid to tell his parents because he thought he would get into trouble.

As we walked into the house, I saw a mouse running in the kitchen and I automatically freaked out and stood on a chair. Everyone was laughing, and I felt so silly. Rite's mother would get very upset if a mouse was roaming around the house. They set up traps and caught it the very next day, to my relief.

Rite's family showed me around the two-storey home, which was very comfy and in a picturesque environment. Our bedroom faced the Atlantic Ocean, and you could see the fishermen out in the early mornings. The fishermen with their licenses were catching cod, salmon, capelin, crabs, and shrimp; and then there were squid jiggers at a certain time of the year. Rite's sister May's house was just across the road from their parents'. Her husband had had emphysema for many years and was on oxygen. May was the best caregiver I have ever known. She would look after those who were sick and helped others in a manner that I have never experienced. My husband was treated like her own child. She always took such good care of him and was so excited to see him. On the first night when we went to bed, the rest of the family would not stop feeding the fire to warm the house because it could get very cold at night. We were not cold because we had probably six quilted blankets on us. They just weighed us down.

Early in the morning, Rite's nephew came up to our room to see us. He was a very little boy who spoke so differently from the average person. The heavy accent was very hard to understand. I've never said, "What?" as many times as when I was in Newfoundland. The children would call you, "Me love." There were also many other things for me to learn.

Rite would get up very early and dig for worms to go catch trout with his brother. Rite always seemed to come home with a load of them. We also went out to the ocean and went boating to catch fish. Rite was quite an outdoorsman. He would bring his .22 rifle to track and kill birds. He was outside at all times. He felt free. He loved fishing, and in Newfoundland, he could catch a cod in seconds. This was really neat.

At one time, Rite and his family lived in Lower Little Harbour, but the government made them all move their houses into Little Harbour. They had pictures of how they dragged all of their houses through the water to the other side. They could walk to Lower Little Harbour, but they were not able to drive there. The area was very mountainous and had blackberries, raspberries, blueberries, and baked apples, and we did a lot of picking. The baked apples were in a marsh where you felt like you were sinking in quicksand. It felt scary.

There was a pitcher plant that I took to bring home until my husband told me that these plants eat bugs. I screamed and threw the plant down. The berries, however, were different. You could really profit on picking a gallon of these berries. Other folks would buy them for a good price. In that area, there were cliffs and lots of walking to do. It was beautiful around the town known as Iceberg Alley. This is where the tourists would come to visit in order to see the icebergs. In fact, we could see them right from our bedroom. They were so beautiful, and sometimes at night you could hear them break up. This was something that I had never experienced before travelling there.

On the island, there were very many souvenir stores. This island had turned into a tourist town. The people made their money through whale-watching tours, and trips to see the icebergs up close. In later years, they opened a winery with at least thirty different wines made from all of these berries. There was a three-dollar fee to go on a tour of the winery. This included samples of as many wines as you wanted. They ship cases of wine to the tourists for a very low cost. They have done very well for themselves.

My brother-in-law Sean had been working at the fish plant through the summers. He was a shrimp inspector. There were very many boats that would go out travelling a couple of hundred miles and return days later loaded down with their catch. These shrimp were huge and delicious, but I realized that these fishermen had very dangerous jobs.

The people on the island definitely had different kinds of food to eat. One was seal meat. This looked disgusting and I never did try it. The sealskins were being sold by the truckload. I had never seen this before, and I had never seen so many people shooting these seals. This was income on a poor island.

We also ate salt meat called "jigg's dinner", which consisted of salt meat soaked overnight and drained a couple of times because of the salt. You would boil it for several hours and add carrots, turnips, parsnips, potatoes, cabbage, and a cloth bag filled with split peas. Rite's mother would make dough boys to put on top. This was probably one of my favourite meals. We ate a lot of codfish, salt fish, cod tongues, fisherman's brews, and seabirds. I did not like the seabirds, especially their livers and hearts. We ate moose, lobster, mussels, squid, and many other different things. It was certainly not food I had ever eaten before. The desserts always seemed to have berries in them. The one thing that I found extremely insulting was when Rite's mother would be passing out the desserts and she would skip me and say, "None for you" because I was too fat. I was again troubled with my weight.

However, Rite's family was generally very welcoming and we truly enjoyed visiting them as much as possible through the years. My in-laws were very loving and caring people. In fact, the people in Newfoundland were all remarkable. There was no place like this one.

When we had to leave, there wasn't one of us who didn't cry. The family was so close and made me feel welcome. I did get very close to Rite's mother, and we spent a lot of time talking about everything. She was a wonderful woman who had worked extremely hard throughout her life and had looked after Rite's father's parents before they died. One extremely hard time in her life was when her firstborn ended up dying at six months old, of liver troubles. I always sympathized with her for this tragedy. To this day, the baby's name is engraved on a headstone in the cemetery, and she will be together with her mother and father when they die.

CHAPTER 9

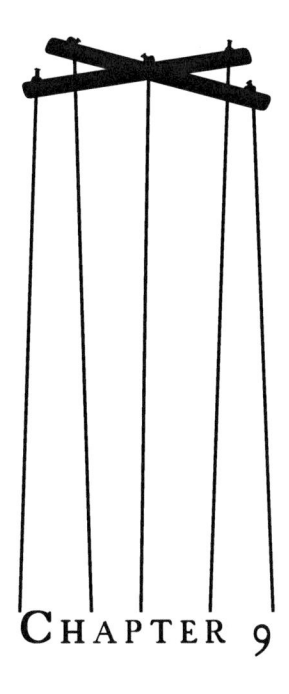

Rite and I finally got back to Winnipeg and were both at work again. We had already begun to think about having a family, but we were afraid that it would be impossible. My husband had been told that he would never have children because he had ruptured his private area twice in one year as a child. We decided that we should try, anyway. I did get pregnant and had a good pregnancy. When I heard the news, I could barely believe it. I even had my friend Candace call the doctor's office to make sure that I had heard right. Little did I know it at the time, but through 30-odd years, Candace has been my longest-lasting friend. We got along very well and giggled and laughed all day long.

Throughout my pregnancy, I lost weight instead of gaining it. Now that I was pregnant, I was even more worried than before about weight gain. It was such an obsession that many people thought I was anorexic. Ben was born on March 19, 1981. We had a little boy, and we were thrilled. At the time, my husband thought that we did not need to have more children and wanted to stop then. I did not feel the same. I would stare at Ben for hours and tell him how much I loved him. He was beautiful. At the time, my sister and sister-in-law were also pregnant. We all had boys just a few weeks apart. I was finally feeling more secure, and this helped to strengthen the ties I had to others.

A few days after Ben's birth, my ex-fiancée, Aaron, committed suicide. While I was at work and going out with Rite, Aaron would always show up at my place of employment. I would get Security to escort him out. He came many times. I'm not sure why he came, but I always ignored him. He definitely had some kind of mental illness that I could not understand, and I felt the need to avoid him. He had made me feel so confused while we were dating. The worst thing about knowing him was the he was such a liar and yet I had believed everything he told me. I was so very gullible and naïve. I felt degraded by the fact that I had actually spent a year and a half of my life being fooled about everything.

Looking after Ben gave me a new purpose in life. I knew that I was going to have six months of maternity leave before going back to work. The fear in me when I thought about leaving Ben was horrible. I wanted no one else to look after Ben because I was afraid that someone would abuse him. This is when I decided to try opening up a daycare. I absolutely hated it because the other children were older than Ben and they were touching things in the house and this made me angry. Ben hadn't reached the stage of touching yet. It did not take long for me to adapt to this. I wanted to stay home, and so I needed to sacrifice myself. I eventually quit my employment at Manitoba Parks Branch at the time when I would have received a promotion. It really was not what I wanted to do, but I had to protect my child from any dangers. This was much more important to me than my own happiness.

I talked with parents who came and went from my home every day, wanting me to do everything for their children. As my daycare grew, I was having a hard time keeping up with all of their demands. Everyone wanted something different for each individual child. I had no rules in place. Parents abused me for years, and all I would do was to smile and pretend to be happy. I was running around in my house, trying to please everyone except myself.

At this point, I ended up developing Obsessive-Compulsive Disorder (OCD). I more than likely had it when I was younger but had not heard of it. OCD is an anxiety disorder that caused me so much stress. I was having a very hard time controlling it. Everything needed to be perfect and I would not compromise with anyone or anything if I needed something done. I was not able to adapt because I had the need to control my own environment. My OCD made me follow rules and regulations, and have compulsions to make lists and schedules. Every Thursday, I would write a long list for every day of the week. This took me about one and a half hours to do. For many years, my husband was getting them photocopied for me so as not to cause me even more work.

Unfortunately, OCD was underdiagnosed and undertreated. The reason for this is partly that many people are ashamed and secretive about their symptoms. I personally tried to reach out to my family doctor, but all he said was that the medication would be worse than the OCD. I could not get help. The drugs used to combat OCD symptoms affect levels of serotonin, which is a chemical messenger in the brain. With my OCD, I found it very difficult to talk about my illness. I had doubts and felt discomfort all the time. I found that I suffered from conditions such as panic disorder, tic disorders, and eating disorders

. It is now considered to be more of a disorder that is neurological and hereditary considering on my mother's side there were many who had these symptoms but were not treated.

Many years later, I was finally diagnosed by a psychiatrist. I saw a psychologist who dealt only with this disorder. I went for cognitive-behavioral therapy in a group setting, which did not help me. Some of the symptoms changed from time to time. I showed an obsession with cleanliness and religious beliefs. My obsessions were accompanied by feelings of disgust and doubt. Things had to be done in a certain manner. This became so serious for me that I was at risk for suicide many times. My psychiatrist had told me that OCD can cause more problems in functioning and puts many individuals through a major depressive episode. There are many people who have committed suicide because of this.

OCD should not be thought of as a clean person doing their housework every week. I have had many people come up to me and tell me that they also have OCD, but truly do not understand the concept behind it. I had to be tidy, symmetrical, and organized. No one could touch anything. My over-attention to details made it hard to live. My perceptions and beliefs were so extreme it affected me to the point where I would to things repetitively. I had a hard time completing a project because my standards were too high. No one could do it like I could. I was so devoted to work and productivity that I had to exclude activities and friends. I had feelings of obsessive doubt and caution. Perfection interfered with trying to finish my tasks. My impulses to complete tasks very long especially if someone was talking to me. I had the need to concentrate extensively on all my tasks in order to continue.

My condition confused me. I had never heard or known anything about it. I felt like an alien. I felt like my brain was a scratched record, forever skipping at the same groove and repeating one fragment of a song. Some good examples of it did to me would be when I would stare at my alarm clock and press the wake up alarm button over and over until it felt right. I could spend half an hour daily doing this every time I walked by my alarm clock.

I would pray, and every word had to be exactly the same every day. This caused me so much distress because I had to repeat the prayer so many times to make sure that I had said it precisely right. I was eventually hospitalized for five months and got help from my OCD doctor in order to stop.

Obsessive cleanliness was another of my problems. I did not want to get my house dirty—not the usual dirtiness that a person would live with, but one that did not make sense. I was unusual, and I was a very private and secretive person. I wore a mask at all times in front of everyone, even my husband. I was so ashamed and guilty of doing certain things, but did not want anyone to know; not even a professional. I knew the things I was doing were not normal, but it was not very severe yet. There were times later in my life when I would see programs on television talking about it. If my husband happened to be watching, I guess he knew how uncomfortable I felt and would change the channel. However, I would rarely watch more than a few minutes of any program. The television would be on, but I never sat down to watch any of it. I would be busy. My mother and her side of the family all had OCD, but no one knew anything about it when I was growing up.

Throughout the years, I also developed several different tics. I would pull on the muscles in my neck and stretch my mouth open to tighten the muscles of my jaw in order to relieve stress. I would make faces, make a sniffing noise or clear my throat in order to relieve stress. The more I did it the more stress I would feel; therefore I was unable to stop for more than a short period of time. I made many unusual faces. This hurt because I could not stop and my muscles would feel as if they had seized. The only time I didn't do it was when I was sleeping. Some days, I couldn't wait to get to bed.

Some of these tics would change from one to another through the years. My mother also had tics and wore out some of her clothes because one tic was stretching out or scratching her shirts. She would then return them to the store and say that there was something defective with the shirts. My brother Emile had Tourette's, but it didn't seem to bother him. The difference between tics and Tourette's are that people with Tourette's make noise. Others could barely hear the little sound I would make except for the sniffling sound and the clearing of my throat. I see a neurologist for my Tourette's syndrome. Usually, Tourette's is diagnosed when the patient is very young. Once again, no one knew anything about it when I was little.

Later in life, I was referred to a neurologist who diagnosed Tourette's. I was put on medication that helps very much. For the problems with my muscles, I get Botox injections from my neurologist for where the muscles tighten up and hurt. Two of my three children also have this disorder. When Ben was younger, he would blink and roll his eyes. Those tics went away as he got older. Myla developed a tic in her stomach. She would pull in and then release her stomach constantly and did so for a very long time. Eventually, the problem went away, but if she is stressed out, it begins all over again. This is very bothersome for her. My youngest child never had any tics.

I also developed outline tracing disorder. This is a very odd condition in which you are constantly drawing outlines of visible shapes with your eyes, hands, and feet. I could just be sitting at ease, only to find that I had been repeatedly tracing the outline of something. I would look at the lines on the wall, the blinds, or the entire area of the ceiling. While driving, I would look at each and every licence plate ahead of me. I would repeat it in my head several times until the next car came along.

Walls seemed to obsess me particularly; especially the outline that things make against the wall. My brain seems to seek out and latch onto the shapes. I do admit that this is not entirely normal, though, because I'm living in two minds at once. Apparently, there is no discernible anxiety connected with this. It doesn't seem to happen more in tense situations than in others. It does go hand in hand with Obsessive-Compulsive Disorder. It is mildly annoying to catch myself doing it constantly. It seems to indicate an over-alert mind in places like bed, in groups, or just when relaxing. It is very rare.

When Ben was born, Rite and I would go out in the evenings, taking Ben everywhere with us. One of our main stops would be at Pierre and Monique's house. She always had parties for us to attend where we could take Ben. Monique was quite family-oriented and would have us over for dinner every Sunday night. We would then watch a movie. I truly had fun on these evenings. She made the best chicken sandwiches in the world. She would always pack one up for Rite's lunch the next day.

When Ben was six weeks old, we went to visit Rite's brother and sister-in-law in Langley, British Columbia. We drove there and found that she also had a baby boy, six weeks older than Ben. I remember having a good time but hearing Rite's family snickering behind my back because I was so fussy. I was extremely embarrassed about the way I reacted towards cleanliness. I could not help it. I began to feel very uncomfortable, but I knew that I didn't have to spend a lot of time with them. Right then, it didn't matter because I was at their place only for a short time.

There came a time when Rite had become accustomed to my not going out because of my OCD. We went out together at times. There were times I wanted to go out with my sister for coffee but could not go because of my OCD. Rite would question me as to why. The reason was because I never left the house without him because of my disorder. It was kept a deep dark secret from the entire world. I felt such shame and guilt that I didn't want anyone to know about it. I would go grocery shopping and tried to please Rite in every way. Everyone thought he was so possessive but it actually was my fault. I could not express myself and this was an extremely distressing time in my life. I was afraid to stand up to Rite until I got help from my psychiatrist, because I was fearful of abandonment.

At the time, I would get upset, but I had so much work to do that I probably instigated his thoughts; therefore I would make up excuses and not get into any confrontations with him. This lasted many, many years. I lived in hell, and I never permitted myself to be with anyone. This was truly very devastating through all those years. I had so much stress and loneliness.

I would sit beside Rite at all times in order to keep him happy and we would kiss in front of my family hundreds of times. Perhaps their marriages were dying, but we kept ours alive. It was all I had.

Rite was very stubborn and always had to be right about everything. I eventually stopped disagreeing with him because I was getting tired of bickering and I did not like to fight. I was always wrong even when there was proof that I was right. He indeed was an extremely stubborn person to deal with and I just learned to give up. He had his own insecurities, and at times he was hard to talk to. Perhaps he wasn't secure but it did make my life hard to deal with. Still, I always felt lucky that someone loved me even though I was fat, and I was grateful for that.

At Christmas time, he would go into an "I miss home" mood. He listened to music that reminded him of Newfoundland and did not talk to any of us. He indeed was very upset with me for not moving there. I made it very clear from the start that I did not want to move away from Winnipeg. I had chances to move to Germany and we chose not to; this is why he was honorably discharged from the Forces. He had done this for me. It took quite a few years for him finally to accept that Winnipeg was his home and he began to enjoy Christmas Eve. Thank God for that! We would go away at Christmas every year and perhaps that was the reason why.

He always looked at other women, but I kept my head down because I assumed he did not like me looking at other men. My life was extremely private and unknown, except in my head. I knew how to be quiet because I felt this way my whole entire life.

Things changed when we got counselling. Dr. Stevens has sure helped us along the way because we are no longer glued to each other like that anymore. I have had to change my perspectives completely. Now, I don't tell Rite what I'm doing or going. If I do so, he usually doesn't even pay attention to me. He really is not interested in what my day was like.

He flipped to the other side and I no longer told him many things because he no longer cared. I kept quiet and didn't bother saying anything about my day because I felt like I was boring him. At times, I would say something about the day and a few days later he would say that I never told him and would get angry. Yes, he was a stubborn person. It is hard to believe, but I want more attention. Now, we have been married for thirty-five years and we do enjoy each other's company. Things can change if you work on it. I love my husband and appreciate all the changes we've made together. Everyone has the ability to change if they want.

Chapter 10

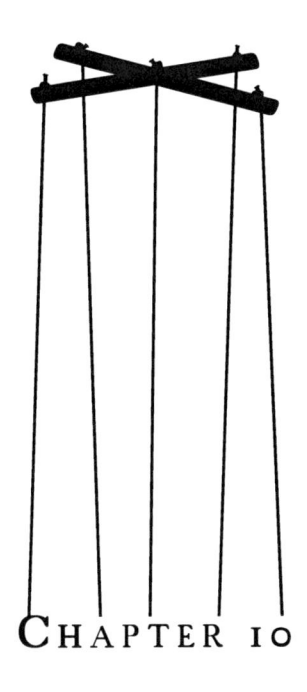

When Ben was just a few months old, Rite started running marathons and went to Tae Kwon Do. He got his black belt, although he ended up with some injuries. He was asked to go to the Olympics in Seoul in 1988. He did not have enough confidence even though I would watch him break bricks and wood with his hands and feet. This was definitely a very interesting sport. After that he started sky jumping in Gimli. He loved this until one time he was doing a free fall and his parachute got all tangled up, so he had to discard it. I knew he was falling too fast and he eventually opened up his reserve chute, which would mean a very hard fall. The owners were worried he was going to land on the highway and it was very busy at that time. There was a country festival going on and Faith Hill was next to sing. I ran with the staff and was told to leave. I was awfully upset with them. Rite continued to sky jump for a while after that but finally gave up the sport. Strangely enough, his brother and family were also there the day his parachute wouldn't open and videotaped the whole thing.

When Ben got a little older, we decided to go back to Newfoundland. Rite's family was ecstatic to see our baby. They spoiled him and gave him all the love a child needed. I had never imagined how good a life a child could have. They read him books and nursery rhymes that I never even knew existed. They rocked him in the rocking chair constantly. They wanted to bathe him and feed him. I was out of the picture. He was the most important little boy on earth. Their love for him was extremely overwhelming. All the neighbours in the harbour wanted to see him. He had the biggest blue eyes you could imagine, and curly blond hair. He was so cute and loving, although he was rough and destructive just like most boys can be.

A couple of days into our holiday the big news in town was that a shark got caught in a fisherman's net and died, and was now on the shore of the beach. We went to see it and Rite took pictures of me standing on it. This was not something that occurred daily. This was exciting.

A few weeks prior to going to Newfoundland we had decided to have another baby. We bought the test in his hometown and it was positive; we were ecstatic, as was his family. I was hoping that it would be a girl. Because of my eating disorder all I gained was seven pounds. I kept my daycare open until the day I delivered Myla. I was in labour not more than three hours before she was born. I did not go to the hospital until the last minute. Nurses and doctors were scrambling around when I had an urge to push. I didn't know what I should be doing, so I pushed. My baby girl was born on April 13, 1983. I was so overwhelmed to find out she was girl. She had a wild temperament from birth. She was my drama queen daughter. I was in the hospital for over a week because I ended up with an infection that gave me a very high temperature. The nurses were really good when I was unable to look after my baby for the first few days. It was hard for them to do anything because this daughter clung to me and me only. She would go to me and no one else. She would wake up several times a night until she was about one year old. She was definitely challenging, and not as easy as Ben to raise. She had temper tantrums every day, which made it very hard to handle her.

When she turned six months, I got very ill with vertigo. I saw a couple of doctors and tried out a few prescriptions, but nothing worked. I had been violently sick with it for three full months, and especially given the fact I had two small children to raise, I wasn't sure if I could live like this.

I was constantly dizzy and my head was spinning. I was always nauseated and afraid to move my head. Because I could not take time off from my daycare or my OCD, I would react to the stress by throwing up several times each day. Even after the children left I was unable to sit or lie down until everything was completed. I no longer felt like I had a life. OCD came first, no matter what.

When I did lie down, it would take a while before my head would settle down and I could feel better. I would wake up with the same symptoms and this was very discouraging. I definitely remember thinking that I would rather die than live like this forever. At the time, my uncle was dying of a brain tumour and that scared me. I was sick with this for years. It would come and go. It was horrible. Now that I'm older, I haven't had the extremely violent attacks, but I do get sick with it occasionally.

It took years to finally be referred to a doctor that specialized in vestibular disorders. The doctor I saw was extremely nice and was from Ireland. My husband had come with me because I wanted him to see and know that I really did feel sick and that this was not my imagination. The doctor at Health Sciences Centre conducted a test with my head. I had something on my head that was connected to a television. At the time, I was not sick with my disease because I had waited so long to see the doctor. He saw nothing going on and sent me for four hours performing different tests. He then told me to call if I was ever sick and he would immediately see me. If I looked up, I would definitely get sick immediately, so I made sure not to do that.

The next time I got sick, I called and got to see him immediately. On that same day Rite had picked up his hearing aids. He kept on putting them in and taking them out while I was waiting to see the specialist. Rite made me so embarrassed because every time he took his hearing aids out, they would squeal loudly. I kept on telling him not to do that but he said that the doctor told him to do this to experience the sound. I kept telling him this was not an appropriate place to do it but he wouldn't listen. I told him to do this at home. When the nurse came to get me she could not understand where that annoying noise was coming from. I told her the truth even though I was embarrassed.

My specialist was able to discover the true problem. On the screen you could see my eyes fluttering extremely fast. This is when I found out

I had a vestibular disorder. He explained to me that the vestibular system included the parts of the inner ear involved in the control of my balance through my eye movements. I was also told that it could be hereditary. My father's side were very ill with this and later in years my oldest sister was also afflicted by it. He had trained a physiotherapist to work with people with this disorder. I seemed to learn how to cope with the dizziness. I knew what made it worse, so I wouldn't do those things. I had taught myself to cope.

Before I even found out about my vestibular disorder, Rite and I had decided to have one more child. It ended up being a girl, and we named her Mandy. I had gained thirteen pounds in this pregnancy. This was the most I had gained out of all my three children. Now it was getting to be a lot of work. I took three weeks off and then I was back at my job again. I never felt like I had enough time to spend with Mandy. There was so much laundry, and I did not use disposable diapers at the time. I washed all my diapers. My husband was slightly disappointed it was a girl. I remember him saying that it was another girl, but not in a happy tone. She ended up being daddy's little girl. Not to say that Myla wasn't his little girl too, but Mandy was very quiet and extremely lovable.

I was very involved in my daycare and didn't have as much time to take care of her. She ended sucking her thumb, even though I tried unsuccessfully to make her try to take a soother. I was way too busy and didn't have as much quality time to spend with her. My OCD had escalated horribly. I was so ashamed of the things I was doing. I got up at 5:00 a.m. and went to bed around 1:00 a.m. for 23 long years.

Mandy played with her brother and sister and obeyed them always. If they were playing, she would always be told what character she was to be. She was always satisfied and never argued.

Later, when she got older, she fractured her leg at Myla's birthday party at the roller rink. I had to take her to Children's Hospital every week for seven months. She had to have her cast changed a few times. Eventually, the casts were not as big as the previous ones, and eventually she ended up with a walking cast. She wore a cast for seven months. We had a lawyer check the floor of the roller rink. Her skate got caught in a hole. A few days later the lawyer went to the rink and took pictures of the floor. The place was shut down soon after. She received a settlement but it was not that much. She needed to go to school in a wheelchair in a handicapped bus. She was so embarrassed. Once her orthopedic surgeon took off her cast she had to walk with crutches for a while. The doctor had written a note to recommend that she not attend gym for a year, but her gym teacher would not listen and made her join in. It was at this time she hurt her leg again and the school got into trouble.

Meanwhile, I was still very busy. I would try to get as much done before the children arrived in my daycare, and then worked through their naps. Once they left, I spent the rest of the evening thinking, checking, cleaning, and doing many strange things. I would even make sure that all clocks and watches were synchronized on Wednesdays. Believe me, it took a long time, because at one point I had other people living with us and I would do theirs also. Of course, they had several watches. Total torture. I would do close to 18 loads of laundry every day. If I had a sock that got mixed up with my tea towels I would have to wash the tea towels again. The Winnipeg Water Works asked us several times if we had a pool.

I had the need to have objects placed in a certain order or position. Tasks or events needed to be completed in a set way. I needed to sort all my clothes by colour and have them placed the same way. All summer t-shirts, long sleeved winter shirts, sweaters, and pants needed to be hung and sorted my way. They were all in order. If my husband happened to take a shirt out, I felt the need to check all through his closet, sometimes once or several times. All drawers were checked every day and sometimes several times a day. Myla would always change clothes when she was older. Sometimes she would change four or five times in the afternoon. I would then check her drawers and closet and perfect them. I always watched what she was wearing. If she would change in five minutes, I would have to go and take the shirt out to be washed and place everything in her drawer.

Mowing my grass would have seven steps. I would mow the lawn, use the weed eater, and pull out any weeds in my flower bed. I would spray the sidewalks in between the cracks with weed killer, and use a knife if there were any present after that. We had a rock bed on the side of our house and I would place the plants in there as neatly as I could. I would do the sweeping and in the driveway, and I would sweep and place the rocks on both sides. Performing the task did not take very long, but thinking it over to make sure I had completed all the tasks would take me longer. I would count walking from the front to the back several times. This was extremely time-consuming and very frustrating. The more frustrated I got the worse it would be and the longer it would take me. My neighbours must have been wondering what I was doing all that time, walking in the back and in the front yards. This was definitely embarrassing.

In my home, I had a magazine rack that had very many *Runner's World* magazines. Every Friday, I would dust the magazine rack and check to make sure that all the magazines were placed in order of date. After that, I would take out all the CDs out of the stand and wipe the stand. Then each and every CD needed to be wiped in every angle. It was the same with our fireplace. I would vacuum the inside and wash all the fireplace tools and container holding the wood. This was absolutely a waste of time because we barely used it.

We lived in a bi-level and I would wipe the black railing in every position. I'm sure some parents must have thought I was nuts, because when they would pick up their children, it would be dripping with soap. Same for the mailbox, whether it was summer or winter.

All my closets needed to be emptied on Wednesdays so I could vacuum and place everything back inside.

I would empty all the children's diaper bags to make sure I took out all the right supplies for the day. I would then fold and place everything back inside very neatly. I felt extremely paranoid that they had placed cameras in their bags or playpens. I did not want anyone to know my perfectionism. I simply was a prisoner in my own home, not allowing myself to leave because I had too many things to do. I was exhausted by the end of the day, but only ended up with four or slightly more hours of sleep. If anyone walked by my TV tables on Fridays, I would have to take them all apart and wipe the stand and every angle of the TV tables before going to bed. It was like I thought the people had contaminated the trays when they walked by them.

I was so sick and tired of living this way. I truly believed I did not have a life and sometimes while washing my floors on my hands and knees, I would think of how my life would end up. I imagined bringing in children with my cane and looking after them and then doing all this work until I died. I'd have to shake my head to stop thinking about it because it was so depressing.

I would empty my fridge every Monday and wrap my hands so I was unable to touch anything once it was washed. I had tea towels wrapped around my hands so I would not touch anything at any time. To put a margarine container away, it sometimes would take me half an hour to make sure the front of the container was in line with the sides. Everything had to be placed with the English side facing forward. I could not let go of the container until it felt right in my head to do so. What a task!

My hands had hundreds of cuts, some of which took months to heal because they were so deep, and I had them wet with dishwashing liquid all the time. At times, I could not even move my hands because they were dry and they bled and looked horrible. One time when I had to go to emergency for something else, the doctors were more concerned about my hands. This was embarrassing.

I cleaned the inside of my oven twice a week, the top every day to perfection because we had a ceramic top. I would look at the top from every angle possible in order not to miss a spot. My kitchen counters, table, appliances were all moved by me every day. Cleaning my kitchen would take an hour and I did not want anybody in the kitchen; otherwise I would have to start all over again. I would pull out all appliances from the walls so I could clean the floor, back, and sides. On the same day, which was Monday, I would empty all my cupboards and wipe them. I would have to take everything out and put it back in again, with the English writing facing the front. If I was to stack a couple of cans of soup, I would have to concentrate to make sure they were lined up exactly they were supposed to be.

It was a boring, stressful, and very tiring and time-consuming way to live. If I could give you a description of everything I did every day, I would be able to tell you every day of the week, the time, and how long it would take me. The only thing I would not be able to tell you is how long it would take me to go out and have fun since it seemed as though I was stuck in this prison forever. I had to check windows, alarm clock, fridge, and oven, touch the elements, comb hair, brush teeth, check the thermostat maybe fifty times, and do many more things before I could leave the house. It always had to be done in sequence. Then, I would put my face in my hands to go through it over again.

Of course, one time was never enough. I would know I had checked everything, but while thinking I would feel unsure whether I did it or not, knowing full well it was done. It could take up to two hours for me to leave; and I couldn't leave until it felt right. I would leave the house checking the doorknobs hundreds of times and then I would walk back into the house because it took me too long to think. I had no time to do anything because I was on a schedule and I needed to pretend I had gone out just to relieve the anxiety. I was stuck and did not know what to do. It took me so long to get out that I had no time to be out. Later in the evening, I would have to empty my purse to clean it because I had carried it with me outside. There was so much tension.

On Tuesdays, I would change everyone's beds. I literally had to wash all the sheets, blankets, comforters, and teddy bears. Another time consuming task. I would also vacuum my basement floor, which was covered with storage boxes and boxes of toys. I would move everything and I would have to vacuum every inch of the basement floor. I would wipe the furnace and workbench and several other things. Ben's bedroom was in the basement and on Fridays it would take me three hours to dust and vacuum it.

I would clean my windows every day. On Thursdays, they were to be cleaned more thoroughly. When it was extremely cold out, I would spend time defrosting the inside of the window with a hair dryer and then wipe and spray them really fast. This took time out of my day. Summer wasn't as bad, except the neighbours would be sitting outside waving to me all the time. I felt crushed but that was not going to stop me. One particular neighbour would tell me how lucky I was to have a husband and three children. She was living with the man behind us after a horrible divorce. I certainly could fool everyone. I always wore a mask to hide all my imperfections. The one good thing was that I never allowed my children to help because I didn't want them doing what I had done my whole life. I always smiled and laughed easily. This was just an act.

Once I got a little older, while driving, I was beginning to worry if I had hit a pedestrian, bicyclist, child, goose, or any small animal. Sometimes, I would see a dead goose on the street and think I had run over it. I would stop to see if I had killed it. If so, I felt extremely guilty and thought I should be punished. My husband always tells me to be careful when I'm driving. Sometimes, I fear that harm will come to me, my husband, children or grandchildren if I'm not careful enough.

Accompanying the fear of harm is usually an excessive feeling of doubt, dread or uncertainty. I often stop my car in an area of safety. I walk around the car to make sure no one is dead. I check underneath the car several times, always worrying that I'm dragging a body. There are times when I drive away, and then I have to go back and check to see if there is a body. I sometimes drive around several times and wait for police to show up. I'm constantly uncertain whether I have hit someone. Sometimes when I run over a bump or train tracks I feel great anxiety and doubt. Checking over and over again relieves my stress. I do not want to give up driving, so I do my best and keep checking. I also listen to the news to hear if there were any hit and runs. Even if I was not in that part of the city I would wait to be arrested.

My children all kept many pairs of shoes at the entrance of our house and I would wash the carpet weekly, and the floor daily. Worst of all, I would take all their shoelaces out of their shoes and clean the shoes with dishwashing liquid. I could never understand all the weird behaviors in my lifetime. Their sandals were all washed by hand and left to dry. Later in life, I would put them in the washer and then let them dry. I was way over the edge and felt so ashamed and crazy. I told no one and nobody knew what I was really like.

I recall a time when I was running a full marathon in 1995, the temperature and humidity was the worst it had ever been. At mile 8, I stopped to drink several cups of water and was worried I might not be able to finish because you are not to wait until you were thirsty. I continued running and people hosed us down and wet our feet. This was not good because if you got your feet wet, they would form blisters. I continued running but had a hard time continuing on when I looked at my feet and noticed my runners were bubbling soap on both feet and would not stop. I hardly could contain myself because it was so funny, but extremely embarrassing. I immediately moved to the curb as close as possible so people would not be able to see too much. At Mile 18, my family were there to inspire us to finish. When I told them about my shoes they were absolutely doubled over laughing. No one will ever make me forget this. I had already run another 10 miles and my shoes still were bubbling.

At Mile 20, the officials shut the race down because too many people had passed out. Not that I was hot because I was being constantly hosed down. We were extremely disappointed and had to get on a bus to return to the university. The organizers threatened anybody who kept on running that they would have their bib numbers removed and said that the water stations were closed. In the bus there were oranges to suck on, but the funniest thing ever was that a man who was overheated had steam coming out of his head. We then ran the track and got a medal, but it was not the same as what I had wanted.

When I took my shoes off, I saw that my toes were covered in blisters. I had lost eight toenails and this was painful. I only had a couple of weeks before we would be running the Grand Beach 10 km in the sand dunes. I was motivated and eager. Nothing would stop me. We trained daily and on Sundays we did our long runs. Every day, I would cycle extremely fast for a couple of hours and do hundreds of sit ups. I wanted to perfect my speed. This was truly the only enjoyment I got out of life. Obsessive? Yes I was.

Now my son competes in marathons. He is extremely fast and part of the Elite Runners. He had joined track through university and had become quite the fast runner. He has won many races and is sponsored by New Balance. He always buys me t-shirts from some of these different runs. He ran the Boston Marathon this year and was placed at the front of the crowd because of his speed. You need to qualify to run the Boston Marathon. I had wished I could go and watch him but it was very expensive. Boston is one of the most prestigious runs of all time. There were 36,000 people running and he came through ahead of 35,760 runners. Not too bad.

Last year, a week after the bombing in Boston, he ran a race in New York and came in third. Every winter he goes with his family to Hawaii. He runs a race there each year and has come in first, running along with the Marines. I have always been very impressed. In Minneapolis last fall he ran his personal best. He will never be the best runner in the world, but he does come in first for many runs and gets monetary prizes. He is planning another marathon in the United States near Maine this coming September. I live through him with running and pray he will always get better.

I was even able to take pictures of those coming in at the Boston Marathon and Heartbreak Hill on my iPad. Around the time he was to finish, my iPad turned off, and I had to turn it off and on again. I had missed him by a couple of minutes and was able to take pictures only of those who came in before and after him. How disappointing! The run was not televised and there was much security. In New York last year, my daughter-in-law fed one of her children a banana and had to hold on to the peel for hours because the security was very heavy and no garbage cans were present.

My youngest daughter is very big into working out. She trains every day for two hours at the gym. She does train until the end of her pregnancies. She is still doing push-ups in her eighth month and running on the treadmill. She also has run a few races and has medalled in them. We all went to Edmonton one year and then Vancouver at Christmas. Ben, Sally, Mandy, and I all medalled in the marathon there. This was quite fun. Mandy is definitely athletic but somewhat muscular. She has been asked to teach aerobics and become a personal trainer. Her body needs to look perfect at all times.

Mandy owns her own hairstyling business and loves what she does. Rite gets his hair cut by her and likes seeing her. I see Myla because she is a hairstylist also, but does not do that for a living any more. She is a manager of a restaurant and gets paid very well. The only reason I see Myla for my haircut is because she is more available than Mandy. I am spoiled on that end. When I want my hair done, I usually ask her and she is available that day to do it. I never have to wait, whereas Mandy has many clients. My children were all different; not to say one is better than the other. Mandy and Myla both aim to please and are very good at what they do. I am very proud of them.

Chapter 11

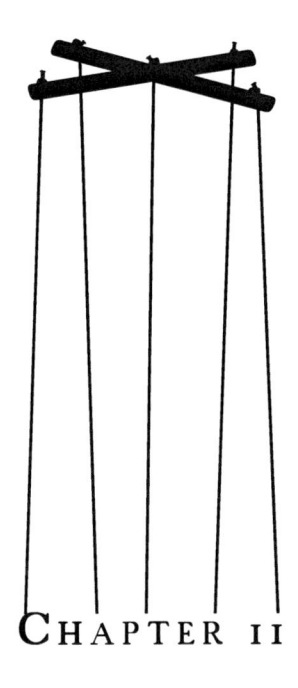

My daycare was keeping me extremely busy. I had some parents who I thought needed to quit bringing me their children because of different circumstances, such as not paying me on time, not bringing their supplies, not picking up their children until 7:30 p.m. These were times I would pack everything for them through the day and send them off with a receipt and stop looking after their children.

One mother treated me very badly when she was pregnant. I thought that usually pregnant women would get upset with someone close to them, such as their husband, but she was extremely nasty to me throughout her pregnancies. I can't imagine how she was towards her husband. She had extremely strange ways and one of her children had weeping eyes that dripped and formed crusts on his face since birth. After a year, she finally brought him to see a specialist to have his eye ducts cleared. I must have told her a dozen times to go see the specialist. Everything was set up for the operation but she got scared and cancelled everything. Later, she finally got it done and it was a miracle.

She always seemed to panic over every little detail with her children, but at times it looked like she really didn't care or want to take the time to see the doctor if things were more serious. She always baffled me and I found her extremely irritating. Her oldest was a boy and then she had a girl. When I was wiping up her son's bum, she would bring her wipes like every other parent. Suddenly now for some strange reason I would have to use the wipes and then wash her daughter differently; first with the wipes and then with a facecloth. What was the purpose? I had been doing this for 23 years and never had a problem with the wipes. I could understand if she was allergic to them, but this was not the case. That mother was always full of surprises, and the extra step was time-consuming and did not need to be done.

I had great references from parents, and treated the children like my own. I knew they were not in harm's way with me looking after them. Nobody would hurt them, and my daycare grew even bigger. I now had set rules in place and parents were to follow them or I would tell them what they had done wrong. I had put a fee in if parents were late after 5:00 p.m. because I was tired of being taken advantage of. I ended up with terrific people, and to this day when I see them, they talk about me like I was the best babysitter. We exchange photos. There are those who were babies when I started and now are in university.

I kept the children clean and I would wash their clothes if they were ever sick. They had breakfast, lunch, and two snacks a day. I was always very consistent and did my best to keep things in order. I had one parent bring her children in late with breakfast to be eaten at 10:30 a.m. I repeatedly told her that breakfast was over at 8:00 a.m. Then the parent thought I would feed the children lunch later than the others. It wasn't a custom-made daycare service. I always wonder what went through these parents' heads. I had some children that clung to me, and others who were very rambunctious. There was one little boy who always touched my hair when I was holding him. He was very quiet and liked to be held.

As my children got older there were a couple of parents who would give them the key to their homes and the stroller, and my children would walk over to look after the other children all evening. My children had lots of babysitting jobs. Parents trusted my children, just like they trusted me.

As my children were growing up, they always had someone to play with. They were all friends. They entertained themselves. I had one child who brought a video named "Cujo" because it was her favorite movie. She was three and the movie was about a dog that had rabies and was trying to kill the mother and son. The movie was very disturbing and definitely not suitable for children. I never could understand what went through parents' heads. They were told not to bring their toys from home because the children would fight. Many of them did so regardless, and I would just put them away so that the children couldn't see. I had plenty of toys for boys and girls. They were never bored. We did activities, baking, went to the splash park, played outside, and many other things. Punishment for them was always time out on the couch. They were unable to play for a few minutes until I told them they could return.

I had one mother who bought everything for her little girl. When my children were older they would end up with cameras, their own televisions, phones and many other teenage things. If this mother was to see that her daughter was interested in any of these things, she would immediately go out and buy it that night and tell me. Wow, I couldn't believe how strange people were. She also would give her daughter bottles of milk when she had the flu. I kept on telling her to take her off the milk because dairy products irritated your stomach when you had the flu. She then told me that the doctor told her she needed her nutrition. I never believed that. After her daughter had been sick for one week, the mother took her to the doctor, where she was told to stay off dairy products. What I had to say never seemed to matter to her.

My children and I would laugh at the size of clothes that the mother would put on her daughter. She was only one year and wearing size 8 shirts. Whatever the child pointed to, the mother would buy; regardless of the size. Also, when she finally started her on meat from the baby food jars, she would gag and throw up because she did not like it. I had told her to stop giving it to her because she didn't like it. I had told her maybe when she was older she would like it. The following day she never brought it but thought she had waited long enough to give it to her two days later. Where was her head? What was she thinking?

There was a time her daughter ended up with a fever of 106 Fahrenheit and I immediately gave her Tylenol and knew she needed to be taken to hospital. At this time, everyone was picking up their children and I had set it up that one parent would take the child to the hospital. When he was leaving, the mother showed up. I had told her the dangers of such a high temperature and to take the child to the hospital. Later that evening, I called to see how she was and found out that the mother had never taken her to the hospital. She had gone home and made supper instead. Very annoying! I had given this same mother some of my Christmas baking, made just for children to eat, for her daughter. I had wrapped it up and I gave it to the mother. They lived two minutes away and the mother had let her daughter eat them all by the time they got home.

Later that night I got an extremely angry call from the mother yelling at me because her daughter was apparently bouncing off the walls. I proceeded to tell her that I didn't give the baking to her to eat all at once and that the mother should have controlled the amount that her daughter was eating. She was very spoiled and the mother let her have and do whatever she wanted. The following morning, I then packed the girl's supplies and gave her mother a receipt for income tax and quit looking after her child immediately. I'd had enough. I certainly did not want to be bothered after hours with such ridiculous comments or to be accused of making a child eat all of the baking I had given to her at once.

A few years later, she and her husband divorced, and he ended up working for my husband. He and his new wife became very good friends of ours. Strange! At one interview with both parents, the mother seemed very kind, but the father was giving me bad vibes. I had already decided that this child would not be a fit in my home. The father got up and went through all of my cupboards and into every room to check for safety. If he had wanted me to give him a tour I certainly would have done so, but he took it upon himself to do it. The following day, I told him that I was unable to look after their child.

The strangest thing was that this father also got hired by my husband to work for the same company. He was an alcoholic. That became clear one day when we were at the airport together. We had gone to see the Snowbirds by the airport runway. My husband worked right off the runway at the time. The man's wife had left him and he had brought his 5-year-old boy with him. As we sat and watched with all of our children, he passed out and his child could not wake him up. My husband finally got him up and then he drove home with his child in the car. He was checking to see if my home was safe and meanwhile he was drinking and driving.

How dare he? He ended getting fired from his job at my husband's workplace anyway.

My daycare was peanut-free, but I seemed to have many children with asthma. One little girl was extremely allergic to peanuts, but other children's parents didn't care. One time I called a parent to see why they were late. He told me that the oldest child was just finishing off a peanut butter toast. Once again, after having given them notices before, I told him that he was not allowed in daycare until his face and hands were washed, clothes changed, and teeth brushed. If this had been their child they would have put me through hell. It wasn't and they didn't seem to care.

Through my twenty-three years of daycare, an outbreak of chicken pox was always a very tough time. It was then said to let your child continue to go to daycare because they wanted the virus to spread when they were young. I had many parents who had a problem with that. I even thought that the affected children should be staying at home because some of them had it worse than others. I had to go along with what the other daycares were doing, and what schools were doing.

I learned how to use an EpiPen and an asthma machine with a mask plugged in the wall. I would put the medication in it until it stopped steaming. One boy sat there and never moved. He was so cute because I would put the television on for him the two times a day he needed to use the machine. If any of the children would walk on any of his cords, he would point to please get off. He was maybe 15 months old.

Nevertheless, my biggest worry of all would be if a child would have been hurt in my home. There wasn't a day that went by that I would not think of this. There were a few bite marks, but you could tell they were done by another child. Biting was not permitted, nor were hitting, scratching, and other aggressions. If any of those things occurred, the child would end up on the couch and not be allowed to play for a few minutes.

Another child came into my home for only a few weeks. The mother was living with her boyfriend and his parents. They were extremely wealthy. The baby would come in the dead of winter with no coat, socks, or mittens; just a sleeper. This mother would forget her supplies constantly and was wearing a winter coat. The baby's feet were blue when the mother forgot to dress her child properly. Of course, she was gone in no time.

Another disease that spread was hand-foot-mouth disease. I actually had never heard of that until that one episode. It didn't take very long to find out what the symptoms of this disease were. The children developed sores on their hands, feet and mouth. We were struck by it in the summer time. It is spread through coughing and sneezing. It usually takes three to six days for a person to get symptoms after being exposed to the virus. This is the incubation period.

At first, I would send sick children home because the child would feel tired or get a sore throat and fever of thirty-eight to thirty-nine degrees Celsius. Then in a day or two sores or blisters would appear on the hands, feet, mouth, and sometimes the buttocks. Some children developed a skin rash or blisters. The blisters sometimes broke open and crusted over. The blisters lasted about a week or so. Some of the children had mild cases, but for a couple of others it was a little more severe. Myla ended up getting this disease. She was always the one most prone to get sick with things. She had a severe case of it and was in high school at the time. She got the disease a few days before school started and didn't want anyone to see the blisters that formed under her nails. Eventually, she lost several toe- and fingernails. She had the worst case out of anyone, although there was one little boy who also lost a few nails.

Chapter 12

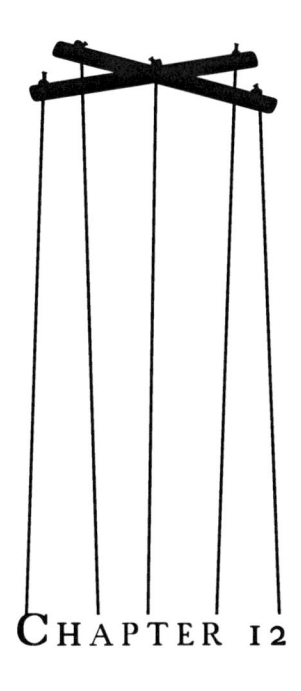

Over the years, we did some traveling. Our children were all so excited to leave on vacation. My husband wanted to take me away from my OCD, so he would plan two holidays a year. We have driven across Canada many times and visited each and every province and were impressed with most of them. Every winter after Christmas dinner we would go to Banff, Alberta, or to British Columbia. We would have all of our luggage packed and at the door for when we came back from Monique's, and we would stop in Brandon. One particular time I looked in the back seat of the car and asked Mandy if she had brought her coat. In disbelief, she told me she forgot it because it was so warm that Christmas. She was all right in Banff and Vancouver, and when we came back to Medicine Hat it was 15 degrees Celsius. We were very lucky that we did not have to buy her another coat.

    I had injured my knee and was concerned about running the Resolution Run on the trip. I tried to train the day before but was unable to run. In the middle of the night I was running across my room back and forth. This is when I said and thought that we had come here for the run and I was going to participate in it even if I would have a hard time. We got to the run site and I ran a little to warm up and suddenly I heard a sound like a rock hitting the curb. It was not a rock; I had sprained my ankle. It definitely hurt. Now I had two injuries. We got in line to run and my mind was set on a "No pain, no gain" run. I finished in good time as always. Who says a little determination wouldn't hurt? I made it across the finish line. You just prepare yourself mentally and do not think of pain. You can reach your goal as long as you don't give into it. I was one of the first women to cross the line.

When we got back I went to see my sports doctor and had to have a cast put on my ankle. I had further damaged it by doing the run.

We experienced some very strange disasters on our holidays. One Christmas we were stopped on the Trans-Canada highway for eight hours because of avalanches. We were the lucky ones because where we ended up stopping was Rogers Pass, which had a hotel, washrooms, and food. They ran out of food but we were back on the highway driving after the park rangers shot down three avalanches. We were very fortunate to have been stopped in front of the hotel. I'm not quite sure what the other people who were behind us did, but it was a long wait that went into the night. Another time, we were just a few kilometers from Banff after driving all day and we ended up having to detour another eight hours because a mudslide had come down and washed out the bridge right before you were to enter Banff. We travelled through the night and we were lucky to have information on hotels. We ended up finding a hotel that had one room available.

Later on, when our children were older, we were stopped right in front of a tunnel which had a burning car on the same side we were to enter it. There were several accidents that had occurred going the other way because of smoke. The police hadn't shown up yet, so we drove through without getting delayed. We got lucky. We drove through a blizzard in the mountains after leaving Lake Louise. We literally were following a semi, but the only thing we could see were his lights. Rite felt extremely pressured and worried. He would get upset with me because I would end up falling asleep. He was worried about dying and here I was, sleeping.

We liked traveling in the United States. Our children have been to many states. One interesting place was Mount St. Helen's. We had brought home pens filled with ashes and several souvenirs from there. Rite liked the outdoors and nature and loved explaining to the children about all different things that had happened in the world. He loved seeing new things every day through our travels and we always took the time to look at everything. We would investigate before we went away; researching things that were of importance and interesting.

We spent a few of our holidays in Seaside, Oregon. This was just a little town located on the ocean. We actually stayed at hotels facing the ocean. We could watch the sun go down and it was absolutely beautiful. It looked like a big ball of fire falling into the ocean. What a beautiful view. However, through my travels I still had problems with my OCD. I would have to clean the shoes on the exact day that I would do it at home. I would have to empty and fix my purse every single night. Laundry needed to be done frequently and this was very time-consuming. I needed to clean all my jewelry and many, many other things. Our suitcases were emptied every day and everything placed back in order again. Then I would have to make sure it was done right because I always had doubts in my mind. It took away some pleasure on my holidays but it was better than being at home.

Our children liked to go swimming every day and spent lots of time on waterslides in hotels. Even Rite and I would have fun doing so. In Seaside, we rented these little cycling dune buggies. It was like a bicycle in the sand and you would go really fast on them. I recall my son chasing after me and I would scream because he would get really close to me and crash. In the evenings, we would go out for supper and then we would go to all the souvenir stores in the town. I still love going there. These were all good memories.

We drove through Yellowstone National Park and the children loved it there.

Chapter 13

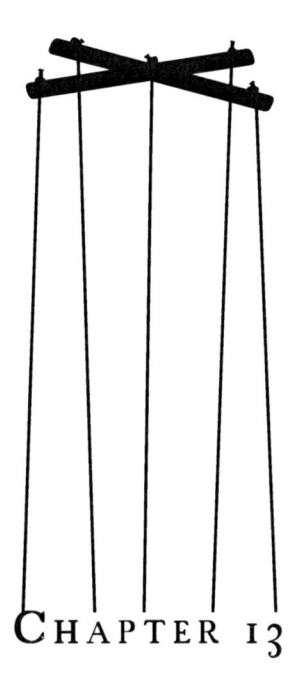

Having my children with me was absolutely the most important thing in my life. I loved all three of them equally, although their personalities were all different. We had so much fun together even if I did have OCD. I always had a great sense of humor. In my heart, I knew and still know that I was the best mom a child could have. I treated them with respect and always listened to them. They were my life. Rite was always working. He would work all day long at his full-time job and then go to his different part-time jobs. At one point, he had seven part-time jobs. He was definitely one of the hardest workers I ever knew; seven days a week and he still works like this now.

He's had several injuries but still works. He has had a cast on his leg, twisted ankles several times, fallen 30 feet, and just recently has cut his inner arm with an X-Acto knife. He needed several stitches for this. The last injury, which happened just recently, occurred when a 120 lb. coil made of steel with sharp edges fell on his hand. He hurt two fingers and everyone thought he should get stitches; but he never bothered because he didn't want to lose time at work. The following day he was talking to Myla and she told him to go to Emergency. I had told him this the night before but he didn't want anything to do with that.

Finally on the following day, after he had been delivering hot tubs all day, I drove him to the hospital and we found out that his finger was broken, just like I had said. The bone was not only fractured, but worse; it was completely crushed. His nail was hanging off already, and he had deep cuts to both fingers on top and underneath. He ignores all the pain and still works. If the children or I needed attendance he was there immediately. We always came first.

When the children got older they all had to get their driver's licenses. First it was Ben, and he liked to borrow our car. He was using it early one morning when he got into an accident at a red light. He was waiting for it to turn red so he could turn, but the girl who should have stopped went through the light at the same time as he thought it was safe to turn. He had totalled our car and we were quite disappointed. We then bought a new car and the owner of Rite's company gave us a few thousand dollars to pay for some of it. He was a very generous person, especially since he knew how hard Rite worked for him. We have always felt blessed that Rite worked for such a nice person.

My children and I were together all day long in their early years, and even with my OCD I never once asked them to do anything because I did not want them to be like me in any way. I did not permit them to clean, do laundry, or even make their beds. In some cases, that turned out to be a problem because they were very lazy if asked to do anything; even something as simple as throwing the garbage out. In some sense, I had spoiled them and they thought they never had to help. Most of the time, it was my fault. I didn't want them to clean for me. To ask them to do the simplest things without bringing out my OCD had become a big problem, and they either wouldn't do what I had asked or would complain so much that I just did it so I wouldn't have to listen to them.

When Ben was younger, he would go to work with Rite so his father could keep him busy. I would miss him. Rite would bring peanut butter or Cheez Whiz sandwiches with him for two. He would actually put it on top of the dashboard in the summer. They would eat their warm sandwiches together at lunch time. How disgusting! Ben would always want to go to work with his dad because Rite paid him a wage every day. Ben excelled in numbers at a very young age. Money was always so important to him. He would count it over and over through the day. His teacher used to call him a mini computer because he was so good at math.

All three children went to French immersion schools. Ben and Myla graduated from College Jeanne Sauve. Mandy had a harder time in school and we put her in an English school when she was in grade six. She had started grade six in French immersion but the teacher was always frustrated with her. I called the principal a couple of times and then we decided to put her in an English school before the end of September. We went to pick up all her things at recess so as not to disturb the class, but her teacher was outraged. She literally threw all her scribblers at us and then turned the light out on us while we were emptying her desk. I complained to the principal about the teacher's rudeness but she never apologized.

Now Mandy was in a much better school and we knew we had made the right decision. She had more help in the English school than French. The only problem was that she was not excelling fast enough. She still did not know how to read. We would read to her every single day. We tried as best we could to get her to read. The school counsellor took her out of class and had a teacher's aide helping her every day. By the time she was in grade seven she wasn't doing any better, although they were working with her. Her teacher in grade four and five would always tell her to wait. She would never return to Mandy because she wasn't going to waste her time on her. She did not care whatsoever, and she didn't want to be bothered with Mandy. This particular teacher would tell her to clean her desk and the blackboard every day. This was all she had learned. I would call the resource teacher constantly, but nothing was ever done. The child psychologist was very interested in Mandy's environment at home.

Meanwhile, in my daycare, I was looking after a little boy who would bang his head on the floor when things didn't go his way. His mother and I discussed this before the child psychologist had come over. We were both hoping he would not do that in front of her. When she came she was very interested in Mandy's Barbie house because she had talked about it so much. The little guy used to hit his head on the floor because he was not having things go his way. All that the psychologist mentioned was that it was his way of expressing himself. When his mom picked him up we both laughed at what he had done, knowing full well that this was the way he acted all day.

Mandy was now going to high school. Her teacher Mr. Norm Bing was an absolutely lifesaver for her. She was put in a class where the other students could care less about school. Mr. Bing took a liking to her because she did not have a bad attitude, but very polite. She was nothing like the others. She was reading and he would take his time to teach her one-on-one. He was amazing! When she went to get her beginner's licence for driving, she failed the first time and was totally discouraged. She didn't think she would ever pass. On one particular morning, Mr. Bing took her out of class to study the manual in order to pass her beginner's test. Then he went through it with her for a few hours until he felt confident that she knew enough. In the afternoon, he drove her for her test and she passed. What an incredible teacher he was! We feel blessed that she had him as her teacher for four years. He went above and beyond the call of duty. He loved Mandy's attitude and was very eager to teach her.

Mandy eventually was old enough to go to Technical College to take hairstyling courses. She enjoyed this very much and was becoming more confident. At the parent and teacher meeting she was expecting her two teachers to say good things about her. Well, as it turned out, through the whole hour they criticized literally everything she was doing. Mandy and I went home crying because this was not what I thought I would hear. A whole hour of criticism. The following day she told Mr. Bing about what had happened. He immediately called me at home to see what had gone on. I could hardly contain myself and cried through our whole conversation. He was outraged at what he was hearing and was angry that both teachers were picking on her, even though she was always such a people-pleaser. They were the ones holding her back. He then called a meeting with the two teachers, the principal, and a very odd guidance counsellor the following day. He was angry. He simply told them that if they would not change their attitudes towards her and take the extra time to teach her, he would pull all of his students out of the Technical School. The principal did sit and have a talk with the teachers, and they were somewhat better after that. They were never extremely nice to Mandy, though.

In November of 1992, we had a long distance call in the middle of the night to find out that Rite's parents' house had completely burned down.

They'd had a power surge near the back door and the neighbor had gone to check it out. He touched the outside wall and he felt the heat. The firemen finally showed up but the house had to be torn down and a new one rebuilt on the same spot. How devastated his mother and father felt. His mom started to get physically sick shortly after that. The stress seemed to be too much for an elderly person. My family donated money and we got them what they needed. The people in Twillingate gave clothes, food, and money, and they even were lent a home until they had a new one built. At the time, the insurance company had gone bankrupt and they had a hard time to get their money back. They ended up with less than what it was insured for. They now needed to build a smaller home. This took a toll on Rite's mother.

When Myla turned fifteen, she was not nice to her sister. She found Mandy annoying, especially since she was into looking for a boyfriend that was of another nationality and didn't want her family to embarrass her. On the morning of a party that we were having for Myla, Mandy fell down the basement stairs while Myla laughed. This was the day that Mandy had actually fractured her leg at the roller rink where the party was held. The party was held at the Saints Roller Rink. Everyone was having fun until I saw Mandy fall and realized that she couldn't get up. The owner went to pick her up and brought her to the side of the rink. He suspected a twisted ankle. She was in so much pain that he carried her to the party site and I served the cake immediately and gave out goodie bags to all of the guests. In the meantime, Rite and my father were called to come back and Rite and I took her to the hospital. That evening when we got home all of my family and friends were there because I had already invited them for Myla's evening party. Myla was very upset and jealous because Mandy had ruined her day and got all the attention.

Mandy met her first boyfriend at Technical School. His name was Keith. It was talent day and she asked him if she could wax his hands. She had a crush on him. He kind of laughed and said that he thought that waxing was too feminine for him. She then convinced him to get it done. They went on their first date shortly after. They went out for several months and without my knowing, exchanged rings. He gave her a men's silver ring, whereas she gave him a gold ring with a diamond in it. It was a ring I had bought her. Keith was still very immature and because his friends were more important to him, they broke up. I would tell Mandy that he wasn't a very nice boyfriend. She agreed with me. The following year she saw him again and wanted to exchange their rings back, but he had lost hers. She kept his and still had a crush on him. She wanted this boy. They ended up going out together once again, against my approval.

Keith was becoming an electrician, and Mandy laughed when he told her his first word as a baby was "plug." He then went on to Red River College and finished with his degree. He was extremely successful at whatever he did. He could fix, repair, and build anything. He was loved as an electrician because he was so talented. He would come over to our house, and on one occasion, he decided to change our lighting in the house. He put beautiful light fixtures in our kitchen and lights in our staircase. I was slightly worried about him cutting the carpet in our staircase. I was specifically worried because we had just put in new carpeting. He cut the carpet and put lights in. It was beautiful. He was very good at electronics and everything he touched. He was a hardworking and a talented individual. I definitely felt he had finally matured.

Over the years as the children were growing up, we would often go on holidays with Rite's brother and his wife, Aline. They showed us around Seattle. They lived in Langley, British Columbia. We had a great time when we would arrive in Seaside, Oregon. This was one place we really enjoyed visiting. We had fun with them on the dune buggies in the desert. We liked travelling with them because there was always something new to see.

We journeyed to Reno with them and took turns to go gambling while one couple would watch the children. Ben was extremely excited to see money coming out of the machines in the lobby. He couldn't believe it. Money was something he liked and he would count it over and over again. He loved numbers and counting and in grade four he wanted to be a chartered accountant, and this was a goal that he pursued in life. Once we parted from Rite's brother we drove through Nevada and stopped to make lunch. We still had a big piece of cheese left over once we had finished, and we didn't want to keep it so we gave it to Mandy to eat. When she was done, Rite crumbled the rest of it into little pieces for the ants. We must have stayed there for an hour watching them carry big loads of cheese on their backs. The children have never forgotten this and still talk about it now and then.

We were continuing our travels into the mountains when our car began to sound like it was going to break down on the top of the mountain. We had travelled a long distance up. Rite was getting worried because the car seemed to jerk. We made it to the top and stopped for a while. One man stoped to see if we needed help. Rite felt very skeptical about him and didn't trust him. The man followed us all the way down the mountain and Rite couldn't think about anything good about him. He felt like this man was going to make us run over a cliff. He thought that the man meant harm to us. We finally made it to the bottom and waved goodbye. The missing family created by Rite were still alive.

We stopped at Jackpot, Nevada, and we were going to get our car checked until we noticed the mechanic was chewing on a toothpick and we were worried he was going to change parts in our car to make money. He seemed so unprofessional. We stayed in the hotel next to the mechanic's shop, which felt like it left no survivors. It was very spooky. We did laundry in this little Laundromat that had signs only in Spanish. Later that night we walked across the street to find ourselves in a building with thousands of people gambling. Where they came from we hadn't a clue. It was just a ghost town and now there were actual people. We never got our car fixed because it was working very well, except when we would climb very high mountains in it.

We would always buy my father's older cars because they were kept in such good condition. One time we had to have our car inspected and Rite had it down to perfection, except for a working horn. The horn did not work but Rite figured a way to fool the inspectors. He would hold a piece of metal on his leg and push it when he needed to honk. We passed the inspection because of Rite's great ideas. My father thought this was an especially funny story.

Many weekends Rite would reserve hotels in Grand Forks. If the children knew we were going away, they would be thrilled. I can still remember Ben jumping up and down because he was so excited. One particular time, we were on the highway and we told them we were going to drive to Grand Forks for a couple of nights. At that time, no one believed us and thought we were pretending. Eventually, they started to believe it when we stopped to show them our luggage. Our daughter finally figured out why she could not find the hairbrush after school, because it was already packed. These were fun times.

The only reason we went away when we did was because Rite worked seven days a week and every evening for us to get by. He was a very hard worker and always supported our family. He especially loved making me happy because when we were on our trips, I could get away from my OCD. Going away was our only thrill we had and we took advantage of it as much as possible. As our children grew, I was making much more money in daycare and was able to save a few thousand dollars every year for Rite's birthday. I would have the money separated into different envelopes and would hand it to him while we were out for dinner. I was always able to save enough money to go away. Better yet, all three children would get something very expensive at the same time. I did this for several years and as they got older they would always be so excited at that time of year. One year, we had bought Ben a car to go to university, and I had also saved lots of money for his education. The girls got televisions, pagers, a stereo system, and many other things. This was an important time in my life because I always wanted my children to succeed in life. I wanted them to do what they wanted because I had never had that opportunity.

My mother and Monique were very negative about Ben going to university. My mother would laugh and smirk and would always comment on where he would get his money to become a chartered accountant. As far as Monique, she thought her daughter was smarter than anybody else because she had succeeded in becoming a teacher. My mother critiqued Ben about this all the time and compared him with Monique's daughter. Little did she know she was giving him the drive to save, work in order to fulfill his dreams. It made Ben even more eager to prove that he was going to be successful, and we did everything we could do to make sure that his dreams would come true. It was the same for the girls. We proved my mother wrong in many ways.

Chapter 14

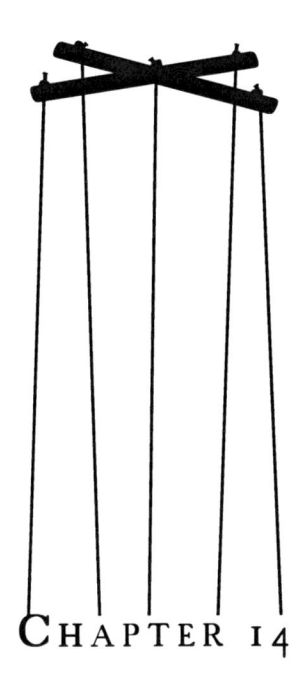

One Halloween, my daughter Mandy got dressed to get candy. No one knew her age because she was so tiny. She went to one house with a couple of her friends. The man who answered the door sexually assaulted her. When she came home she was trying to explain it to me but in a very vague way, saying that there was this weird person who gave her candy and wouldn't let them leave. I questioned her story, but it didn't seem all that important. I couldn't understand what she was trying to tell me.

The police showed up at 11:00 p.m. and they wanted to talk to Mandy. We woke her up in her Tweety Bird pajamas. She was then told that the police had picked the man up and that he was already in the Remand Centre. They questioned Mandy and they said the man seemed to like all girls with the same profile. All had long blond hair and were of the same height. He was employed at the Legislative Building. When the police left, they gave us their names on a card so that I could contact them to see when the man was going to be attending court. Every time I called, the case was always remanded to another date. In the end, he got off but had to do some community work. We were very disappointed. This took about 18 months before he was sentenced.

Every Friday night we went grocery shopping and I was allowed to leave my prison for a short while. All three of our children ended up having their partners live with us at this time. Mandy was the only one that would go back and forth from Keith's home. The other two stayed with us one hundred percent of the time.

Food was plentiful and I would buy everything each person loved separately. I spent thousands of dollars on food because I would always buy the new things that would come out and I was always out to please the others because I loved them like my own.

Ben met Sally at the Commerce Social from the University of Manitoba. Ben was very shy and wanted to meet a girl, but she wasn't shy and went after him. He was thrilled. Even before the social, she had checked out where he lived. Her intentions were to meet him and go out with him. Ben fell in love immediately with a beautiful girl that we all loved. He had just met her when we were leaving for Banff at Christmas. I felt bad that we had to go away at the beginning of their relationship.

Ben was anxious to get back to be in her loving arms again. They were a terrific couple and fell in love quite quickly. They dated and when summer rolled around we allowed Sally and Myla's boyfriend to come with us to Newfoundland. We rented a large van and left on a Friday night after Rite was finished work, along with my cleaning the house. I was so excited about this trip because it was going to be different. Our first stop was at Subway just at the end of our street. It wasn't even a kilometer going that way. We were all laughing because we had just piled in and then we were all out in less than a minute. We wanted to eat something fast so as to get on the road as soon as possible. Subway was one place Ben and Sally enjoyed very much. I think Ben could have eaten there every day. We ate and headed for Dryden. This was our final stop for the night.

We stayed in a hotel and Myla's boyfriend Jeff got everything out of the back of the van. He was so loaded down with suitcases and bags, he could hardly walk. We were all laughing at him with his eagerness. He was very appreciative to be coming with us and was always very respectful. We all went to bed and Rite and I would get up early to get ready first while Ben went out running. We would always go out for coffee first while the others got ready and Ben would always be last after his morning run. We then headed for Ottawa. Our hotel room was a suite with many beds. We had two washrooms so we could go get ready faster.

We ended up getting a call that Rite's brother had hit a moose driving on the highway in Newfoundland. The moose's hind end went through the windshield and fractured all the bones in Rite's brother's face. The moose had a bowel movement on him and then died. My brother-in-law was very lucky to have survived. He was able to get out of the car and wave people down. He was brought by ambulance to Gander's Hospital and then flown to St. John's hospital where they had all the specialists. We wanted to rush to see him, but could not get there any faster because our ferry was booked and you needed to make reservations ahead of time. We then headed for old Quebec City. It was beautiful there and everyone went out in different directions for their own romantic supper. We met later to go back to go to the hotel. Everyone toured on their own that evening.

The following day we made it to Moncton, New Brunswick, where they had the fastest tides in the world. The higher waters in the bay cause the water in the placid Petitcodiac River to roll back upstream in one wave, which can range in height from one inch to twenty-four inches. Just as spectacular is the rapid and dramatic change in the river itself. At low tide the muddy river bottom is often visible, but within an hour of the arrival of the Tidal Bore, the water level rises some twenty-five feet, filling the river to its banks. There are scheduled times for this event, but they are only approximate. Depending on many factors, the Tidal Bore can vary by fifteen to twenty minutes before or after the scheduled time.

The Hopewell Rocks were what we wanted to see. Before going to the Hopewell Rocks we would check the schedule to see when it was safest to walk on the ocean floor. It was incredible and very unique. This presents a unique opportunity to walk on the ocean›s floor when it was low tide. At one point in time, we waited very close to see the tide rise before we went back up. You literally could see the water rising at your ankles and everyone just stood there until we thought we had enough time to get back safely. There were signs on the beach at different locations telling you when it was safe to leave. Otherwise, you would get caught in the waters and probably drown. Sally was extremely interested in this because she was studying it in university.

We then went to Prince Edward Island and crossed the Confederation Bridge, which is 13 kilometers long. The bridge connects New Brunswick to Prince Edward Island. As you get off the bridge there is a tiny little village that is quite unique to see. We stopped and had mussels, but Myla and Mandy found them disgusting. Sally loved them. P.E. I. is an agricultural province. The sand is red and this is the home of potatoes. There are McCain's plants there that make most of the French fries for the area. We went to Charlottetown and around the island. We then drove that same day to get to Halifax. It is very hilly and there is lots of scenery in Nova Scotia. It was amazing! At one point, we met Ben and Myla's principal on the street. This was quite unusual, since we rarely met anyone we knew on holiday.

There are quite a few toll fees to cross the bridge. Rite didn't know exactly where he was going and went on the same bridge nearly four times, paying the toll fee each and every time. Ben and I were laughing so much, but Rite was frustrated. We could not contain ourselves, and he got very upset with us. Later that evening we were still laughing.

We went to visit the Swissair monument at Peggy's Cove. Everyone who died had their names listed. It seemed pretty gruesome to come to such a place, but we were all interested in seeing the area. This was where a plane had crashed from JFK airport en route to Geneva, Switzerland in 1998, and the people felt their homes tremble as the plane crashed into the water a few kilometers away from the Halifax airport. They had smoke on the plane and were cleared to land there. However, the plane crashed in very shallow waters and all 229 people on board died. This crash had a great impact on the local fishermen. They led the search for survivors, and residents welcomed the victims' families to stay with them.

The following day we headed out to Cape Breton. We drove around the Cabot Trail which is 185 miles long. We travelled in a loop. We had stayed in Baddeck and we drove, stopping several times to take pictures and feast on seafood. We visited the Alexander Graham Bell National Historic Site in Baddeck, where the phone was invented. Once we got around the Cabot Trail, we arrived in North Sydney to catch our ferry the following day. We did not get much rest that night. We had to wait in line to catch the ferry, even though we had made reservations months prior to our getting there. There were so many cars. It took about six hours to get to

Port-Aux-Basques and drive to Corner Brook. We were unable to make it to Twillingate because it still was a few hours away. We left early the following morning and when we arrived, we were greeted by Rite's family. We all were ecstatic.

Twillingate is known as iceberg capital of the world. In the town reside approximately 2,500 people who once thrived on the cod fishery. Since 1992, they have not been allowed to catch cod and so the town turned to tourism. Twillingate Island is composed of several communities.

Once we arrived we had to go pick up Rite's brother at the hospital in St. John's. He was getting better but his face was swollen and bruised. He was lucky to be alive.

Every year in the month of June, Rite's supervisor would host a lobster night. We were able to get them flown in from Twillingate. His supervisor would order maybe 40 or more lobsters packed on ice and seaweed. Rite has always cooked every lobster for years. We planned our 10-year anniversary in Twillingate. Those who wanted to come had a great time. Before we got there we went to Cape Spear, which is the easternmost part of North America. It was very foggy, and we walked on many trails.

Everyone wanted to go to the island of St. Pierre Miquelon. This island was owned by France, and you needed a passport to get on the ferry. Everything they did was like being in France. No one spoke English, even though they had a lot of tourists. You had to walk wherever you were going. It was an extremely hilly and steep walk with our luggage. There was one taxi available in town. It was now also a tourist town with a few restaurants and mostly Bed and Breakfasts. You had to make reservations for your meals, otherwise you couldn't eat. They would serve one table per meal and it didn't matter if you ate fast; they did not replace you with anyone else after. We bought everything in euros, and in the afternoon all shops and restaurants were closed while everyone had their siesta.

They had the most unique cemetery I had ever seen. Everyone was buried above ground and there were hundreds of headstones. On each and every one, flowers were placed upon them, even if the person had died years ago. We had gone on a weekend that they were celebrating the opening of the fishing season. They had a parade and a mass for the fishermen. The prayers were for those fishermen at sea and their safety. This was quite unique.

Once we got to Rite's home, we found out that his family had made sleeping arrangements for everyone. Some people were scattered but everything was close to us. The family had also arranged a party for us to celebrate the lobster catch. On the night of the party we all drank and ate many lobsters. We could not leave because the supervisor's wife had taken everyone's car keys so we wouldn't get stopped for drinking and driving. We had to crash in whatever spot was available. The lobster parties still continue, and we will have another reunion there in a few more years.

Chapter 15

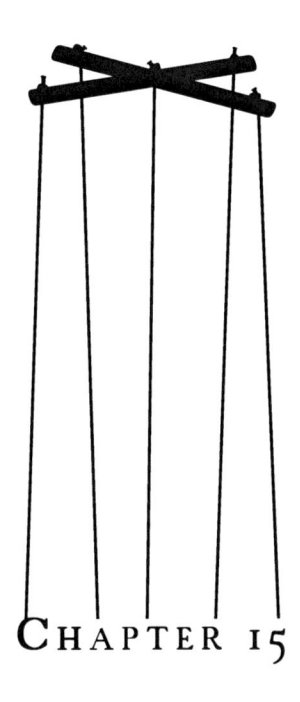

After we returned from our trip, we got back to our routine. Although we had been running for a while, we really started to run marathons. I was a runner in my teenage years but never thought I would end up doing well enough to qualify for the Boston Marathon. As I got older and the children were older, I tried running one kilometre nonstop. It was easy, and I built on that. I wasn't running for speed, but for the endurance aspect of it. Within one week, I had already started running a half marathon through training. It was so rewarding; you had to either love it or hate it. Well, in my case I became obsessed with something healthy, and it was very good for me mentally. I was actually able to get out of the house to train every day. Some days, I would get up extremely early to get my run in first thing in the morning. I would get home and cycle for two hours as fast as I was able to. I wanted to build muscles in my legs in order to run faster. After all of this I would do three hundred different sit ups.

I was in great shape and I felt healthy. I finally got thin enough to wear a size zero. I had never weighed this little in my whole life. I even had abs.

The secret to successful marathon training and half-marathon training lies in staying supremely motivated, training smart and safe, and maintaining proper nutrition. When you learn what is driving you, then you can use that to push yourself through willpower and determination. You will build the foundation that will get your subconscious mind working for you, not against you. In short, you are in for an incredible experience. If you want to experience something, run a marathon.

Running is something you will like or not. Every individual is different from one another. Training can be hard but is worth it when you see the finish line. Believe in yourself. Once you learn the right way how to train for a marathon or half-marathon, you will begin to believe, and then you will realize your goal.

Whether you are training for a marathon or half-marathon, it takes determination and willpower to get you through training on the big day. You have to let your mind lead the way and not your body. Never let the body tell the mind what to do. The body will always give up. It is always tired, morning, noon, and night. However, the body is never tired if the mind is not tired.

Rite and I spent much time training every day. Sunday was the day we would do our long runs. They ranged from fifteen to twenty miles. It was good preparation for the Manitoba Marathon. Finishing the marathon was all I wanted, and we didn't care how long it would take us. At that time, we ran together as a couple. Later, as we started to be more competitive, we ran for speed. This was more of a challenge. Ben came in first in many runs, and I was always so proud of him. He has hundreds of medals that are very big in size and unique. When Rite and I started running, Ben had already reached a level not too many people could compete with.

Ben had also started to work in a running store and was selling their merchandise. He also taught beginner runners how to train to finish a 10 km run, 1/2 marathon, and a full marathon. He would hold classes twice a week while attending university. Sundays were everyone's long run days, starting at 8:30 a.m. Here people ran at their own speed but for longer periods to increase their stamina. Some would enter races to boost their self-esteem by just trying to get their personal best. It gave them a sense of pride when they had completed it. Ben was sponsored several times, but now he is sponsored by New Balance.

On his way to work one day as he was turning into the parking lot, his car caught on fire. He was able to get out and grab all his university things. The firemen showed up shortly afterwards, but his car was completely in flames and was totalled. The fire had started from the engine. This happened at a very busy intersection in rush hour. It was on the news because the intersection had so much smoke and the police were preventing people from driving in that area. Now, Ben needed more money to buy another car, along with paying for his university. His willpower got him through everything. He was a hard worker and succeeded whenever he put his mind to it.

Ben introduced Rite and me to running the Timex Series. This was Canada's only national road race series. The Timex Series encompasses 9 series in most provinces across the country. It was developed by Timex in 1989, in conjunction with the branch associations of Athletics Canada. The TNRRS has over 110 races with an excess of 150,000 participants. The TNRRS gets more participants yearly. There are many more people who train for running now than in the past. It also gives many the opportunity to be competitive. This series was different from anything I had ever run. There were 5Ks,10Ks,15Ks, half marathons, and ten mile runs from Winnipeg Beach to Gimli. There were harder and hillier runs in Brandon, and even a 10K run in Grand Beach in the sand. The races were usually on Sundays and even though I had Obsessive-Compulsive Disorder, I still seemed to fit it into my schedule. Once home, I would have to complete my two hours of cycling and three hundred sit-ups. Only then could I continue my day with all the work involved. Running was extremely good for my mind. I still would have to do everything but it seemed to make me work faster. I was competitive with certain women in my age group. We all wanted to be first and this was a challenge. No one knew who would be first, second, or third. Each medal seemed extremely important because not everyone could reach the level of medalling. I truly loved to run and feel like I have lost a big piece of my life since I have been unable to do so.

Every fall, the officials would add up your points to see where you placed, and I ended up receiving three awards in three consecutive years--little trophies with my name engraved on it and the place I had finished that year. Award night was exciting and we were all invited to eat pizza. I couldn't believe that I was running competitively and winning awards.

I was thrilled. Running had turned my life around and given me self-esteem, and somehow got through my OCD at the same time. It was not to say I was getting much sleep, but I was able to function with both.

Ben got Sally into running also. She had a very good speed and was extremely flexible in every way. She didn't run very much for a few years because she had three children. She has just started running again but is very busy with her children. She also went to dancing lessons as a child and never gave it up. She still takes classes but now teaches ballet, tap, and jazz. She is an awesome dancer and so elegant. She was even doing ballet at eight months pregnant, in a recital. Unbelievable! She takes her oldest child with her on Saturdays as he is also into dance, together with Mandy's eldest daughter. In her first two pregnancies Sally had boys and in her third, a girl. I am quite sure Ben and Sally's daughter will be joining dance, and she already wears all different colours of tutus. She is under one year old, but she has a headband and sparkly shoes matching her clothes every day. She smiles all the time and is so adorable. Sally is a great mother that pays very much attention to her children, and to Ben. They are the perfect little family. It is so nice to see this in this day and age. Once her youngest child is in school she will go back to teaching once again.

Chapter 16

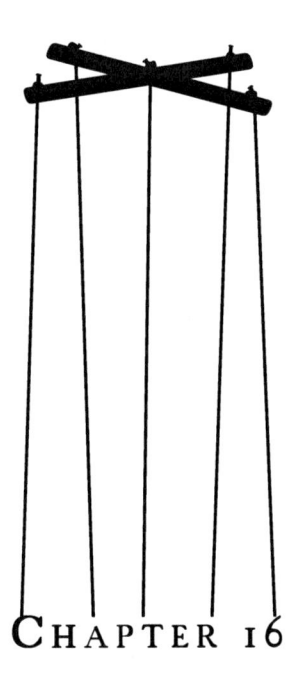

One spring, at the time when our running series were to begin, my father was shoveling snow off the roof of his house when he accidently fell and landed on concrete patio blocks. He was able to get up and my mother called for an ambulance. The paramedics let my father walk to the ambulance and when they got him to emergency, the triage nurses sat him in a wheelchair to wait like others. He became extremely pale and was sweating profusely. At the time, he had already been diagnosed with cancer. The oncologist had given him five years to live, because he had been diagnosed with multiple myeloma. He was getting very agitated in the wheelchair. My mother informed the nurses, probably in a very abrupt rude way, but they ignored her because of her attitude. She was told to sit down and wait like the others.

By that time, all the family had showed up at emergency and we all knew that my father never complained about pain, but we could see it in his face. My older siblings went to talk to the nurses and he was immediately seen by a doctor. He was then put in intensive care for three weeks because he had sustained so many injuries. The doctors couldn't tell us if my father would live or die and we were all seriously affected by it. He had a collapsed lung and they needed to put a chest tube in. Even though he never complained, I do remember him telling us that it was painful when they inserted the tube. Nothing this serious had happened to our family before, and we stayed there in the family room for weeks.

We could only see my father one at a time. His shoulder had been crushed, but the doctors could not perform surgery on it because it was too badly damaged. He had a fever that spiked very high for three weeks and this was very dangerous. Eventually, he got better and was put on the ward with the other patients. He would say the silliest things when he was given morphine. He hallucinated about the craziest things and was very paranoid that the doctors were all under cover and using him as an experiment. No matter what we told him, he was convinced that this was going on.

After several weeks in the hospital my father was discharged. We were very happy to see him back, but my mother put him to work immediately. If he was cleared by the hospital, then in her own sick mind she thought he was able to do housework. He was off from work and she used him to her advantage. He was not going to be sitting and recovering, but helping her out instead. She never showed any sympathy and was a very cold and uncaring individual. She showed no compassion. At each and every one of her siblings' deaths I never saw her shed a tear. She was emotionless.

A short time later, my father had a heart attack and needed surgery. The doctors were waiting for a bed at Health Science Centre but he was to stay at the St. Boniface Hospital in the meantime. They did not want him to stay at home because they were monitoring him. My father was always the caregiver and if he saw a patient that needed anything he was always there to help. This was his demeanor. He prayed all day and night. He was a special person to everyone. One time in the hospital when we went to visit him, he was struggling with a wheelchair because a person wanted to use the phone booth. There was my dad helping her up and opening the door for her to sit down. He then put on the brakes on her wheelchair. He was helpful like this to everyone throughout his entire life.

One particular day in the middle of the week, we were in a rush to see my father at St. Boniface Hospital. We were running late because I had so much to do that day. I had injuries to my knees. Doctors had accidently discovered a bone cyst in my knee and were very honest with me by telling me it could be cancer. I had a couple of bone scans and it was not cancerous and I continued running.

Of course, on that particular day, I had seen my family doctor and was told to stop running for a few months in order to let my knees heal. I did not listen and instead asked Rite to pace me faster that night because I was indeed going to train through the winter, as usual.

I had some kind of internal resource when there was a stressful situation. Running was all part of it. After a very stressful day there was nothing better to get rid of my anxieties than to go for a run. I was focused and felt in charge of my mental and physical state, and it was giving me more energy. I thought of nothing else except my speed, my health, and the smell of freshly cut lawns or the sounds of the birds chirping. In the winter, there were not very many people out in the mornings when it was -40 degrees. I could hear myself breathing, and the sound of crunchy snow from each footstep. The fogginess of the cold made the trees so beautifully white and I would appreciate being outside in this cold weather and still feel warm. I had made many friends as we would run by each other and it gave me satisfaction about my fitness and health. I indeed wanted to get my speed faster and worked at it by doing intervals, running up the garbage hill, and also by cycling and doing other exercise. I was hooked, but it was a good feeling. I loved running in the winter. It was so peaceful and I was living in the moment.

On this particular day, September 30th, 2002 at around 7:50 p.m., it was getting darker outside because of the season. I was following Rite and going through a green light through St Mary's and Novavista Drive when I turned my head to the left and saw a car turning, and realized he didn't see me. In my head, I was thinking, "He is going to hit me." Before I was able to think those last few words the car came at me and hit me on the left side of my body and head. The impact was so intense that it flipped me over his windshield so that I broke it and then I rolled off unconscious in the front of his car to the street. As I landed unconscious, I hit my head and it began bleeding. I lay in the middle of the road and Rite thought that the man that hit me was going to leave. Rite stopped him. Once I was conscious again, my husband came running to me and he was holding my head up because it was bleeding profusely. The first things I checked were my legs because I didn't want them to be hurt because of my running. I could not get up and felt like I had broken my arm. The firemen came first, and then the paramedics and the police. Rite used someone's cell phone and called Ben. Ben appeared within seconds and called Sally at work to come home. I don't recall seeing Myla with her boyfriend nor Mandy and Keith. The paramedics put me on a backboard and put me in the ambulance. They started an IV going in my hand. I felt something different with my breathing and I was coughing. Once I got to the Victoria Hospital my family was surrounding me. Mandy was crying.

I then went for x-rays, which were excruciating, and they told me I had a fractured scapula, four fractured ribs, and a collapsed lung. My father was informed at the hospital he was in and started having chest pains. They had to give him something to stop the pain.

I definitely knew that getting a chest tube would be painful because my father had already said so. I knew they would freeze the skin, make an incision, and then ram that chest tube into my lung. This hurt very much. They put my arm in a sling and stitched my head, but there was nothing they could do with the fractured ribs and scapula. They were to heal on their own. All my running clothes were cut off and I was disappointed about losing my shirt. I had gotten it from a race and I always ran with it. I could not sleep because of the pain and position I was in.

Rite finally left in the middle of the night and discovered that he had a parking ticket where Ben had parked our car. I stayed in Emergency for at least 24 hours. They finally let me go pee in a bedpan, which was impossible for me to do. They then put a catheter in and I felt relieved. They hadn't emptied my bladder for twenty-four hours. They gave me morphine as a painkiller. They put a morphine patch on my scapula. I eventually got a room with another lady. I lay there sleeping as Rite sat by me with Myla. Later, Pierre and Monique showed up for the second time. The mother of the patient in the other bed thought I had too many visitors and said so verbally to Monique. She then started arguing with her and threatened to hit Monique. They were making such a commotion I began to cry. I was being disturbed and I only wanted peace and quiet because of the pain I was in. The nurses came in and told the woman that she was being very inappropriate and moved me to a private room. My family was then able to visit whenever they wanted. All of my children showed up every day with their partners.

Each morning, Myla's ex-boyfriend Jeff would come to see me. He had lived with us for three years and Myla had broken up with him just one month prior to my accident. I remember him crying and my heart was broken because I knew he still wanted to be with Myla. He was from Vietnam and I loved him so much. He was a very sweet young boy that was sent to Canada by his mother when he was fourteen. Just recently, he told Myla that he would like to meet up with us again. I was thrilled but we haven't connected yet. I'm sure we will soon.

I would go for x-rays every day with an oxygen tank. They were checking to see if my lung was getting better. At one point, they clamped the oxygen. They were checking to see if I could breathe on my own. I wasn't getting enough oxygen and they needed to unclamp it again until I got better. I had a student nurse looking after me for a week and then a young paramedic who was so eager to help. I remember my vestibular disorder started to bother me and I knew I was going to throw up. The paramedic jumped over my bed to get a large stainless steel bowl for me. Vomiting was excruciating since my insides were not healed yet. I wanted to be taken off all medication because I thought this was causing me to throw up. I was taken off and refused all pain medication completely. I wouldn't even take Tylenol 3s; absolutely no painkillers from that day on. I would rather suffer with pain than with my vestibular disorder.

In the hospital the physiotherapist that would come to see me wasn't very nice. She was rough and rude. She kept on complaining about all the flowers in my room. This was not my fault and I felt she had no right to say anything about it. Certainly, other patients had received that many flowers before. Once I was able to breathe on my own, the specialist came to take the breathing tube out. I asked him if I could see it, and looked at it in disbelief. It looked like a large hook. I'm not surprised it hurt when they put it in.

I was still not able to walk on my own because of my vestibular disorder. The hospital staff kept on trying to get me to walk as I tried to keep my eyes opened. I was way too dizzy and shaky to do this by myself. Through the day they at times had me sitting up for a while. The young paramedic would be running everywhere in order to help me. He was definitely going to be good in his career. He would place water and my phone next to me without me ever asking.

We had tickets to go see Great Big Sea and I missed the concert. Myla and her friend had it announced on the radio, describing what happened to me, and were hoping the musicians would have come to see me. Myla and Rite needed to wash my hair while I lay in the bed. It was quite funny. They said that the water was bright red from the blood and lathered shampoo into my hair. Rite would never have graduated as a hairstylist because he was dropping shampoo all over my face. Suddenly my face got covered with a towel and I was laughing at how awful he was washing my hair. Myla stepped in and took over and did a pretty good job. My hair was clean now, and she combed it into a ponytail. I felt cleaner. Every day I would get a sponge bath, but the young paramedic insisted I sit on a commode and he would shower me. I told him Myla was coming to give me a shower. There was no way I was going to be showered by someone that looked the same age as my son.

Finally, Myla showed up and gave me a shower. It felt so good and refreshing. It could never have felt this good with the paramedic. She also fed me because I was unable to move very well. She seemed to really care about me and came every day to help me. Rite had a hard time sleeping at night through this time. He actually slept with my ponytail holder, which was covered in blood. He was devastated by what had happened. Mandy did not sleep in her bed for four months. I'm not sure why! She was extremely sad to see her dad sleeping with my ponytail holder. She was also sad that I was in the hospital.

After a couple of weeks I had my first bowel movement. The toilet was filled with blood and I knew I was to keep it but flushed it anyways. I waited until I had a female nurse that evening to tell her. My trauma doctor came to see me the following day with three other people. I was so embarrassed. He did not want to do additional tests because I had gone through enough trauma. He told me keep my bowel movement the next time I would go. I went again, but flushed it anyway. This was way above my comfort zone.

The day after the accident we had decided that Mandy would look after my daycare until I got better. I did not want to shut down my daycare and everything went smoothly, just like always. Mandy had done everything that I did prior to this because she loved taking care of the children. She as always was so very kind and treated them very well. She would play with them and would make sure they shared. The parents were also happy with the arrangement. All they cared about was not having to change daycares. Mandy took time out of hair school until I was better. She did this for four months but was paid very well for her services. She then returned to school to become a hairstylist.

She was very good with hair and could give you the best head massages of everyone I had ever encountered. She worked for a few high-end salons and had that personal touch with everyone. She smiled and did as they asked, and Rite and I were very proud of her. Her clients loved her and treated her very well. Eventually, when she was pregnant for her first baby, she decided that Keith would build her a salon in their own home. Keith was very talented and could build and design anything he wanted. He made sure that Mandy would have a beautiful salon with all the accessories, and more. Her salon is beautiful and most of her clients followed her. I could understand why they would because of her wonderful personality.

On the first night I got home after my accident, I was absolutely uncomfortable in bed. No matter which way I positioned myself, I could not get comfortable. I could not sleep, probably because my bed could not be raised up and in the hospital I had slept with seven pillows. I sat in the chair in the living room with Mandy sleeping on the couch. We talked for four hours. She was devastated by the accident. We talked about what happened in detail and she was very sad and upset. She didn't like the idea of Rite sleeping with my hair elastic, which was a scrunchy, now covered in blood from the accident. He had felt guilty for running ahead of me. This made Mandy very sad. She was also saddened by the way I looked. My body was bruised from my head down to my knees. I wasn't able to lift my arm and could not do anything for myself. Whenever I needed my hair combed or washed, Myla or Mandy had to do so. It took months before I could raise my arm high enough to do it myself.

While I was in hospital, Ben had to go to Victoria, British Columbia with his doctor friend to compete in a race. They came to see me early in the morning and when he got back he told me that he had done his personal best for me. Before the run he had said, "This one is for my mom." When he returned he whispered in my ear that he had bought an $8000.00 engagement ring for Sally. I was so touched by this that I cried. I loved my future daughter-in-law more than anyone could ever imagine. It was to be a surprise. He never told us the day he was going to get engaged but I suspected on the night that it happened. He had a room booked at the Fairmont, on the top floors. The staff attended to all of his needs. On the upper floors the couple had appetizers before dinner with a drink. Then he and Sally went out for dinner while the staff got into action. When they returned she walked into a room of many, many candles lit and a scroll for her to read. The last thing it said was, "Will you marry me?" and Ben was down on his knee. It sounded so romantic and the staff listened by the door and eventually asked if she had said yes. She called me immediately and told us and we were so very happy.

Her parents were in denial. They thought that when we would get back from Newfoundland that Ben and Sally would have had enough time with each other. They actually thought their relationship would come to an end. For some reason they didn't like Ben. He was devastated by this. He was in university becoming a chartered accountant and Sally was becoming a teacher.

Ben was an extremely quiet individual and very polite. We have never known the reasons why Sally's father and mother hated him so much. They wanted her to go to the lake with them and she refused because she wanted to be with Ben. The father immediately got upset and told her to leave and threw everything outside on the front step. She had asked him to keep her pictures on the walls and she would come and pick them up at a later date, but he tore them all off. She then went to her aunt's house for a couple of days but had no other place to live. It was at this point, Rite and I had about fifteen minutes to decide if she could reside with us. Seeing both of them broken-hearted, we decided to let her live with us. There was only one stipulation. This was that they gave me three hours every week to dust and vacuum their bedroom.

Through all this chaos with having two extra people living with us, I still had to go to physiotherapy and to see my orthopedic surgeon. I was also getting help from my husband's chiropractor. On my first visit he wanted x-rays of my entire back. I was to go to some other place in Winnipeg. He had a very young guy direct me there. I just followed him. While waiting this young boy told me that he had a deal with Dr. Lucas. He said he supplied the doctor with weed in exchange for free services. He was also into cocaine, which explained his strange behavior. On my second visit, I went with Rite. The doctor would put some kind of electrode on my scapula. He kept telling me I was beautiful. I was feeling quite uncomfortable with him. He would leave the room, telling Rite the same thing. One time, he asked me to work for him for $12.00 an hour. I told him that I made much more than that running my daycare. He then said that Rite was a lucky man because he had a good wife to have sex with and I was able to support him financially. He then took the electrode off and snapped my bra. I was in shock and never did go see him again. I should have filed a complaint against him but was so deep in pain at the time, I just let it go.

At this time, my father had his open heart surgery. There were complications and the doctors needed to operate on him again for a further eight hours. Each time was getting more critical and we were afraid he would die. Once again, the medication was making him hallucinate and he was telling Emile and me things that the hospital staff members were doing. He was convinced he had to sleep in a chair through the night in the staircase. Emile was facing him directly and couldn't keep himself from laughing. I was also laughing but I was on the side of the bed where my father couldn't see me. Tears ran down Emile's face and my father got really angry at him. I guess he didn't respond to well to pain killers.

Meanwhile, life at home was stressful, especially since we had decided to keep Sally for the three years she lived with us. I ended up getting better physically but was still very uncomfortable with all the strange things I would be cleaning. It was exhausting. Myla's old boyfriend did not seem to bother me. Everybody moved in at our expense. Sally was kicked out of her parents' home at the end of November and was worried about her tuition for university in January. The parents made it very clear that they weren't going to be paying for it. I didn't want her to stop in the middle of her education, but to continue and finish it. She gathered enough money to pay tuition, and had a job at a teacher's store right next to our home. She did very well for herself. All of her living arrangements were free. I would make supper, wash her clothes and buy more food for everyone. I truly loved her from the bottom of my heart. Myla's next boyfriend moved in and eventually, Mandy's boyfriend also moved in half time. It was a fifty-fifty stay between his house and ours. All my suppers were labelled with each person's name on top of the food in the plate that was wrapped in Saran Wrap. I would do this because some liked vegetables and no meat.

Others would prefer mostly meat and so on. I was catering to their every need. Everyone worked different hours and they would come home to warm up their suppers and put the used dishes in the dishwasher. I would then wash the dishes before bedtime.

All there laundry was done by me and I hung it up in their closets. I would buy them special things every week. Ben would get at least fifteen Gatorades a week. Everyone got what they specifically liked. I would ask them individually and they would put in their requests as Rite and I would go grocery shopping at times when it was -40 degrees below. The two of us would bring all the groceries in and no one else helped. Rite was getting angrier and angrier by the week. He couldn't believe no one would get up off the couch to help. It was only common courtesy. However, I considered this my fault because I didn't want them to turn out like me.

At Christmas, for gifts in their stockings, I would spend approximately the same amount of money for everyone. At least $200.00 went into each one and then there were presents. They were most definitely spoiled.

As I was recovering from my accident, I began to feel extremely depressed. I had heard about a twenty-one-year-old boy whose girlfriend had broken up with him a year prior to the accident. He had toured France on his bicycle and was put on anti-depressants. One Sunday between St. Mary's and Pembina Highway he jumped in front of a semi. This is when I realized I needed help. At the time, I was going for light therapy at the Victoria Hospital, near where the incident had happened. On Monday, Tuesday, Wednesday, and Thursday, I could see where he had died because of the blood on the highway. On Friday, it was raining and the blood was washed away. Some people in my daycare knew his family and told me about him. This was an eye-opener for me to go see someone about my problems. I felt like I had changed, and decided that mental illness was nothing to be ashamed of.

I had been told by my family doctor about speaking to a psychotherapist. I ended up going see her. This was the second attempt at talking about my OCD. She listened and put me on Paxil. On the package, it was labelled that the drug helps OCD. I finally thought I had found a cure for it. Little did I know that there was not one specific way to get help. I didn't tell the doctor much about myself but I gave her hints of some important issues that needed to be talked about. One was that I couldn't understand why

I suddenly hated and despised my mother and that Pierre should have been convicted of sexual assault. This is all I said to her but couldn't tell her what happened to me. I started seeing her in April 2003 and never told Rite about it because he would have thought I was seeing her because of our marriage. There was nothing wrong with it, but I knew this would be what he would be thinking. This was not the case; I was just simply depressed all of the time and I couldn't control it. Myla and Mandy would look after my daycare as I went to my appointments. Rite knew nothing.

Dr. Lea Morris was one of the kindest woman doctors I had ever seen. She was a medical doctor that worked in psychotherapy. She explained to me about the trauma of my car accident, in detail. She explained that the trauma from this event had caused me to feel shameful, helpless, and powerless. This traumatic experience completely overwhelmed me. She put it very in very straightforward terms that a traumatic event of this sort was beyond my control. She told me that I more than likely had survived sexual abuse and physical abuse along with neglect. She then explained to me that such a traumatic event could cause normal people to block the experience from their memory or try to avoid being reminded of the trauma they experienced as children. I had simply blocked it out of my memory and avoided any reminders. This was how I survived. My lack of processing the trauma meant that it was present within me for years and that I didn't feel the event for all of that time. My body had a way of coping with very difficult emotions that I had not dealt with and later impacted my life.

I knew I needed to feel whole again. The trauma had changed me and I was worried I would never feel normal again, and grounded. I couldn't seem to find my way to feeling whole. The impact of these traumatic events in my childhood delayed memories from my consciousness. This is how I survived. I needed counselling and to talk about it in the open. One of the most important steps I learned only later in life was to trust someone and be comfortable with them in order to heal.

By the end of August, I had gone to see the psychotherapist again but things didn't turn out as I planned. Right before I left, she asked me if I would be ok. I had a delay in my thinking and paused for a second before I said, "Yes." My agreement with her did not sound positive enough. She would not let me leave the office because she wanted me to be assessed by a psychiatrist at the Grace Hospital in the emergency department. I told her I would be all right, but she did not believe me. She would not let me leave. All her appointments were cancelled because of me for the rest of the day. I pleaded and I remember crying because I did not want Rite to find out. He would have thought I was in the process of leaving him and this would cause many problems. She called Mandy and told her what was going on. Mandy was upset so Dr. Lea Morris gave her cell number, home phone number, and office number. She was a wonderful and caring doctor. She finally got a hold of Rite and she told him the news. He was in such disbelief he fell onto the couch as she talked to him. Now everyone knew what was going on and I was extremely worried.

Within a few minutes Rite showed up and came in and kissed me and told me that he loved me. I was quite surprised. The police showed up and asked me if I would run away, because the doctor had informed them that I was a fast runner at the time. This was said jokingly. They let me go with Rite and met us at the hospital. I was then put in a family room with Rite to wait for a psychiatrist. It became very hard to explain to Rite what was going on. Dr. Leech, the psychiatrist on call, told Rite to leave the room so she could speak to me alone. She wanted to know why I was there and what I wanted. I was unable to express myself because I had so much to talk about and I had no idea where to begin. She was a very serious doctor who did not smile. I hadn't come here willingly so I could not tell her why I was there, and told her I did not want anything. I was wasting her time and she gave me a very harsh look of superiority. She was cold and unfriendly, and I felt extremely intimidated by her. I ended up telling her that I was not suicidal and did not say anything else to her. This was my saving grace so I could be discharged and return home.

I think a bartender would have given me better advice than that doctor. I had so much to talk about with Rite and the family that I wanted out of the hospital. She let me leave, not knowing anything about me. Now I had to deal with Rite and try to explain to him why I was seeing a psychotherapist. He immediately thought it was because of him. He thought I wanted to end our relationship. This was not the case. I tried to tell him some of the reasons, but he tuned me out and only thought it was because of him. There was no way to convince him or talk to him. We ended up being silent towards each other and I was unable to solve anything.

My LIFE Not Mine to Control

All of this happened on a Wednesday. On Thursday, all hell broke loose. Rite made up a whole bunch of comments and was very angry. He got Mandy to drive him to a liquor store and then a hotel. He never came home. I was feeling devastated and worn out. That evening, I went for groceries because I wasn't sure if I could keep myself safe or not and I wanted to make sure the children had everything they needed before my untimely death. I remember getting the groceries and stopping to park and think about what was going on. I stayed there for at least an hour, just thinking about my life and what had become of it.

I got home and Ben, Sally, and Mandy were there. Mandy told me that Rite was in a hotel and I was somewhat relieved. I unpacked the groceries as all three of them sat around the table talking about Rite not being there to support me. Mandy eventually went to bed, and I stayed up till 2:00 a.m. with Ben and Sally. Ben seemed to have many issues about Rite. He indeed was quite angry at him. Rite worked a lot for the family and never seemed to have time for his children, although he thought he was doing the best for them.

Ben and Sally both went to bed and I decided to clean my fridge. When I had everything emptied from inside of it, it looked like a shell. I cleaned and washed everything without touching anything with my bare hands. Myla walked in at 3:00 a.m. and was wondering why I was up at this time cleaning my fridge. We both went to bed until I had to get up for the children in my daycare. It was not going to be a busy day. Life itself became more arduous and grueling than running a marathon. I was unable to concentrate and follow all of my OCD rituals because I was so confused and upset. Around lunch time, I threw all my pills on the bed and counted them. Little did I know then that this would never be enough to kill myself.

I called Dr. Lea Morris and told her how I was feeling. She wanted me to go to Emergency and had already called them. She asked to speak to Ben, and he was talking about his issues for a very long time, including mine. Rite worked very much and Ben didn't like it. He explained how I was a prisoner in my home for the last 23 years because of my OCD. Dr. Morris could barely hang up on him because he was so emotional. Ben called Rite to tell him I was going to the hospital. Rite came home to drive me there and begged me not to go. I was too distraught to listen to him. I saw the psychiatrist and was admitted immediately. Rite was very upset as

I was being wheeled to psychiatry. I was extremely scared when I saw the doors had "PSYCHIATRY" written in bold. I stayed in my room with Rite as I watched one person rocking himself outside. I was scared and regretted ever have been admitted. Rite had to leave while the staff filled out forms with me. They eventually gave me a tour around to show me where everything was. I was scared and did not leave my room. I only wished I could go back home. This was not the place I wanted to be.

Eventually, my psychiatrist, Dr. Leech, came to talk to me. I felt extremely uncomfortable with her because of her demeanor of superiority. I felt she was looking down at me because she was the doctor and I was a patient. She was in charge and she was telling me what was wrong. I mentioned my children and she clung to this, blaming everything on them. These were not my troubles and I did not trust her. I was unable to tell her the deep dark secrets of my past. This hospitalization was only for three weeks. I made a couple of friends while being in there. One girl was a cutter who self-harmed and would show what she had done to herself. I couldn't believe someone would do that. The other was a lady approximately my age, whose name was Martha. We exchanged phone numbers and later became friends for a while. The oddest thing I had ever heard was about a girl who swallowed cutlery. I was in disbelief and knew I was in a really sick place. While four of us were sitting down for breakfast, I jokingly said that we should bring her a tray of cutlery for breakfast. We all laughed and then she approached us to see why we were laughing. She wanted to sit with us. She seemed to take a liking to me and told me the dreadful details of her life.

I had to see Dr. Leech a couple of weeks after my discharge. We talked for a couple of minutes and that was the end of my treatment. No referrals to my family doctor; no medication or anything. She assumed I was cured.

Chapter 17

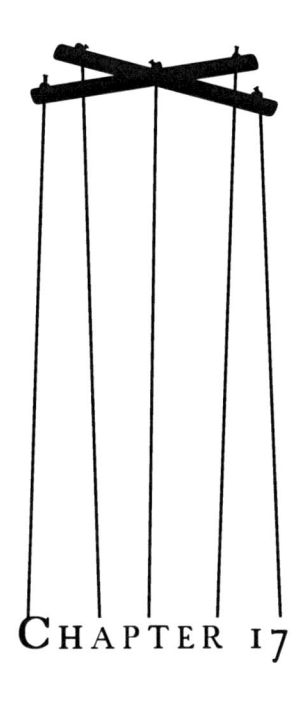

At the hospital, I picked up many pamphlets about mental illness and read them. I understood that depression wasn't just a temporary mood disturbance or a sign of personal weakness. Many people like me feel ashamed or afraid to seek help. I always made light of my symptoms, which led me to suffer in silence. It is always important to remember that depression isn't a character defect or something that you have brought on yourself.

As I read these pamphlets, I recalled reading that one in ten people in Canada have experienced an episode of major depression. Unfortunately, people like me avoided seeking treatment; I was worried about what others would think of me. I felt isolated and alone. My one personal piece of advice is to seek help before your condition worsens. There are many people in the world that suffer in silence.

In my view, it is very important to discuss your symptoms with your doctor. When I did that, it made me feel better, and the doctor also referred me to a psychotherapist who was absolutely wonderful. She sat and listened to what I needed to say, although I wasn't very trusting for many years. I felt sad every day and lost interest in my favorite activities. I also felt worthless, guilty, ashamed, and could not concentrate. I had thoughts of suicide but never thought I would have attempted it. My symptoms seemed to have started after a traumatic event and this caused me to begin to recall my past.

Through the many years that I had Mental Illness I always knew that is was a chemical imbalance. I knew very little about serotonin and dopamine but knew that this was the problem with me. I had researched everything I could about mental illnesses and depression. I certainly fit the criteria.

Martha, the woman I met in the psychiatric ward, turned out to be a very strange lady. Once we were both discharged she had started calling me every single day. It was later after the children were gone and Rite was working overtime. I would do my cycling every day. I used an X-Acto knife to cut myself. This was a very bad behavior right from the start. I feel like I needed to punish myself in order to feel good. I did this for several weeks and I was beginning to feel out of control in mind and body. I would tell Martha that I was cutting as I was talking to her. She tried to discourage me but I could say the same thing about her wanting to commit suicide. She had a stockpile of pills.

I remember Rite calling me several weeks after I started to cut myself, and I could tell he was quite appalled about it over the phone. He called the Mobile Crisis Unit and explained to them what was going on. They finally reached me and wanted to come over. I told them I would meet them at the end of the day. I got into their van and was put into Emergency once again. I had cut myself all over both my arms. The next day Dr. Sean Stevens was on call. I told him that I was unable to speak to Dr. Leech and I needed to be very careful about what I would say to her. She was very opinionated and cold. She was a very hard person to talk to. I wasn't about to tell anybody anything if I didn't trust them. I asked him if he could be my doctor because I felt more comfortable with him. He told me that they do not do "doctor hopping", but I could ask her. Instead of speaking to her face to face, I wrote her a letter asking to be transferred. She came back to see me to tell me that Dr. Stevens would take over. I was shocked and relieved. She wanted to know why I wanted to change and I told her the truth. She has never looked at me in the eye since. I have never wanted to deal with her again.

When I got admitted into the hospital, I was able to see Dr. Stevens every day. He was trying to get me to talk but I was still afraid. I feared he would not believe me and I had deep trust issues. I was extremely quiet, filled with so many secrets that had never been told throughout my entire life. I believed that if I told anyone they would just turn around and think I was crazy. Through life, no one cared in my family, so why would a doctor even care for a second? They would just laugh at me and ignore everything I said. Some of my communication was done by writing to him because I felt such shame. I would write very minimally so as not to be made fun of. He seemed like a nice doctor, but was he really?

On my weekends off, I was sent home from the hospital and now it was nearing Christmas. Martha had come over and my children found her to be a very strange lady. They tried their best to like her and be sympathetic but she would do things that were very appalling to them. I would go over to see her on some days. She was very strange. I didn't have any other friends because I had secluded myself from the world for twenty-three years. I needed a friend.

We talked about my loss of my daycare and the amount of money I had been making. I was able to buy $600.00 worth of groceries with my money. I was able to save and buy things. Everything drastically stopped the moment I was admitted to hospital. Rite had closed my daycare. I had lost everything and didn't know what we were going to do. Rite and Ben had gone out for a run when Rite asked Ben if he could give us fifty dollars a month. He also wanted Sally and every family member to do so. This definitely was not enough but it would have helped ever so slightly. On a weekend home, Ben told me that they would do it for me, since he was having issues with his dad.

Before I was released from hospital, Ben and Sally both decided to move out on their own into an apartment next to the Grace Hospital. I was extremely hurt by Ben because he never came to see me once through all my hospitalizations in all the years. He lived next to the hospital, but for some reason or another he never came to see me with Sally. Maybe it was the stigma of mental illness. Also, Sally's family started coming around for some reason or another and gave them some furniture and other things to get started. Christmas was slightly different but they came no matter what. I tried to explain to Ben and Sally that more people were realizing that mental illness is not a character flaw, but simply another form of illness that can happen to anyone, even a psychiatrist. I had nothing to be ashamed of.

Martha came up with a great idea for us financially. She thought we could move in with her. I amused her by playing along, but she was dead serious. Her plan was to take our bunk beds into her apartment and she and I would sleep in one room. Rite would be able to sleep in the other room. She had strange thoughts, beyond the fact that I still had children living with us at home. At one point, we were all together at Myla's work and she told Rite that he wasn't going to be around forever. Very creepy! We felt like she was going to poison him.

I still had her over one day around Christmas and she came through the door with bells on her feet and dressed like an elf. Even though my children were already old enough to see something was drastically wrong with her, they were still respectful. She bought presents for everyone. Most of it was used and junky. The one present I recalled the most was a damn-it-doll. On the tag was marked "To Martha from Jane." It was a re-gift, given to Mandy. Mandy thought this was the weirdest present she had ever received and threw it into the garbage. Just as a joke I had tucked it under her pillow that night. I could hear her screaming and we all laughed at this. Since Christmas was so close I decided to take it out one more time and put it in her stocking. We all started laughing and I finally threw it out. No more pranks!

We had a wonderful Christmas with all our children and their significant others. However, I felt like something was drastically wrong with Ben because he stopped calling or seeing us and was pulled to Sally's side of the family. We barely heard from him for nearly ten years. To this day, I don't know why all of this had occurred. I'm not sure how I got through it, but I was extremely sad and deeply hurt. We've never known the truth behind this to this day.

Once Ben moved out, Mandy decided to buy a house with Keith and so we decided to sell our home and buy a condo near the University of Manitoba. We profited by selling our home, and Rite was very sad to be moving, but I felt like I was leaving my prison. We got a two-bedroom condo but thought about how much Myla and her boyfriend at that time would fight. They were way too loud, so we gave her money to move out on her own. She was independent now and loved the idea.

Shortly after, I was hospitalized for overdosing on Tylenol. I also was self-harming in many ways. This was my way of coping with my life and my increasing troubles with Martha, who had started harassing me. It was not that I really wanted to die, but I was just expressing myself. I wanted help and didn't know how to go about it to get it. My husband called Dr. Stevens and told him the strange situation I was in with Martha. Dr. Stevens talked to me and gave me 15 minutes to get rid of her. I was dumbfounded because I didn't know what to say to her. I had never done anything like this before. Dr. Stevens told me what to say and to hang up once I was finished taking to Martha. I did what I was told and hung up on her. Martha never harassed me after that. Not even once.

In hospital, while being admitted, I overdosed on Seroquel. I had brought my bottle of pills from home into the hospital. I don't recall doing this but Rite said that the nurses were all fighting me down. I was absolutely out of control but I have no memory of this. I did not like to be restricted because of my past. I had enough of that growing up and this would freak me out. I didn't like the nurses holding me down. I was told by my psychiatrist not to overdose in the hospital again or I would be discharged.

I was still in a major depression with many secrets I did not divulge. I was so afraid and ashamed, I felt like the worst human being on earth. I didn't want to share everything that had happened to me for fear of being made fun of, not being believed, or having people thinking what a horrible person I was and that everything was my fault. At this point, Dr. Stevens asked me what I thought about electroconvulsive therapy treatment. I knew nothing about it and he explained to me exactly what the procedure was all about. My psychiatrist explained to me that Electroconvulsive therapy is a procedure in which currents are passed through the brain, intentionally triggering a brief seizure. ECT seemed to cause changes in brain chemistry that can quickly reverse symptoms of certain mental illnesses. It was used when other treatments were not successful. There was much stigma attached to ECT. This stigma was based on early treatments in which high doses of electricity were administered without anesthesia, leading to memory loss, fractured bones, and other serious side effects. ECT is much safer today and is given to people while they're under general anesthesia. Although it still can cause some side effects, it now uses electrical currents given in a controlled setting to achieve the most benefit with the fewest possible risks. Since my medication had failed to ease my symptoms, Dr. Stevens thought this would be a good form of treatment. It was also considered useful my when severe depression posed a threat to me, considering that I was suicidal and had attempted to kill myself a couple of times. At the time, I was in a deep depression, unable to share many of my feelings. He thought it would get me back to the point that I wouldn't be so depressed and I would be able to talk.

Prior to treatment, I was given a muscle relaxant and wheeled to the area of the hospital that ECT was performed. Because the muscles are relaxed, the visible effects of the seizure would be limited to slight movement of the hands and feet. The electrical current passes through the brain, causing a seizure that lasts typically for twenty to ninety seconds. I would wake up five to ten minutes after. Later, I would not remember the treatment or events surrounding it. I was given treatments three times a week for a total of ten treatments. Although they say you will have temporarily memory loss, I experienced some total memory loss surrounding that year. I do not remember my son getting married, a trip south to the United States, and one of the classes I had taken when I became a Mental Health Support Worker. The worst thing of all was that it did not help me in anyway. What a waste, considering I had lost some of my memory forever.

Once discharged, I decided to put on a run for mental health and took on the role of race director for it. Since I had been afflicted with this illness the most, I decided to put on a sanctioned 5K run and 3K walk for the Mental Health Education Resource Centre of Manitoba. I was even going to challenge myself in the run. I had stories about my accident and my injuries advertised in the newspapers and television. I had reporters from both newspapers come over and I had pictures taken, while I spoke about my illness and the stigma that was attached.

At the time, I was hospitalized but still made thousands of calls. I wanted it to be perfect, and Athletics Manitoba helped me out with equipment needed for the race. I was the director and did all the fundraising I could possibly do. I had worked very hard on this project. I was going to do the best I could to raise as much money as I could. We made t-shirts with "Mental Health" and the year written on them. On the back were listed all the sponsors. Since it was a part of a Timex Series, we got three watches to give away. Molly Maid was my biggest sponsor, paying for all the medals. We had medals made for the three top female and male winners, and the top prizes given were monetary. We also had medals for the three top women and men in each five year age category. We were given coffee from Tim Horton's, juice from McDonald's, and huge support in the form of fruits, water, and bagels with butter and peanut butter, all donated from different stores. There was more but I don't remember everything.

Dr. Lea Morris attended the run to explain to people what mental health was all about. She was such a special person in my life and she took the time to do this for me. Once she was done, I handed her flowers and a coupon for brunch for two at the Fort Garry Hotel. It was a success and I was able to donate all the money to the person in charge of the Mental Health Resources Education Centre of Manitoba. They bought books about mental illness to put into their library. They wrote my name in the beginning of each book, stating it had been donated by me. The following year I had Stride Ahead involved while volunteering for the Schizophrenia Society. On that year, it was also a success. However, Ben never showed up.

I volunteered quite a bit at the Schizophrenia Society office and Mood Disorders centre. There came a time when the Executive Director of Eating Disorders committed suicide. Since this was a building for people to come to for help with mental health issues, everyone was surprised. Four days later, the Executive Director of S.P.E.A.K. also committed suicide. She had started this program for parents who had children that committed suicide. It was a support group, but I guess she wasn't able to set herself free from her son's death. The staff immediately called the Mobile Crisis Unit to come because they were worried about me, since this could be a trigger. I had not mentioned anything regarding suicide, but the team came for a visit. They called Dr. Stevens and all he had to say was that I knew what I should do. I was left alone and went to both funerals. The offices were very quiet and grim for a while after that. It was very sad to see their names scratched off the windows of their offices, as if they had never existed.

I would do different things for the Schizophrenia Society every day, such as making calls, getting prizes, making baskets for the silent auction, and getting things ready for the big day. They had several fundraisers, a walk, a Gala Dinner, and a golf tournament. I was in charge of all the fundraising. I also would help to set up and clean up after all the events.

In 2007, I won the Volunteer Award. I was thrilled and shocked that they had picked me. This event was on the day they had their Gala Night Dinner and the dinners were $150.00 a plate. I also received, in 2006, the Mental Health Heroes Award. The Minister of Health was present and the Governor-General gave us each our awards. This was because I stood as an inspiration and source of hope to those who had suffered a mental illness and continued to deal with it.

On the night of the Gala Dinner there was a silent auction and a live auction. Rite bid in a live auction for a trip for four to go to Churchill, including accommodations, train fares, and four tickets for the Tundra Buggy to see the polar bears. We took Myla and Bill with us. We went in the month of November on our anniversary. We mixed drinks and alcohol in bottles to drink on the train. It was a two-day excursion on the train, where our meals were also paid for. We all enjoyed being on the train because it was everyone's first time. The train broke down and we sat on the tracks for eight hours. Everyone on the train gathered around us and others drank everything they were selling at the bar. We were all drunk. Myla had bought us a big bottle of champagne for our anniversary. Now that it was past midnight, she decided to sneak in the back of the train and went and got it from where our luggage was stored. We all shared it and we didn't even mind being stuck on the tracks because we were having so much fun.

Myla and Bill were having the time of their lives. Myla had two little girls at that time and was worried she would miss them. She missed them, but she was relaxing and enjoying herself for the first time in a few years. She always was the child that needed the most attention. She sought it in every way. She was very kind, generous, and giving. She would get mad easily but forgave very fast. I was so excited to be away with my daughter and son-in-law. This was great and these were times I appreciated the most. Myla would get excited to go anywhere. It could be just a sleepover, but she always had fun. The train conductors finally announced that we were going to get off the tracks and be brought by taxi to a hotel in Thompson. We all got to shower and sleep in a bed for the night instead of spending it on the train. That evening, most of us met at the bar and finally we all went to bed. We got up and they announced to us that we were going to fly us into Churchill. We were all excited about that. We met a young girl from

Korea who spoke very little English. She had not made any reservations for her stay in Churchill, so we helped to find her a room at the place we were staying at. She stayed with us for four days. She called Rite and me "Dad" and "Mom". Myla had made a new friend from a different country and e-mailed her for a very long time afterward.

In Churchill, we would call the front desk at the hotel before we ventured outside because you couldn't go out if there was a polar bear walking around town. Those that were caught were put into polar bear prison and tagged. If they were to do it again they would be moved in a different location. We did go out to try and see one on our own. We would go near the water and look for them every day. We never saw one while we were outside walking. Little did we know how large they were and how dangerous they had become at the time, because it was their hungry time of year.

There were two restaurants in town with excellent food. It was very busy and all the townspeople were the ones eating. There weren't too many visitors but many people from different places would go there to work because they made good money and didn't have anything to spend it on. They were simply there to save money.

At lunch time one day, Rite told us that at the other side of the restaurant was Chantel Kreviazuk with her children. She was married to Raine Maida from Our Lady Peace, a band that we always listened to. I knew he was right because he paid very good attention to what people looked like and was never wrong. Myla and Bill didn't believe him, but finally Myla had the courage to go up and ask her if indeed it was her. Yes, it was and now Myla wanted to take pictures of them together and Myla was so excited. We left the restaurant in awe. Why in the world would we meet someone like that up north where very few people lived?

Myla went to every store in the area to find things for her children. It didn't matter if there were only two or three stores there. She was out shopping and had a great time. We tried to make reservations for the Tundra Buggy for which we had four tickets, but we were unable to do so because Chantel and her crew had it for a few days. We were very disappointed, considering that it was part of the package Rite had bid on. This was the reason for our coming here. We couldn't find anyone to take us to see the polar bears. Some individuals would charge an extremely large amount to take you to them and wouldn't guarantee you seeing any.

The man that was running our living arrangements did not want to see us disappointed before we went home. He got a friend to take us where there was much security. He had the codes and rights to get past through to where the polar bears were. There was an area that had hundreds of dogs running around. They would be fed daily by some other individual that had a "NO TRESPASSING" sign up. He would feed the dogs and always left food for the polar bears. This way the bears would not eat the dogs. You needed keys to get through a couple of gates. The person taking us had the keys and was able to bring us to a good location. There were two bears playfighting. We couldn't believe how big they were when they stood up. They were fighting for a good half an hour and we were able to take pictures of then in all different positions. This was definitely worth sixteen hundred dollars for four days. In the past, this package would go for thirty-eight hundred dollars and basically that's how much it would cost an individual to go there and see everything in Churchill. What a deal!

Chapter 18

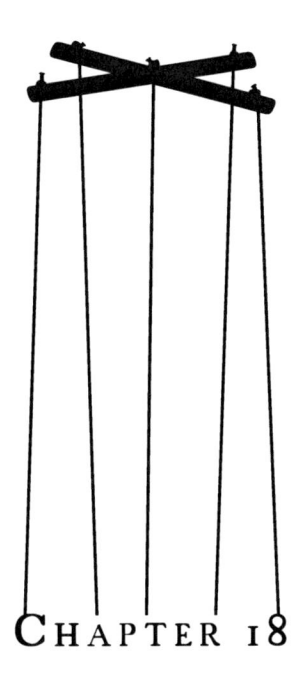

Back at home, I returned to my usual problems, like my suicidal feelings. I had attempted suicide many times, and going on a trip was only a temporary relief from my feelings.

On one of my suicidal attempts I had taken a whole bottle of aspirin but thought I had bought Tylenol. Rite got a hold of me on the phone just as he was getting home from work when he felt like something was really wrong. When we talked, I was on the other side of the city and he told me to stay until he arrived. I was parked in a parking lot. Little did I know, but Rite had called the paramedics and told them where I was. He gave them my license plate number and the make of my car. As soon as I noticed an ambulance near my car I immediately rolled up my windows and locked the doors. They parked directly in front of me so I could not get away. One of the paramedics was holding onto my car as I looked in the rear view mirror and drove off. I then had the police looking for me but they never found me. I ended up going to Ben and Sally's building and buzzed their apartment. There was no answer, although they were there. They did not know what had happened and I eventually met up with Rite and was brought back to the Grace Hospital. This is when I found out that I had not taken Tylenol but aspirin. I had many bags of intravenous and when I left I was swollen and could hardly get my pants up because of all the fluid.

Through one of my hospitalizations, I noticed information posted on the wall on how to become a Mental Health Support Worker. You had to have a mental illness in order to apply. The deadline was posted and I was a couple of days late. I talked to Dr. Stevens about it and he suggested that I try it out, and gave me a letter of recommendation to give to the Canadian Mental Health Association of Winnipeg. It was being funded through them and Red River Community College. I went directly to the address where I was supposed to mail it. I knew I was late and wasn't sure if they would accept it. When I dropped it off, no one said anything. A few weeks later, I received a letter to go for an interview. I was ecstatic. I told Dr. Stevens I had an interview lined up with CMHA. He was happy for me because this was something positive in my life.

I went to the interview, feeling confident that it would work out on my behalf. There were a few people in the interview room. They asked me many questions about why I would be interested in becoming a Mental Health Support Worker and I told them that I found this to be a mission in my life; to help others in any way that I could. They questioned me on the mental health runs I had coordinated myself. They seemed very interested in this and knew how eager I was to help. They told me that they had received one hundred and fifty applicants. What they were going to do was pick forty of those to go to school for three weeks and then they would decide who would be best suited to take the course. There were only twenty spots available.

I was picked to be one of the forty and was slightly nervous about going back to school again because I was already in my forties and hadn't been in school for a very long time. I went for three weeks and never missed a day, being very dedicated so I could be picked to become a Mental Health Support Worker.

Shortly after, I was notified that I had been picked to be one of the twenty students to enroll in the Mental Health Support Worker Program, which was funded by CMHA and Red River College. I was thrilled but slightly nervous and worried. They paid for all our books, binders, pencils, and other materials. I asked them if we needed to know how to use a computer. They said there was no computer work involved in this course. My psychology professor was from the University of Manitoba. She was very professional at her employment. The other two teachers were workers from CMHA. I'm not sure if they had their teacher's degree but one of them didn't seem as professional as the other. I've never known whether they were workers from CMHA with a history of teaching. Nevertheless, they knew quite a bit about mental health issues. This program had started two years before but was not successful in terms of the number of people graduating. There had been complications and the instructors had changed things; now they were offering it again after two years.

I felt that one of the teachers named Zen really did not care for me. At the beginning, I was still cutting myself. I hid my arms but she knew what I was doing. She called me aside and told me to stop or I would be expelled. In the first half of the year, my grades were high. In the second half, the instructor just didn't act like she was very fond of me. Perhaps it was because suddenly we had to have all work done on the computer. At the beginning of the course this was definitely something I was concerned with. The people I asked had said there was no computer work to be done. Now suddenly we had to have our work printed. I found this to be very unfair and panicked and was extremely anxious because I had absolutely no knowledge of computers. Everyone else seemed to adapt somewhat to the few old computers in the class. The school had a limited number of computers and some students had time to start their homework but not finish it. I'm not sure where they got the rest done.

The owner at Rite's place of employment decided to buy me a new computer and printer for home. I was more than grateful for this. He was always looking out for Rite. Now, my only problem was learning how to use it. I had asked my son-in-law, Keith, if he could show me. He did his best but I was having great difficulty using it and trying to figure out how to work it. There was one essay I had completed after several hours. It was quite lengthy and I typed slowly to make sure there were no errors. When it came time to save it, I ended up deleting it and I was totally devastated, with my heart sinking to the pit of my stomach. I didn't know enough about the computer and it was creating a lot of trouble and stress for me. When it came to computers, I wasn't so keen on the idea of having to use them.

Psychology continued as usual and was very interesting, with a professional professor. I was able to do very well in this subject. I did my first practicum with the Mood Disorders centre and loved it. This was definitely what I had gone to school for. This would have been a dream job, but they were not hiring. The Executive Director in charge took me to Selkirk Mental Hospital in ETU. This was very interesting. Our class went to the museum where they had straightjackets, beds built like cages for schizophrenic people, and old electroconvulsive therapy machines on display. It was very scary and I pitied the poor people who had gone through all of this. Lobotomies were done back then and it was startling to know how people turned out after having one. These were such archaic procedures. Back at the Mood Disorders centre, one of the Outreach Workers named Helen was the one to train me. She was quite knowledgeable. Helen definitely had her down periods where she was unapproachable. I had no idea why but knew to stay away from her. She facilitated different groups. She showed me the process of what to do when I answered the phones and sent out information to those calling. Their filing system had everything you needed to know about mental illnesses. Some calls were more serious than others, and I was trained in how to handle these calls. I was also given the opportunity to facilitate depression groups.

On my return back to school we had begun the other half of the year and had lots of homework and reading. There were times I would be reading and ended up falling asleep at the kitchen table. My husband insisted that I had to go to bed because I wasn't retaining anything at this point. I had some very long days and it was very tiring. Close to the end of the term before we were to graduate, Zen came in in a foul mood. She said she was leaving because she did not want to be there, and gave us all this homework to do for the day. She had abandoned our class first thing in the morning.

I was dumbfounded at the prospect of her leaving us. Everyone started chattering about her and I said that she was a bitch. Truly she was. One of the other students went to report what I had said to her and within a few days I was reprimanded and wasn't allowed to attend class for a week. They hadn't even confronted with me whether I had said this or not. This was signed by the Red River College and the CMHA. I was never able to defend myself, and who says this person was telling the truth?

When my week was up, I was already very worried about what I had missed and was distraught by this whole event. You could tell the other teacher named Michelle did not look like she agreed with Zen but this was her co-worker. I was hospitalized because of all the stress and told by Red River College to write a letter of apology to them and Zen. I was to go to Red River College with my letter and then give it to Zen. I did this, but it was close to two weeks before the school administrators would meet with me. I was devastated and had a lot of catching up to do on my own. I had three adult children who had all graduated from high school, and I knew from them that some of these teens would do and say far worse things and never be reprimanded in their schools. I felt that Zen should have been the one to get in trouble. A teacher cannot get up and leave her class for the day because she had mood swings. This was unacceptable.

I'm not sure how they were able to dismiss me for so long without even checking the story out. When I got back Zen dropped my grades in the classes that she was teaching me. I had an A in the first term and now she simply could change them according to what she wanted. Her goal was not to let me graduate. I did end up graduating because in all the other subjects, I had high grades. In the end there were some students who did not graduate at all.

Zen decided to choose where I would go for my next practicum. Most students did not want to go to the place she chose. The name of the place was Doray Enterprises. The staff were incredibly nice and I was offered employment once I graduated. I was a Supervisor of a certain number of clients. At least one good thing came of my studies. After I graduated, there was never a Mental Health Support Worker program put in place again. It was not a success.

I liked my time at Doray Enterprises because the clients were so very cheerful, as well as the staff. This was a high-paying job, but I was already receiving disability benefits and therefore just volunteered there. I facilitated group sessions with many who had Obsessive-Compulsive Disorder. I taught them how to let go of things and to change. They were all eager.

I also volunteered at Schizophrenia Society, Mood Disorders centre, and the CMHA, doing research. I kept myself and my mind busy.

During those years, I agreed to write out my story in short form. It was a co-operative approach to recovery called Partnership for Consumer

Empowerment. It took us four years to complete our stories before we were able to start our presentations to graduating nurses, police officers, and many others. The first day we launched it was during Mental Health Illness Week. There were four of us trained to share our life stories. We had a large audience with press and television coverage. We all did well and were sent to different places to do our presentations. We travelled through Manitoba and stayed overnight at some locations that were further away.

My teacher Michelle from the Mental Health Support Worker Program also sought me out to do presentations for her at several places. I remember a man who lived in a housing co-op who had his hair all disheveled and looked like he hadn't combed it for a long time. There were many bedbugs in these co-ops. I will never forget how awfully his life had been impacted by OCD. He was a hand washer and could not use his bathtub for fear of dirtying it. He had no appliances because they were too hard to maintain. He vacuumed every day but was very unhappy. At the end of my presentation, he came to speak to me and began to cry. My heart was broken for him because I knew exactly how he felt with this disorder. He was very thankful that he was not alone and shook my hand.

I did some of my presentations in psychiatric units in different hospitals in the city. These were slightly shorter talks and not as many people attended them. There was always someone with lots of questions to be answered. I would do so with the best of my ability and explain to them what OCD was about, or try to answer many of their questions about abuse.

I also volunteered much of my time doing the Hearing Voices Workshop. This workshop was for those people who were graduating as nurses, police officers, social workers, parole officers, and other related jobs. They would have to listen to voices with earphones to simulate what a real schizophrenic person might hear. It is much harder to concentrate with these voices. The participants were then assigned to do different tasks while they listened. The voices were very disturbing and the staff members were very hard on them. It was simulating what a schizophrenic person hearing voices went through. After we were done, the director told them that we all were just acting because that was how people were treated. I would usually do the role of the impatient, rude psychologist and later do my presentation. Many of the participants were very interested and I was to stay in case someone would want to know more about what I had written about my own experiences.

I was in and out of the hospital several times for quite a few years. I've been very suicidal and have attempted to kill myself many times. When I would arrive at the hospital they would take me in immediately so I could get hooked up to an IV. I became very ill each and every time. I overdosed on just about everything and anything. Dr. Stevens had even told me not to overdose on Clomipramine and Lithium but I never cared. He told me that these two would kill me. I had to drink the charcoal they had mixed and even if I refused, the doctor would tell me to drink it or they were going to put a tube in my nose and pump it into my stomach, which would be more unpleasant. I drank it; it was black as coal and thick and gritty. My mouth, tongue, and teeth were all stained black. How disgusting!

There was also a time I overdosed on Clonazepam at a hotel in our city. I acted extremely cheerful in front of my husband but intended on taking an overdose of Temazepam later before bed. I had called the Mobile Crisis Unit on my way to the hotel. I called on my blue tooth with my number hidden. They were looking for me but I told them that I was not going to be at home and that there was no way of reaching me. At the time, my cell phone was not under my name but Myla's. I eventually hung up on them and went into the hotel where Rite was waiting for me. My cell phone did ring once, so I turned it off.

Whenever we were away, Rite never answered his phone if it was family because he wanted to be alone and enjoy our time together. That particular day Myla called and for some unknown reason, he picked up the phone. Myla told him that she had had two police officers at her door, thinking she had overdosed but she explained it to them that it was not her but her mother. The police showed up at the hotel and called the paramedics to come. As they arrived, they asked me to get on the stretcher, after which I don't remember anything else at all. At one point in the ambulance, one of the paramedics hit me on the chest very hard to wake me and asked me something and then I was unconscious until the following day.

When I woke up, I did not remember anything at all. I was hooked up to an IV, had a catheter, and was dressed in a hospital gown. I couldn't remember what had happened except I know I felt at peace while unconscious. When Rite left the following evening, I decided to get my bank card out of my purse. I got dressed and went to the washroom and pulled out my IV. I simply walked right out and went to the IGA close to the hospital, finding it closed. I then turned in the other direction to walk over to Superstore, which was a little farther away, only to find it closed. It was only then that I realized it was Sunday. I had lost track of my time. I decided to walk to Shopper's Drug Mart, but it was quite a distance from where I was and knew the police would be out looking for me. I finally got to a Petro Canada and bought a Slurpee and every small bottle of Tylenol they had. I went outside and ingested them all. Upon my return to Emergency, Rite, Myla, and the nurses were there and were all very angry with me. I was put in hospital pyjamas and had a guard with me 24/7. I would be seeing the doctor the following day. Rite was to take my clothes home so that I could not escape again. I had different guards through the night who were all friendly. The last one was not a guard but a worker who normally disinfected the rooms in Emergency after they were used. He stayed and talked with me for three hours.

On Monday, Dr. Nest came to see me and I immediately asked to speak to my doctor, Dr. Stevens. Dr. Nest told me he was not coming and discharged me. The last guard who sat with me for three hours came with me to psychiatry. I then saw Dr. Stevens talking to some other people in the waiting room. When he was done I asked to speak to him and he ignored me and said he did not have time and turned and walked into ETU. I stood there waiting for him to come out and one of the very nice psychiatric nurses came to talk to me. I was crying because Dr. Stevens had totally ignored me. He then came out and I asked one more time to speak to him. He told me he was too busy and would talk to me another day. This was not good enough for me because I felt like I was in crisis. He waved to me with his back turned saying goodbye when I lashed out at him and told him he would never see me again. My mind was centered only on the waving hand.

I knew once I got my clothes on I was just going to end my life somewhere in a field. I was adamant and the date I had chosen was August 20, 2011. This was the day I was going to die. It was also my abuser's birthday. When Rite got to the hospital with my clothes he announced that he had taken a few days off. Now my plans were on hold and I supremely disappointed. Rite always knew when I was desperate.

We left the hospital and Rite called the Mobile Crisis Unit and they told him to return me to the hospital. There was no way I was going back since they didn't do anything with me taking two overdoses through the weekend. They wanted nothing to do with me.

Rite then called the police and they suggested I go to another hospital, which I did. They admitted me for one night until I saw the psychiatrist. We talked and he suggested I make an appointment with him A.S.A.P. I was angry because I was trying so desperately; trying to seek help and all doors were being shut. I felt so desperate and alone. Rite called and got me an appointment to see the doctor that day. I was then immediately admitted and somehow found some relief that someone would help me. I had severe problems with my thyroid which caused me to be somewhat psychotic. I am not normally psychotic but at that time you would never have known it. The desperation I felt was like nothing I had ever experienced before. I stayed in the hospital for about twelve weeks while the doctor started treating me for my thyroid. He called for an endocrinologist to come and see me but she spent five seconds with me. I was hospitalized three times because of my thyroid.

My family doctor was absolutely useless and had referred me to see an endocrinologist, but after four months I still hadn't heard anything from the new doctor. She then was going to refer me to another doctor and I would have had to wait again. She did not care about the state I was in and had never checked anything on me while I was on the examining table. I had arthritis and I would have to wait three hours in the waiting room to see her. For what, I really did not know. Perhaps she did not like working with people with a mental illness. One Christmas, she was talking about depression at this time of year, even though I hadn't said anything about that topic. This is when she explained her family dynamics and how she wasn't able to see her stepdaughter and grandchildren who lived in Minneapolis because her stepdaughter and her husband had split up. I wasn't there to listen to that and I could care less which family members were going to be depressed.

Mandy got me in to see that doctor years ago, and Mandy liked her but not the long wait with her children. There came a time when the doctor asked Mandy how I was doing and said that it must be very hard to have a parent with bipolar disorder. I was not diagnosed with this and the doctor was not keeping her confidentiality. I also called the doctor to get help during my chronic depression and told her receptionist I felt like I was on death row. She in turn gave me an appointment six weeks later. Now, that's uncaring. I ended finding a much better doctor and got Mandy to see her, too. No more waiting three hours.

The third time in hospital, the psychiatrist who was replacing Dr. Stevens gave me a referral for the endocrinologist to come and see me again. My numbers were way off the charts for my thyroid. I had been itchy all over for close to a year and this left me with deep gouges everywhere on my body. I ended up going to see my dermatologist in order to get help. I spent months going for light therapy at both hospitals. It was making me very anxious because no one could help me. The reason I was itching like this was that Lithium had become toxic to me because of my overdoses. I was on Lithium and for some reason or another I didn't seem to be absorbing the thyroid medication, so my family doctor kept on increasing it.

Once the doctors found out Lithium was toxic to me, I was taken off immediately and several blood tests were done over the next couple of days. Dr. Stevens told me that I might have damaged my kidneys and would have to go for dialysis. He also mentioned that I could have brain damage. He was extremely angry with me and threatened that he would only see me every six months for ten minutes for a prescription. I knew he was exaggerating by telling me that I would need dialysis or that I had brain damage. I couldn't believe how uncaring he had become and I was deeply hurt. If he did not want to see me anymore then he should just have dropped me as a patient right then and there. He should have discharged me.

I felt like I could no longer trust Dr. Stevens and once again, I became very quiet and depressed. I was so upset by all of this that I once again took extra Lithium but never told anybody. My blood was back to normal, so when I did it again no one noticed. I felt I should punish myself for having made the doctor so angry. Death was what I wished for. In the end no one found out about the second overdose of Lithium. I'm not sure why they didn't notice, since I was living in the bathroom all day long. Not a living soul cared whether I was alive or not. Once I stopped taking the Lithium I became my thyroid medication became toxic to me because I was ingesting too much of that medication. I had now become sensitive to both medications and had severe reaction because of this. This lasted for over a year, but the endocrinologist who was supposed to be treating me did not care anyway. She apparently did not like treating psychiatric patients because of the stigma given to mentally ill people.

Chapter 19

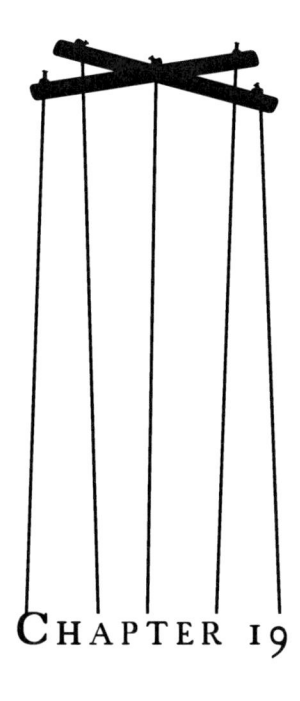

I have been hospitalized so many times the staff and some patients all knew me. Some of the psychiatric nurses were good but there were those that really slacked off on their jobs. Some seemed extremely lazy and wouldn't even introduce themselves at the beginning of a shift. I would have to go ask who my nurse was in order to get my pills. This often happened in the evening shift because you couldn't get your medication until it was time to go to bed. One nurse who came after a long weekend did not say anything to me, only three words, "Here we go", while handing me my pills. That's it. How were they supposed to be helping people if they weren›t talking or asking questions about the weekend and reporting the patients' responses? Whatever this nurse wrote down was obviously fabricated because the nurse never did talk to me. I could have taken my own pills; I didn't need them handed out to me. I knew what I was taking.

The lazier nurses often seemed to be the new ones. They would treat you like a two-year-old who was brain dead, even though I more than likely knew more about life than they did. The older nurses were more compassionate and were probably trained to treat people with dignity and respect. They were more "old-school" but I guess instructors don't teach nurses bedside manners anymore. Each nurse is assigned so many patients on their shift, and is supposed to talk to all these patients for a certain length of time; but not many did. They seemed to enjoy putting a patient in lockdown and I was present many times when they would be doing so. They felt in control and superior to that patient.

To spend all of this money staying in the hospital was ridiculous because I wasn't getting any extra help that I should have, except from Dr. Stevens. He came to talk to me just about every day. The medical system was paying for our stays on long weekends and holidays but yet, we were sent home. What a waste of money and time!

There were cameras in both lockdown rooms, but sometimes their screens were moved so that the other patients could see what was going on in the room. There were times I had seen naked people. How humiliating for them. The nurses were so very unprofessional. There was one particular nurse who smiled all the time with her big teeth showing, but if you were getting out of line her demeanor would change instantly. She really should not have been working in psychiatry. She was impatient and her temper would blow in a simple second. I always smiled at her but never caused any trouble because of her attitude. If I wanted to talk to her about something that bothered me, she gave me one chance and after that I was not to repeat myself. I was not to go down that road again. Is this what you call good care?! She was basically telling me to shut up.

One evening two patients and I witnessed a nurse slapping a young female patient three times across the face. This patient never talked and the nurse was upset with her for whatever reason. We all saw the nurse slap her across the face, although the young girl slapped her back. We then told one nurse in the lounge and he did take a look, but came back after the other nurse told him everything was under control. At that point, she brought the patient into a room and closed the door. I didn't know abuse was part of recovery. I heard one nurse call us "you people" like we were not human. We were all crazy and they treated us like that. The nurses spent much of their time behind the desk, working on the computers for their own use and laughing really loud. This was very annoying to me when I felt extremely depressed.

Dr. Stevens would tell me there was no reason for nurses not to take time to talk to their patients. They were supposed to fit it in on their shifts. However, some of them would completely ignore you if you needed anything at the nurses' station. They wouldn't even look at you and you could stand there for half an hour. If you were not assigned to them that night, they would treat you like you were invisible. Great help, since they all tell you to come to the desk if you feel suicidal. They said that there was always a nurse available. What lies!

The nurses were definitely eager to look through your belongings to make sure you didn't bring anything harmful. If I wanted to self-harm, I would bring in knives, blades, pills, and anything I wanted to use to hurt myself! One time I went outside and took someone›s cigarette and burnt myself with it. The following day Dr. Stevens jokingly said to me that he had heard that I had started to smoke. This man had lots of black humour that sometimes would offend me.

I eventually would let Dr. Stevens know how I felt so I could keep our doctor and patient relationship healthy. There were things he said to me that were very disturbing to the average person and I would never write about it because it was all part of his black humour that was quite offensive. There was a time I was so hurt by his comments it took me several months to forgive him and forget about it. Those who I spoke to about it were all disgusted by his comments. He had gone way too far. This was his attitude, simply dark, and trying to make light of difficult situations. He actually really was funny, kind, empathetic, caring, and an excellent psychiatrist. He has helped me so much through the years and always recommended people for me to talk to. I think I had a love/hate relationship with him because of my Borderline Personality Disorder.

Even just being in the hospital was an education for me. During my first hospitalization, I saw many things that I never knew existed, whether it was cutting, burning, hair pulling (tricotillomania), or hitting oneself.

One of my friends, Sandy, was scarred all over both arms. She cut herself with a scalpel but would often tell me she didn't remember doing it. She would not find any blood anywhere in the house. Her arm would be bandaged until she got to the hospital, where the doctors would then stitch it up. One time when she went to Emergency, the doctor did not freeze the arm because he thought if you could cut it then he should be able to stitch it without freezing. I thought that this was absolutely cruel on the doctor's part. You more than likely wouldn't treat an animal like that. Sandy was horrified at the prospect of no freezing but let them do it. She was once a paramedic so she knew where she should cut in order not to die. Her arms were shocking; I've never seen arms as scarred as that before.

We hung out for a couple of years. She had hopes of becoming a doctor and was extremely intelligent. There were times she would freak out at university; she would tell me she would have to leave the class because everybody's faces were bleeding through their eyes. She was definitely psychotic and very sick. I had a hard time believing her stories, but who am I to judge others? I have never been psychotic and never lived in that world. It was very hard to understand. Sandy and I eventually stopped being friends when I once again was hospitalized and she called me to tell me she could no longer hang out with me because of her own mental health. Our friendship was now over. This was probably one of the best things that has ever happened to me. She was an unhealthy person to be friends with and once again, my family did not want me around her.

I did a lot of self-injury. Self-injury can be defined as any intentional injury to one's body, usually leaving marks or tissue damage. Most people who engage in self-harm do it when they are alone so they are able to hide their behavior.

Self-harm can happen to anyone. Many people engage in self-injury in order to make themselves feel something. The actual pain of harming is numbing in comparison to how you feel inside. This behaviour occurs often when someone has been abused physically, sexually, emotionally and has a feeling of abandonment. Many of those who have experienced this become abusive towards themselves because they were never allowed to show their anger throughout their childhood. When I injured myself, I felt really alive because I could feel something. I was able to feel the pain outside instead of inside and I controlled or managed the pain, unlike the pain I experienced through physical or sexual abuse. While harming I felt numb and depersonalized. I felt self-hatred and felt like I needed to be punished for having feelings that I was not allowed to express when I was younger. These feelings were an outgrowth of abuse and a belief that the abuse was deserved. I would always wear long sleeves, even in warm weather. I did not want to expose myself to anyone, even my psychiatrist. I had low self-esteem, difficulty handling feelings, and I felt very lonely.

My main injuries in self-harming were taking overdoses, cutting, and burning with cigarettes or salt and ice. I would get second degree burns doing so. It was painful only after I did it, but felt numb while I was doing it. Some of my skin has been permanently damaged. To me it was like a trophy so I could recall all the pain I have felt my entire life. I would just have to look at my arm and I would immediately want to scar it bigger and bigger because I didn't feel deserving of having a good life. One time, my family doctor had removed a large cyst in my knee and stitched it up. While I drove home, I simply pulled all the stitches out but my knee was bleeding down to my feet and I could not stop it. I returned to Urgent Care the following day, where they packed my knee with bandages. When I took the bandage off, I saw that it was several feet long.

I was to go back to the hospital every day to get my wound checked, but I never returned. I would kneel down in my flower bed with all the dirt and my knee got dirty, but I would not wash it. I went for arthroscopic surgery on my left knee. I asked not to be given any relaxant because I wanted to watch the surgery. They put the television facing me and I watched and heard everything going on. I had some arthritis on the bone and they shaved that off.

I was in recovery until 7:00 p.m. that night. It was a day surgery. It was Friday and the staff all wanted to go home. My knee would not stop bleeding, but they told me to come back if it got worse. I went home on crutches but never really used them. It was too hard to walk with them. I spent just a couple of hours cleaning the next day and then lay down until Rite got home. The bandage was saturated with blood and I needed to go back to the hospital. I was to keep my leg up but my housework always came first. My therapist found this odd because she tried to convince me that I no longer needed to suffer. I knew she was right but still went on the dark side and punished myself. I can never explain it because none of it made sense. I felt extremely different and, as Rite would tease me, that I was a strange animal. I certainly was.

Mandy was very upset with me for having tried to commit suicide. I had hurt her deeply. Keith did not believe there was such a thing as mental illness. At church they would have meetings every week and he mentioned this to others. He was told that there was such a thing as mental illness, but he had never encountered anyone with this problem. We didn't see Keith and Mandy as often as his parents saw them, but it seemed as if I had created this problem among us. However, it was their life to live their way. I had no resentment towards them and felt that they were adults and were able to make their own decisions at that time. My love for them was never altered. Mandy is still my little angel.

Chapter 20

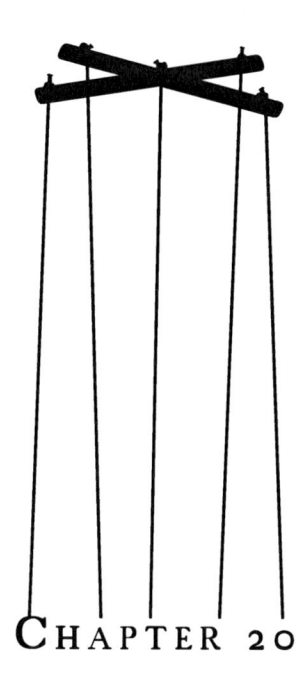

In 2006, my father became very ill; not that he wasn't sick before that, but now his cancer had spread to his prostate. He had outlived the five years the oncologist had said, and now it had been fifteen. The doctors performed surgery and removed the tumour. He did not get better, but instead got sicker. He was going for chemo and this made him very weak and tired. Eventually, they discovered he had cancer in his bladder and performed a urostomy so the urine could flow there instead, and his bladder was removed. He was so unhappy with this. It leaked and he never was the same.

After the surgery, the doctor had told my father that he did not think the cancer had spread to the walls of the bladder. We were all relieved by this news. My father had to go for chemo again and became weaker and weaker every day. My mother did not have any sympathy for him. She only cared about herself and no one else. She thought he was exaggerating about how sick he felt. He would be throwing up but that did not stop her from going for coffee every day at her favorite coffee shop. He literally had to drive and pick her up every day. She was so demanding and in control. She had no feelings and didn't care about anyone else.

Once my parents would get home, she would complain about how her legs hurt. He was to make supper, do dishes, and clean the kitchen as the queen sat in her chair. She would order him to get her a glass of water, clean her glasses, do housework, run her bath, do laundry, and so many other things. She had no heart and thought that my father was there only for her convenience.

On September 3rd, 2006 Myla and Bill got married. Myla was already pregnant and they wanted to get married before my dad got any sicker.

On the day of Myla's wedding, my father called her to tell her he would not be attending because he was so sick. She was disappointed but understood why. My eldest brother George would not let my father miss the wedding, and he forced him to go. George went over and dressed him and by the look of the wedding pictures he looked like a dying man. He was unable to eat but did try to have a bowl of soup. It was so pitiful. He had lost so much weight and he had big bony hands with no fat on them.

The doctor took more tests because my father really wasn't getting better. The doctor found that the cancer had indeed spread onto the walls of the bladder. It was now spreading everywhere. My poor dad who was always so kind and wonderful to everyone was now suffering unmanageable pain. He must have been hallucinating as well, because he once got out of bed completely naked and started to walk down the hall of the hospital. We laughed, but knew that this was really not funny. He tried his best to keep his spirits up but eventually he was put into Riverview Health Centre palliative care, where he knew he was going to die. I remember when they needed to put a diaper on him for his bowels and he wanted nothing to do with that. He had told us previously if he ever got that bad, that he would rather die. He signed papers indicating his wish not to prolong his life if he was dying. We watched him suffer for months and cried each and every time we saw him. Rite was so close to him, and his heart was broken. In the meantime, my mother got sick with a bladder infection and was telling all of us that she was much sicker than my father. She was hospitalized in another hospital. How dare she? He was dying and she was more concerned about her pain than his. It shows you what kind of person she really was.

On December 6, 2006, Myla and Bill had gone to see him in the morning. He was not speaking anymore and his breathing was laboured. Myla was eight months pregnant with her first baby. My father held his hand on her tummy and held Bill's hand and passed away. We were all called and felt so lost without him. My father was 81. My mother never did cry, but was worried about how she was going to take care of herself now that he had died. Everything was about her.

Everyone ignored her and no one felt anything for her. She was so cruel. At his funeral there were 350 people who attended the church. My father had wanted an open coffin and then to be cremated. When it was time to leave the church, I could not look at him enough. I wanted to see him forever. I eventually walked away with his image etched in my head and with tears streaming down my face. We all cried for days, and we celebrated the lunch after church in my dad's style. We had a hot dinner with everything you could think of and had bought cases of wine with his name printed on each bottle. This is what he would have wanted because this is the way he was. He liked things done large, and had done so all of his life.

Many friends I had made from volunteering had come to the funeral. I was overwhelmed by how supportive they were.

In the following years we celebrated my father's death by getting together for dinner. My brother had video of him when he was in the hospital and it played all evening long. This was truly heart-breaking for the entire family. My mother was to be placed in a nursing home and we had to have their condo sold. My other siblings had to get rid of everything in the condo. My mother hated being at the nursing home. Very rarely would she have someone to come and visit her. Myla had always felt sorry for her, and so she would pick my mother up several times a week. They would go shopping and out for lunch. My mother was blessed by having Myla pick her up to go out.

One time, I had gone shopping with them and my mother was screaming at Myla's oldest daughter because she was crying. My granddaughter was very young at the time, but I had never felt so embarrassed as when my mother yelled at her and told her how ugly she was when she acted like this. She would deliberately say it over and over and make sure everyone in the store heard her. She was also antagonizing my granddaughter, which made it worse. I just wanted to walk away from my mother and pretend I didn't know her.

Another time, I was along with them and Myla mentioned Pierre, the pedophile. Myla was saying that he had sexually abused several girls. My mother seemed extremely surprised and wanted to know who. I gave Myla a look to be quiet. Myla had to go in and get her walker for my mom while my mother tried interrogating me about what had happened. She was now 85 and I was not going to speak to her about it. I felt so disgusted by her because throughout my life she had known, but now that she was older she wanted to know the facts. Those were my secrets and she would never know.

In the nursing home, my mother would start calling all of her children and demand that they bring things for her. When she called it had to be done now, and she refused to wait. She did not like the nursing home washing her clothes, so Monique and I had to do it. This was pure misery. Eventually, Angel and George had enough of her and didn't do anything for her. George was supposed to be executor of the will, but she had it changed. She liked hurting people in every way.

I could never say no and continued to do everything she asked. It was tiring and I hated it. She would call for cases of 24 bottles of water, diet drinks, and lots of food. My brother and sister put in a little fridge in her room, and after that, she would not eat anything from the nursing home. She often ordered out even though the nurses were trying to get her to stop doing that. No way! She was taking so many vitamins that they filled a whole Safeway bag full. The staff had confiscated it and she only spoke badly of them. Most of the nurses were from Africa and spoke only in French. My mother's attitudes came out when she was dealing with the nurses. If she did not want to be changed at night by one of them, she would blatantly say so and insult them because they were black. This woman needed a rude awakening.

My nephew was getting married in Hawaii and they all wanted my mother to go. The only issue was that no one wanted to take care of her. They got a plan together and asked one of the nurses to come to Hawaii, all expenses paid. She was eager to go and look after my mother and to push her in a wheelchair. She would put my mother to bed and go out to enjoy herself later. My mother did not like this and said so.

On the last day, this nurse would not push her wheelchair anymore. I guess she had been abused enough. Once back at the nursing home my mother only spoke badly about her to everyone. She got so angry at the nurse that she even hit her. They had to move her to another floor and my eldest brother and sister had to talk to her about the incident. She was told if she ever did that again that they would kick her out of the nursing home. My sister told my mother that she would be placed at any nursing home available in the city where they might even have bed bugs. My mother always tried to get the doctors' attention whenever she wasn't feeling well. They took days to go and see her. They didn't care about her. She was nasty and did not know how to ask for help politely. They ignored her and didn't care.

Eventually, Myla was pregnant again and she had another little girl. I was able to be in the delivery room for all her children's births. This was quite interesting, and I felt honored that she wanted me there. She even wanted Rite to come in, but he was not comfortable with that.

My mother got very angry with Myla when she had her third child, a little boy. Myla was too busy to pick her up and could not push a wheelchair and three children all at once. On Halloween that year when the baby was six months old, Myla went up to my mother at my sister's house and asked her to look at the baby because he had a costume on. My mother refused to look and simply said that he was ugly. Myla was very hurt by this. This was her baby. My mother walked into my sister's living room and sat down. Rite and I were sitting in there too. My mother started insulting Myla in every way for no reason. She told Myla she was stupid and had a lousy career. Myla shot back that my mother wasn't exactly highly educated. She hadn't even graduated.

Myla was shocked by what she was saying and my mother got up to hit her while she was holding the baby. This was one year before she died. She even got mad at Monique and her daughter a few months prior to that and hit her daughter's hand. Her daughter hit her hand back and my mother said that was abusing the elderly. She wanted to call the police. They gave her the phone and called her on it because through all the years we had all been victimized by her. This time she cried and my sister refused to wash my mother's clothes or have anything to do with her for months. I was the one that did everything for her during that time.

I eventually was hospitalized and Monique had no choice but to deal with our mother's needs. I was not held captive to the many demands for a few months. When I was in hospital none of my family ever came to visit me except Angel, Emile, Myla, and a few times Mandy. Of course, Rite was always there. Before my dad got really sick he came only once with my mother. I felt so ashamed of them coming and met them on the main floor. My dad could not understand how his daughter was not perfect and had a mental illness. This was too much for him. I also had feelings that he did not love me but loved Rite. It was disturbing.

On my mother's 87th birthday, Monique decided to throw a big birthday party for her at the nursing home. Her birthday was on September 26th, 2011. She was very pleased because we celebrated it with her. By the end of October, on a Sunday later in the afternoon, Rite called me to tell me that my mother was sick and had been brought by ambulance to the Victoria Hospital. Monique had contacted the doctor and was told that my mother had a bladder and kidney infection. She was started on antibiotics. Myla hadn't talked to my mother for a year but went to see her at supper time. The doctor talked to Myla and said that they were taking my mother off all medications because they didn't think she would live through the night. We all visited her that evening in disbelief that this was actually happening. I felt some deep relief inside of me. She was lucky to be dying so peacefully.

Myla was upset because the following day was Halloween, which marked the anniversary of one year of not talking to my mother. While we were visiting together, we told my mother to smile and all of us gathered around her to take a picture. Each and every one of us was smiling, including her. My sister Monique now says that she forgives our mother and that she felt sorry for her, and she was included in this picture with her daughter. It's easy to say how forgiving you are when you don't have to do anything for the person.

Monique was no different from anyone else in my family except she was a martyr and made sure everyone knew that she was doing everything for our mother. She was wrong about this, since we all had our duties, but of course she always made it sound like she was the only one and told everyone this. No matter what I did, Monique always had to be right. Monique was tired of all of our mother's commands, too. She wasn't innocent in this regard.

My mother did not die that night, and on Tuesday evening Myla decided to go talk to her, even though my mother wasn't responding. No one had told her she was going to die and Myla thought it only right that she should know. She didn't know if my mother could hear her, but she talked to her for a lengthy period of time. She told her that Grandpa was waiting for her and as she looked outside the hospital window, she told her that it was alright to let go because Grandpa's star was shining very brightly. Myla had a star picked out for him and would talk to it every night. She missed him and felt very confident that this star represented him.

While all of this was going on, Myla and I were wondering how long my mother was going to live. We were heading out for the States in a few days and everything was booked and paid for. We could not get a refund.

On November 2, 2011, I had gone to see my mother in the afternoon and said hi to her. My sister Angel and brother George were there with an aunt and uncle that hadn't visited her at the nursing home. I felt very uncomfortable that they were there. They did not belong and neither one of them got along with my mother through all those years. Why would they come now, when it was too late? I definitely had troubled feelings about them being there. I told Angel, when I first saw our mother, it looked like she was not breathing and that her colour was not good. Angel kept on telling me to sit down because the nurses had just left after suctioning her lungs so she could breathe better. I sat down and George was cracking jokes every second. All we did was laugh since we really did not have feelings for my mother. He had us in stitches.

I got up twenty minutes later and once again told my sister that it did not look like our mother was breathing. Angel finally got up to see her and tried to get a pulse, listened to see if she was breathing, and then told us that she would be right back. The nurse walked in with her and listened to see if she had a heartbeat, but then announced to us that she had passed away. Before the nurse even left the room, George was laughing and joking that she had been dead from the time I got there. It was like a comedy movie, but in real life. Sad to say, but no one cared; and we were finally done with this chapter of our lives.

Once everyone got there, no one really cried but I'm sure we all felt a little guilty about what had become of our lives. This was not the way people reacted when one of their parents died. We all went for supper together that night. It was like a celebration. Her funeral had all been planned ahead of time, so there wasn't too much for us to do. We had her cremated and Monique insisted that we put out a big lunch. She was always in charge when it came to food. None of us could ever disagree with her because it was always her way and she controlled all these things. I stepped aside, knowing very well there was no point in arguing with her because she was always right and everything had to be done her way. I didn't think anyone would show up at the funeral but Monique called everyone to tell them. Many came out of respect for my dad.

Earlier in the year, we had found out that Pierre had been diagnosed with rectal cancer. He had part of his intestine removed and ended up with a colostomy. This apparently was a real inconvenience and the bag leaked like my dad's, except this was not urine. He had to go for radiation and chemotherapy and got very ill. He had lost so much weight that at my mom's funeral he came to kiss us all and I couldn't believe the changes in him. I'm not sure if I would have known who he was if they hadn't pointed him out to me. He had lost his hair, lost a large amount of weight, and looked extremely old. No one had warned me about him because no one cared about what happened to me as a child. They loved him and they didn't care about what I had to say. I had been betrayed my whole life.

Myla and I did end up leaving on the day we were scheduled to arrive in the States, except we got there late because it was the day of my mother's funeral and burial. We left directly after that and had a great time. Monique has said that our family was not present because they all got together for dinner that night. Rite had attended and we were present for the entire funeral but I didn't think the dinner together was a part of it. I have never felt guilty about going away on that day; after all when my father's mother died they were leaving for Hawaii and did not cancel their trip. They didn't even stay for the funeral. I learned from them.

Chapter 21

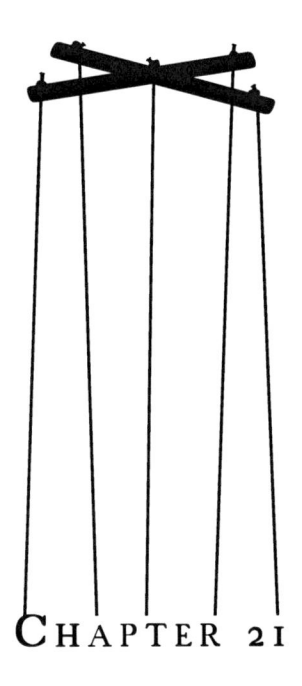

My mother's commitment to her own health was inconsistent. At the time of my father's retirement she wanted him to quit, but he had mixed feelings because he liked working as a dietician at the Taché Nursing Home. He liked working with the nuns and patients. I was even given the opportunity to work with my dad as a teenager while in school. Of course, I had the best position there and everyone knew it was because he was in charge of hiring and firing. He only quit his career because of my mother.

She now had nothing to do because she made him do everything around their condo. Her legs were failing because she never got up to exercise them. He would try to convince her to walk up and down the hallways because he did not want to see her cripple up. My oldest sister Monique was on her case all the time, but she would just smirk and laugh. She was not going to listen to anybody and I personally did not get involved because I was the youngest and no one ever took me seriously. They would listen to my older siblings, but not me. Remember, I was stupid, although I was the super, super sucker that should have had this tattooed on my forehead, because I obeyed everything she commanded. I jumped when she told me to jump and I did everything she asked me to do. While they were on holidays in Hawaii, Rite would drive and pick my parents up in the middle of the night and I would have to clean their entire house, then condo, before they got back. No one ever returned the favour when we would go to Newfoundland because the flight left at 3:50 a.m. We always took a taxi. No one was there upon our arrival back home.

My mother was definitely mentally ill, but no one did anything about it or helped her through her entire life. She lived in denial. In fact, I did not know this until a few days before she died. We would all meet in the family room and discuss things that one or the other of the family was not aware of. Again, I seemed to be kept in the dark because I was the youngest. It was then that the family began to talk about our mother's past and there were many things I had never heard before. I did find out and heard about all the various aunts and uncles that had mental illness on her side of the family. Many had OCD and it trickled through the family.

Chapter 22

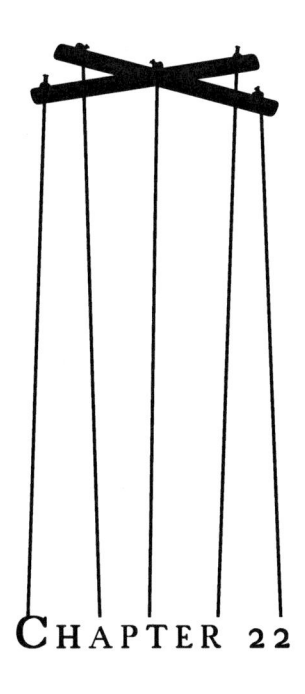

There was one time I felt like I was losing it. My doctor decided to talk to me about the suicidal, selfish person I was being. I immediately and definitely used the defense mechanisms that I had learned. Normally, I was able in my own mind to reach compromising solutions to conflicts that I was unable to resolve. This process was usually unconscious and the compromise generally involved concealing from myself the internal drives or feelings that threatened to lower my self-esteem and provoke anxiety. I repressed and withdrew from my consciousness any thoughts about the suicidal person I was. I only pushed this down or repressed it into the unconscious part of my mind. That happened when the doctor confronted me. I had projected this form of defense in which my unwanted feelings were displaced onto the doctor because I felt he was a threat to my external world. I was threatened about my own angry feelings and accused him of harboring hostile thoughts. I denied the conscious refusal to perceive that painful facts exist and felt like I had depersonalized to protect myself. I wasn›t going to allow him to talk badly about me because I had suicidal feelings. My mind was set on suicide and being stuck in that deep hole of darkness. There was no escaping it. I could not crawl out, and I felt that no one could ever help me. I couldn't think of anything else except to die. I felt disconnected or detached from my body. I felt like I had died and was floating on top of my body, watching myself. When I depersonalized I didn't feel like I had feelings and my emotions would disappear, but I felt great anxiety.

Depersonalization disorder is often triggered by some sort of abuse and in my case that's exactly what happened. I mostly felt extremely disturbed, and felt like I was losing grip on reality. I felt like I was dreaming. I was feeling that my body controlled me and that I was shaking inside. This upset my stomach. I could only spend time in bed to calm myself down. Some days, I had a hard time getting up to do my OCD rituals. I was exhausted and drained. I definitely thought my psychiatrist did not care and I did a lot of drinking in order to numb myself.

I wanted to punish Dr. Stevens for saying I was selfish. I had thoughts of overdosing in hospital during the evening so they could find me dead in the morning. I wanted to piss him off and make him mad. When he told me he would hunt me down in hell if I ever did this, I became even more hurt. I didn't and still don't believe in hell and thought I had a good comeback. I thought if he was going to criticize me, then I would put a wall up because this was another one of my defense mechanisms, along with writing an extremely long list of negative things about myself. I felt like I should be tortured for getting so upset and my only way was to think of suicide. I felt that I was not living in reality but totally in someone else's body.

I did not know I had a Borderline Personality Disorder. I was having problems with my emotions and behaviors. I had intense emotions and mood swings. I felt like I would go back to the hospital to die in my bed, and wanted Dr. Stevens to feel guilty. Once I thought it over, my thoughts changed and I figured if I was going to kill myself, I would do it secretly and in hiding. I felt like I would not have impacted Dr. Stevens or any staff at the hospital if I died. I knew he would get mad but I had then decided that I would do it when people least suspected it, when I would be smiling and everyone thought I was better.

I felt so empty and hurt that self-harm was a thought, but death was where I was going. I have felt that I have been criticized so much in my life, but I have never done anything about it. I've always worn a mask and put up with it. I was now getting upset; I stopped talking but felt very hurt. If anyone hurt me I pushed them away. I did not run back to them like in the past. I ended relationships and considered myself worthless and not deserving of anything good coming my way. I thought the worst of myself and put myself down beyond belief. My mother had ingrained this into my head and after all these years I couldn't seem to change. I knew I needed to work on this intensely with some of Dr. Stevens' guidance. I once again apologized to him for my behavior because I felt extremely bad for doing this. It's like I was living in two bodies; a good one and a bad one. I really didn't like the bad one. Once again, I apologized because Dr. Stevens was definitely on my side and was a highly qualified psychiatrist. I really had nothing bad to say about him. I was creating my own troubles and I was my worst enemy.

Dr. Stevens had given me homework as to what Borderline Personality Disorder (BDP) was. I fit the criteria. I knew it was a serious mental illness that made me play head games with people of authority. I was upset about every negative aspect about myself and he would disagree with me to make me angry. I wasn't able to see his point of view on things and I simply refused to. Instead, I would get so upset that I would write a long list of horrible things about myself that I knew weren't true. My mood would change and I would become unstable and at times detached. I was extremely impulsive and would self-harm without even thinking about it. I wanted him to feel guilty about it. I was putting it on his shoulders if I would extremely self-harm, trying to get him to care. It never worked. He was always right and I finally succumbed to listen and understand instead of disagreeing with him. He certainly made it very clear to me what I was doing that I became conscious when I was put in a situation. This was the most tragic outcome of any mental illness. Psychotherapy was definitely a helpful tool for dealing with Borderline Personality Disorder. One thing I dealt with through psychotherapy was self-harm. I felt like I was self-harming to help me regulate my emotions, to punish myself, and to express pain. I did not see this as harmful. I had been doing it since I was eight and it was habit-forming. From the studies I read, I also learned that women were more likely than men to have co-occurring disorders such as major depression, anxiety disorders, and eating disorders. I had all three.

At one time when I had gained weight my psychiatrist would tell me to tape my mouth. I fought with this disorder my entire life. I definitely thought he did not understand, and I thought of myself as a fat pig, rhino, elephant, or whale and would call myself these things in front of people and Dr. Stevens. I felt like he simply laughed at me and did not care, and was just seeing a very obese person sitting beside him in a chair. Whenever I went to see him, I did not like to mention anything about weight because he immediately would tell me to weigh myself on his scale. I absolutely refused each and every time because I knew what he was looking at and felt like he was repulsed by me in his own head. I went as far as wearing a shirt that had an elephant design on it to prove who I really was. I felt excessively hurt if anyone would put me down or say something. I would always twist it so that I would get hurt.

There was a time Dr. Stevens was trying to convince me how I would hurt people if I committed suicide. I didn't think so! He then asked me why I never asked him what he would think if I did commit suicide. I then asked, and he told me he would be very mad and sad and that he wouldn't be at his next golf game and would wonder where he went wrong. I was deeply touched by this at the time. I thought he was such a caring doctor. As the years go by, I know that these were just words to help me get by but were not really meant sincerely. Why in the world would he care about any of his patients? He was making money off of me and if I died I would be replaced with another patient. As far as golfing, I'm sure he would have gone that day and I would have been just another statistic. I still feel betrayed by him and his staff, although I think he was working with me to get better.

I needed to trust Dr. Stevens, Karen, my social worker, and Cheryl, my therapist from the Laurel Centre for Sexually Abused Women. At one point in time, Dr. Stevens waited while I called the Laurel Centre to get involved with them about disclosing my sexual abuse. It had been so many years and I needed professional help in dealing with the sexual abuse. The Laurel Centre's mission was to resolve long-term consequences related to unresolved trauma. It was a centre that had therapists work with you on child sexual abuse. It also worked with co-occurring disorders, which would include abuse and addictions of any kind.

The Centre opened in the 1980s, dealing with women who were struggling to overcome the trauma resulting from childhood sexual abuse. I was unable to deal with the pain in my younger years. They helped me cope, teaching me mechanisms to understand the ways in which the abuse affected my life. I identified ways to deal with my feelings of sexual abuse. This helped me alleviate the guilt and shame I was feeling and gave me strength and survival skills to keep going on. The therapists were there to help me feel better about myself and develop a sense of dignity and self-worth. They understood my mixed feelings about talking to anyone about what had happened to me because it hurt too much.

As an adult survivor of childhood sexual abuse, I only experienced difficulties later in life. I felt worthless, depressed, suicidal, and lonely; I self-harmed and isolated myself because I was different and felt bad. I had many nightmares and flashbacks, and felt like I needed to please anyone and everyone. This was all I knew. I did not trust anyone and felt somewhat responsible for the abuse. I had individual counselling for four years and I went to all the group sessions they provided.

I had formed a great deep bond with Cheryl, and I was never able to share my secrets with anyone else in my life. She was non-judgmental, and I never felt uncomfortable telling her anything because she took me seriously and tried hard to help me change the patterns of negativity in my life. Cheryl had so much knowledge and explained to me that eighty percent of victims were abused by a family member. She also said that since I was abused as a young child, I was more likely to develop psychiatric disorders later in life. I was able to make sense of the long-term effects of my depression, anxiety, dissociative disorder, and my suicidal tendencies. Dr. Stevens made me feel like he did not care about me at times, and I eventually learned this was because I had Borderline Personality Disorder. He needed to reassure me over and over again that I was being heard and that he did care about me. This was all I had to hear at the time to believe he had my interests at heart.

I went for dialectical behavior therapy at the Health Science Centre for a very long time. It was supposed to be effective for helping people manage overwhelming emotions, and help those people handle distress without losing control or acting out destructively. I had been greatly affected by the trauma and neglect I suffered as a child. Trauma literally caused me to be more vulnerable and I created all my negative emotions. In my groups, we were to learn about distress tolerance, mindfulness, emotion regulation, and interpersonal effectiveness. I was learning the concept of mindfulness and this was keeping me aware of the current situation.

The therapy was designed to teach me skills to control intense emotions, self-destructive behaviours, and to improve relationships. It was to help me overcome conflict, and feelings of being upset so I could alter the course of my relationships. It was to help me to get through overwhelming emotions. I coped by spending a great deal of time thinking about my past. I isolated myself to avoid distressing situations. I made myself numb by drinking alcohol and self-harming. I punished myself by controlling my food intake and overdosing. I was addicted to the natural painkillers called endorphins that were released when I hurt myself. I tried to distract myself by volunteering, looking at my grandchildren's pictures, and trying to comfort others with a mental illness. Even though I tried hard to understand all of this, I found it hard to do and actually felt extremely stupid in the group sessions that I was attending. They were moving too fast for me or perhaps I wasn't ready at that time.

Later, with Cheryl's extreme patience, she was able to make me understand very much about dialectical behavior. At times, I would not understand what she was talking about and I felt no shame telling her so. She was always so kind and patient, and explained anything she had said until I understood what she was talking about. I was able to comprehend all of these things better when we spoke on a one-on-one basis. Cheryl was absolutely calming and never made me feel stupid in any way. It took me three years of waiting to get into the Laurel Centre, and it was definitely worth the wait. The groups they held were not just for me. I went to every group they had and learned so much. They would give their clients three years with a therapist, but my time had been extended another year. I couldn't believe it, but I had many issues to resolve at the time and I considered myself extremely lucky to have the extension. I wasn't sure who I would be able to talk to after my time was up. It was a very disturbing thought for me. I did not want to feel abandoned like I had felt as a child. I had more needs to be addressed than the average person because I had highly changeable moods. I would go to the centre at times feeling extremely suicidal and very alone. I only wanted help and at times I would disassociate if we were talking about something uncomfortable. Because of my Borderline Personality Disorder, I had been hospitalized and had some of my medications changed. I knew what I was doing with my self-harm and suicide attempts, but still got trapped in the midst of the behavior.

This year, I will be out of psychotherapy with Karen at the end of June. She is now retiring and no one will be replacing her. A few months later I will have my term ended with Cheryl. They both played a big role in my life for many years. I shall miss them both, but I know I have to be strong and push myself to get better day by day. This is probably a very positive thing for me. Recovery is a process, and I have come a long way.

Thinking back, I certainly reached out for help in every way possible. I saw my family doctor, after which he referred me to a psychotherapist. She was absolutely wonderful and had me assessed by a psychiatrist in emergency. Just by chance, I was extremely lucky to see another psychiatrist in the hospital because I was not comfortable with the first one and did not trust her. The first time I met Dr. Stevens was in emergency after have taken an overdose and cutting my arms. He was on call that week. When he came to talk to me, he woke me with a soft touch of his hand. I immediately knew I had the wrong psychiatrist from the beginning. He was not like Dr. Leech. He let me speak and did not have that look of superiority and coldness. I asked him if I could have him as my psychiatrist because I had only heard good things about him. He replied that they didn't condone doctor-hopping, but told me it was my responsibility to ask Dr. Leech if I could switch. I wasn't able to tell her in person, so I wrote her a letter because I was scared of her. She did return and told me that Dr. Stevens would take me on as his patient. I was ecstatic. Although, I had to explain the reasons why I wanted to switch to her. I simply said that she and I were not a match. Through all my years of getting help, I realized that trust was a main issue with your psychiatrist. I was hospitalized, which helped, and opened many doors to psychotherapy, sessions of which I went to several times a week and never missed. This was a good chance to share all the anxieties and feelings I was having. I also went to Transitions a couple times a week for years to help me with all my addictions, and the reality of dealing with both mental illness and addictions. They are usually connected to each other. It took me years to even speak because I had to make sure they were trustworthy. It took a very long time in seeing Dr. Stevens before I could actually speak. I was afraid and I wasn't very co-operative when he spoke to me. He simply questioned me at each session, which were an hour long. At times, I gave him information but mostly sat there staring away from him. If not for his persistence and patient demeanour, I was lucky to be kept on as his patient. I then started writing about things that happened my past. After he would read my notes, he grilled me with a long course of questions in which I only had to answer simply, or nod my head yes or no. Later on in the years I had asked him why he kept on trying to help me, and his answer was that I always went to my appointments and he knew I wanted the help.

When I became a Mental Health Support Worker I had one of my practicums at the Mood Disorders centre. I was astounded at the wealth of information they had about every single mental illness. They have support groups if you are depressed, and I facilitated some of them.

I couldn't believe the resources out there and where someone could go if they needed help. The Manitoba Schizophrenia centre was located in the same building, and the Executive Director is also the Executive Director of the Schizophrenia Society of Canada. He works extremely hard and puts all his strength and heart into mental illnesses. He was such an inspiring person to know. He even wrote me a letter about his life as a child and into later years. This was a very sincere person and I appreciate everything he has done for me. He would come to visit me at the hospital when I was admitted. Not just anyone would do all of that for someone. I had also bonded with someone else from the system now.

The Obsessive Compulsive Disorder centre was located in the same building, which held group sessions with a psychologist who was trained to work with OCD patients. I did improve somewhat in the group sessions, but once I worked one on one with him, there was not much improvement with the medication I was given. It took a long time for me to figure out which ones helped. Once I was on the medication, I felt some helped more than others. I was able to change some of my compulsions. I completely changed in many ways. Although I will struggle with this disorder forever, I am now able to get out and enjoy myself at times.

I also called the Mobile Crisis Unit, which came to my home when I was self-harming. They were very professional and knew when to bring me into the hospital. I got lots of care from them. If not admitted to hospital, I would then be admitted to the Crisis Stabilization Unit, until there was a bed at the hospital. They now have built a new centre called the

Crisis Response Centre if you have any type of mental illness. You get to speak to a clinician, and if she feels you should talk to a psychiatrist then she refers you. I had overdosed on 158 temazepams and they did not want me going home because of the seriousness of this. There were no hospital beds in Winnipeg in Mental Health so they had no choice but to send me to the Crisis Stabilization Unit. I was really anxious, and only wanted to be admitted by my psychiatrist, but they built this centre for people like me. My psychiatrist was no longer able to admit in emergency. Although I was upset about this, these were the changes they had made, and thought that all psychiatrists were trained in the same way. Although I disagree about that because only my psychiatrist knows everything about me and so you would never know if the person you were talking to was sympathetic to your case or not. I was definitely lucky because I was able to speak to two wonderful psychiatrists. But I do believe they do not always click with your personalities.

There was also help for eating disorders in the building for those who were anorexic or bulimic. I was amazed on how many services they provided in one building. They did have an office, which was called S.P.E.A.K., which was for those who were suffering from a loss of a loved one to suicide. This was one great place to get help, and I attended many groups there after becoming a Mental Health Support Worker. All groups were free except the Anxieties Disorder of Manitoba group session, where there was a fee, but they were very helpful and effective. I went and did everything I could go to in order to help myself. It was a very long journey, but I was hoping that I would become a whole person for the first time in my life, and I would succeed.

Chapter 23

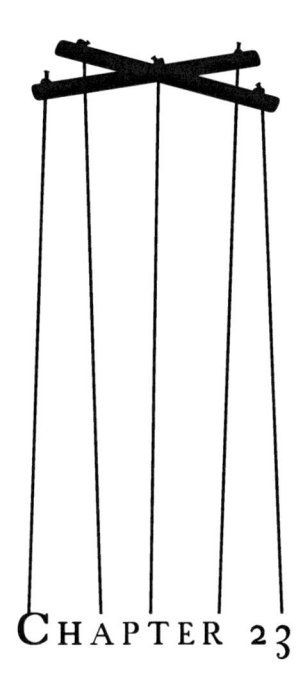

As I had in my previous hospital stays, I made friends with some very different people. Some were very kind, and some were extremely sick. I had made a very good friend by the name of Ashley. We both had Dr. Stevens as our psychiatrist. Then there was another lady in the hospital, and she was about the same age as we were. She had been in the hospital several times. Her name was Cindy. They both were very nice and I enjoyed talking to them both. The three of us became friends quite easily. We seemed to enjoy each other's company and we got to share our problems together.

Cindy and I had so much in common. We both thought about things in the same way. We both had the same beliefs and seemed to share many things about mental illness, although we were not diagnosed with the same disorders. She was bipolar and I had Obsessive-Compulsive Disorder, Borderline Personality Disorder, and major depression. Ashley was a depressed person who had no friends, and her family did not seem close to her. She had a sister who lived in Winnipeg who had her phone number blocked so that Ashley could not contact her. Both her parents lived in Victoria and she did not see them very often. Ashley had never been married and had no children, whereas Cindy was married and had two children.

Cindy was not a very assertive person and I felt that people seemed to talk about her and laugh at her. She took quite a few prescription drugs and sometimes seemed mentally way out of it. She abused her drugs and had for years. Although I barely knew either Cindy or Ashley at the time, they still seemed to be good friends. Once Ashley and I started talking more together we seemed to have bonded. I had no idea at the time that Ashley had actually told Cindy that she was going to be alone one day like her. Her children would grow up and move out. Cindy got very upset with this and they had a disagreement about whether the three of us could get along and do things together. After that, Cindy just seemed to disappear without my knowing any of this and how hurt she felt.

I was now spending quite a bit of time with Ashley. We became best of friends. We were hospitalized three times together. The third time, I felt so much sympathy for her because she really didn't have anybody in her life. She was a Royal Winnipeg Ballet dancer and then a physiotherapist working in close proximity to where I lived. I'm not sure why she lost her job as a physiotherapist, but I imagine it was because of her depression.

During our third hospitalization, Doray Enterprises told me that they wanted me back to work with them as a mental health support worker. I had done one of my practicums there and the clients seemed to cling to me. These clients all had mental illnesses and would go to do some work there for only seventy-five cents an hour. They were happy with that because it got them out of the house or group homes, and they were all provided with bus passes. The money they made paid for their cigarettes and they were able to socialize with each other. It was a very good program. At Christmas they were all taken to a hotel for a turkey dinner, and each and every one of them would receive $50.00. They were in their glory. It was wonderful to see. Doray Enterprises had called me on a couple of occasions to work for them, but I was already on disability pay.

Ashley was looking for another kind of employment and I suggested that Doray Enterprises hire her. Lucky her; because of my recommendation they did. She was ecstatic and so excited to do something different.

She found out while we were having coffee at Earl's. She came out of the area where she had been talking on her phone and danced all the way back to our table.

During that hospitalization, Ashley's roommate was bitten by bed bugs. She was extremely anxious about this. It had taken the hospital staff several hours before finally they found them. Everything was stripped from the three people in the room and put outside where it was -40 degrees. Bed bugs only die from extreme heat or cold. I couldn't believe how calm I was, but nevertheless I changed my bedding and found out from the nurses where to look for the bugs. They also gave us information about what bed bugs look like and where they usually hide. That night Ashley's room had been stripped of everything, but the patients all got new mattresses and the staff seemed to have it under control. The person with bed bug bites was a nurse and was into cocaine. She certainly tried to convince me to try it. I never did but found it quite sick that she had this stashed in her room and no one had reported her, because she was telling everyone.

Ashley had mentioned to me that she once was an alcoholic and had gone to AA for a very long time. She had been dry for several years. Once I got to know her more she finally told me that she was involved with this man who lived on a farm. He would come to pick her up on some Saturdays and take her back to the farm. It seemed kind of odd that he never took her out anywhere else. Maybe she spoke of going out once with him to me. He was obviously just in it for the sex. She seemed blinded by all of this and would tell me how they would get up in the morning and he would make her breakfast, and then dinner in the evening. She seemed to be thrilled just with the notion of him picking her up. He was also an alcoholic but did not want her to go to the same AA group as him. Strange, is what I thought! She had gone out with him on and off for several years. They always seemed to get back together eventually and I'm not sure, but perhaps this made her feel important.

People at the hospital would all think he was her dad. I had never met him and just thought he probably looked old. She had only one other friend who was a lot older than her, too. He had lost most of his sight and she would sleep with him also.

At one point, she told me that her friend was not allowed in her house, although he would come over and cut her grass. He found it somewhat strange that he was not allowed in. The reason was that she did not want him to see the inside of the house because she was a hoarder. I guess I can't blame her; I would feel the same if my home was in such disarray.

One or the other of Ashley's friends would get mad at her and it seemed like a game of switching and bouncing around from one to the other. She ended up quitting work at Doray and worked for CMHA. She thought this would be a good choice to work there. She ended up hating her job and got depressed again, getting fired once again. She would miss many days of work. She landed back in the hospital but had started to drink. I really didn't know much about her except the fact that I felt sorry for her. She now had no money and ended up cashing in her RRSP's.

She would buy hundreds of dollars' worth of clothes and waste money on getting her body waxed, gel nails, brows done, false eyelashes, facials, and different kinds of massage therapy. One of her massages cost her four hundred dollars. I couldn't believe it. She was worried about money but was wasting it at the same time. On that particular week she had spent seven hundred dollars at the hair salon. The staff would convince her to get different things done, and she would do them.

One day when I drove Ashley home from the hospital to pick something up, she was in shock. She came to get me to see the inside of her house. I couldn't understand why. She wanted me to see it. The house was definitely run down but it also was somewhat decent. Her father had come to see her at the hospital and had also gone to her house and looked into her windows. He saw that there was junk everywhere. While she was in hospital, he had paid people to clean up her house. She was upset that he had done that, but was also happy to see her home clean again and everything put away or thrown out.

Ashley turned out to be my best friend at the time and we hung out together every day. There was one problem for me with the friendship, and that was the money. I needed to spend so much money on gas to pick her up and then drive home. It was phenomenal. She gave me money to fill up a couple of times, but I lived very far from her and would go to see her every day. I would take her shopping and take her to Unicity to pay her phone bills. We would go grocery shopping together and I would have to drive her back home and carry her groceries in.

Little did I know then, but she was the biggest liar I had ever encountered. She lied about everything. There were three instances when I would go to my condo and bring things up. She always told me she would wait. Each and every time when I got back into my car it smelled like cigarette smoke. I obviously knew she smoked, but wouldn't have expected her to smoke in my car. One day when I arrived unexpectedly at her home she had a cigarette in her hand and she started apologizing. She had an ashtray completely full of cigarette butts. I'm not her mother or her keeper, and she should be old enough to know that she can smoke without lying about it. Her house was beginning to look like she was hoarding again. I don't know why, because all she had to do was maintain it. I saw her bathroom one time only and that was after everything got cleaned. Directly after that, I could not go to the washroom in her home. She told me to go to Tim Horton's.

She didn't have any light bulbs that worked in her whole house. She had the television on and one tiny little lamp in one of the bedrooms upstairs. Other than that, they were all burned out. I have never seen anything like this in my life. Ashley then wanted me to change the light bulbs. I would stand on a chair and try, but I was not tall enough and she refused to stand on the chair for unknown reasons. She is extremely tall and would have been able to see inside the fixture. We finally went out and bought two lamps for the living room. She had no cutlery or dishes and did not cook for herself. In fact, you couldn't even get to the stove because so much garbage was littered throughout the house. She had mold growing underneath some things on the floor. Her front entrance had hundreds of different pills scattered on the floor. She would not let me throw them out. She wanted to separate them collectively into their own bottles. Even after three months they were still scattered all over.

There came a day when I decided to empty and clean the fridge. She found this overwhelming. We first needed to empty the fridge of all the moldy things. She had a gallon of milk that had dripped all the way down the fridge. The milk was so sour and extremely thick. It was disgusting. I couldn't understand how anyone would want to live this way. We threw many things out and then I proceeded to empty everything and wash the fridge. At the bottom was something that looked like rust, but as I picked at it over and over again, it started to come off. It smelled of sour milk.

As I was cleaning, Ashley went to sit in her staircase and cry. She was overwhelmed, but she never once came to help me. I found this very strange, considering it was her fridge. I got everything clean and placed her good food back in the fridge. It looked so clean that we would look inside a few times in disbelief. I just wanted to help her out and make her house into a real home. She was very grateful and thankful that I had done one thing at least. We were to proceed very slowly. I then worked to clear and clean her counters. She had bought a microwave, coffee maker, and toaster. I washed and cleaned all the counters and placed the appliances on the counter. The kitchen finally looked decent; but that was all I really ended up cleaning in her home, because she always wanted to go out. We had at first planned we would do some cleaning for at least one hour a week, until we had finished.

Weeks went by and Ashley never seemed like she wanted to do any cleaning anymore. She was enjoying her freedom in the world. We went shopping a lot and she would buy hundreds of dollars' worth of clothing. She then would place it on the floor. The bags were never opened again except for the fact that they were all dirty with cat hair. Even the bags were getting dirty.

She then began to drink behind my back and no one knew. She would drink vodka straight from the bottle. One night she was so drunk that she fell down among all of that disarray and split her head open. She needed several stitches to her head. A couple weeks went by and then she fell again, seeming to have crushed her shoulder. She was in a lot of pain. She was already in the psychiatric part of the hospital. She had returned from a weekend pass and was in a lot of pain. The psychiatric nurses were not much use because they had been working in that department for a long time. They weren't trained for fractures and wounds. She finally had it operated on, and the doctors had to use sixteen screws to put her shoulder back together. She had damaged it extremely badly.

She continued to drink during her weekend passes and was told by Dr. Stevens that if she drank again, it would be an automatic discharge. She was waiting to go to rehab and he let her stay in hospital until she would have a place at rehab. Yet, she continued to drink and was automatically discharged.

Ashley would tell me that she was not drinking anymore, but when I picked her up one day a neighbor noticed me walking up to her house.

She came running to me because she was wondering why Ashley was lying on the street in the snow. The neighbour then told me that she called the police. When I got there Ashley lied and acted like nothing had happened until the police showed up. At this point, I was only allowed at the back entrance. She had gone upstairs, but when the police showed up, they wanted me to follow them. I told them that she didn't allow me in her house, but they told me to go with them. Ashley was ok, so they took my name, etc. and left. She never told me anything about it. In fact, she denied doing anything like that. I knew she was lying.

Several times when she told me she wasn't drinking anymore, I went to pick her up and she staggered through the snow to get to my car. She fell down several times. This was not what a sober person would ever look like.

Ashley was really taking advantage of our friendship. I picked her up every single day, even though she lived quite a distance from me. I spent thousands of dollars on gas visiting her and taking her out to buy groceries, but she simply didn't seem to care what I was doing for her. She just kept on taking and taking and not being appreciative of anything. It took me a very long time before I could ever see the light of what she was doing. She was manipulative and conniving to everyone. I guess I should have seen the signs, since her family rejected her. In the winter, she even convinced my husband to shovel her snow for a fee. She knew he had injured his back at work and had a hard time working, but once again everything was for her.

She did not have insurance coverage for her medications, and I felt sorry for her. When we both got out of hospital I gave her a large bottle of Prozac and Clonazepam because I had a new prescription and I had these left over at home. She ended up getting drunk and for some unknown reason she had scattered all of her pills on her bed to make it look like it was a suicide attempt. I'm not sure who she called but she was passed out and the fireman who got there first used an ax to get into her house and broke her front door. They found her with all the pills and the paramedics brought her to the hospital, only to find out that she had never taken any pills but was simply drunk. She was playing games with the system and was also very jealous of me.

She played these games for a few weeks and was picked up by paramedics several times in a short time. She received the bills for all the ambulance calls, but she didn't care and never paid them.

My daughter set Ashley up with her boss at work. She didn't call him for a while. She seemed decent to him until she phoned him at 3:00 a.m. He was not impressed and knew she was drunk. She said that she was going to apologize to him but never did so. Once, she called me seventeen times in a night, because she was depressed and drunk. Rite was livid and told me to tell her not to call our home again. She abided by that rule, but just for a short time.

Myla, who is a hairstylist, highlighted Ashley's hair, cut it, and put hair extensions in her hair to make it look thicker. My daughter is very kind-hearted and didn't charge her. We would visit her on some occasions and my daughter let her come over. We once watched a movie she really wanted to see. My daughter would make supper and always give her a dinner to take home. Ashley always accepted everyone. Were we ever suckers!

Even on Christmas Day, Myla had Ashley over for dinner because she didn't want her to spend it alone. Myla and I brought her presents so she could fit in. Ashley did buy a few little things for Myla's three children, but we were still being taken advantage of, even if it was my fault.

One day on our way out from her home, the postman told her to empty her mailbox because he couldn't fit anything inside of it anymore. She never bothered with the mailbox, and even when she did empty it, she wouldn't even open her bills. Her mail would be piled high on her coffee table, unopened. I know for certain she had a $2,500.00 bill from the paramedics. She could care less and didn't pay her bills nor answer her home phone ever. She made sure that no one could leave a message because she would leave her answering machine full at all times. She hadn't filed her income tax for about six years. I'm not sure how she got away with this, but I do know she didn't answer her door either. She had cats, but she never took care of them. I never saw a litter box. I would imagine they would go anywhere and everywhere. I would take her to buy cat food several times but that was it in terms of taking care of them.

Ashley had a lot of problems. She indeed wanted to be admitted to the hospital because she had called someone, but I'm not sure who it was--perhaps a crisis centre or the police themselves. Maybe she wanted me to call, but I never did. Another unusual thing she did was to walk into the Assiniboine River. She definitely was seeking attention. Her story was that she made sure that no one was around. She took off her expensive shoes and watch and left them on the shore. Why would she care about these items if she were going to drown herself? She walked into the muddy water, and then a fisherman came to her rescue.

I recall her telling me several times how good a swimmer she was. I'm not sure how far she went into the water, but she told me she had her head under. I could never understand how a fisherman could get to her if she had walked in that far. She certainly had time to drown by the time he could get to her rescue. She never fought with him either. She was saved. The paramedics were called and she sat down beside the shore. She told me how peaceful it was. She fought to get *into* the ambulance because it was so peaceful.

The whole thing seemed unbelievable to me. Ashley never forgot about her shoes and watch. Someone that distraught would not even remember that. When she was pulled out, she was covered in mud and at the hospital they threw her clothes away. She was seen by a psychiatrist and after paramedics had been called for her five times, she was discharged once again. She was telling them nothing but lies, in my opinion. Because the hospital staff had thrown out all her clothes, she was sent home by taxi in a hospital gown. Her toenails were disgusting because they still had mud in them. She told me all about it, but right from the start, I never believed her story for an instant.

Another example of the strange things she would say was when she decided to drive to Portage La Prairie to stay in a hotel to read a book. She told me that along the way, near Headingley, it was pouring rain so she stopped on the side of the highway. A man got out to see if she was all right. If it was pouring rain that heavily, why would anyone stop to see how she was doing? People would normally drive by, knowing full well why someone had pulled over. She said that she thanked him and he left. He must have noticed the alcohol on her breath because the R.C.M.P. stopped behind her a few minutes later. Again, why would they stop? In her car apparently lay very many bottles of pills and a book on the passenger seat. The police gave her a Breathalyzer test, but apparently she was not strong enough to blow into it. They tried several times and she had charges laid for drinking and driving. They took her to the hospital, but she was released at once. Her lawyer fees were phenomenal and she did have to pay this time. She lost her license for one year and her car was impounded for three months. I drove her to bring her car back, but to this day, I don't remember who parked it in the garage.

I had to take Ashley out of town to Headingley, which cost me more money, for her to have her mug shot taken and be fingerprinted. She didn't seem to mind, but I was embarrassed for her. We got to the station and we were both in the R.C.M.P. car on our way to get all of this done. This was the first time I had been in a police car, ever. Ashley was actually talking with the police officer, and he was very friendly. I just wanted to get out of the car. She had no shame whatsoever.

Another strange incident that happened after her arrest was an attack. She had gone shopping at Giant Tiger and an aboriginal male was walking behind her, and then approached her. Apparently, she yelled at him the word, "No!" very loudly and he pounded her face on the cement. He did not take anything from her, which was very strange. He had no reason to do that unless he was deranged. She took the bus home covered in blood, but the bus driver never said anything and she in turn told him nothing about the incident.

When I called the following day, Ashley would not answer her phone. I was worried and drove to her house. She would not answer the door but I could see her head and hair on the couch. She had sustained a broken nose and bruising on her face. This happened on a Saturday night and maybe she needed time to make up a story on Sunday, since she probably fell down from drinking. On Monday we talked, but what she had told me did not make any sense. I asked if she had called the police and naturally she had not. I kept on insisting she go to the police station. Finally, on the following Thursday we went to the police for her to report it. They didn't seem to believe her and told her that they wouldn't be able to do anything. This was so strange, and I was getting extremely tired of all the lies. Some I could prove and others seemed odd, but I wasn't able to really say anything. Ashley thought of them in a drunken state, I imagine.

Ashley eventually went to rehab for twenty-eight days and when she got out she was put into a home to recover even longer. I think it cost her four to five hundred dollars to sleep and eat there. Within a few months, things started to go bad with the staff. They would run out of food before the end of the month. She would have to pay for her own food. Food she had to refrigerate would disappear. She was allowed visitors only at certain hours. This centre was run by a few twenty-year-old girls.

On the day that Ashley had her surgery for her shoulder, the doctors had her wrapped and strapped her to an ice machine that needed to be assembled. Since I was the only one they told how to use it, we headed back to the centre where no one was present. She lived in the attic and she had to scoot up the stairs on her bum. The following day I went back to the clinic to get a piece that was missing. I came back with it to find that someone was trying to help her; they had all the bandages unwrapped and therefore she could not use the machine properly. As I was attempting to help Ashley, a staff member came up and told me it was not visiting hours and I was to leave. I explained to them that I was the only person who had been shown how to use the machine. They didn't care and wanted me out. I was not allowed to come in to put her to bed the night before, but there was no staff present even though they knew she was going for an operation. They kicked her out and packed all her things in a garbage bag. She was missing quite a few things. One was a coffee maker she had purchased on her own. I'm not sure if she ever received it back.

Through time, I had noticed that some of the Obsessive-Compulsive Disorder symptoms I was experiencing got her thinking she had the same symptoms. I would tell her something that no one ever did and she would tell me she was doing the same things. I was getting help for it, whereas our psychiatrist did not find it a big deal for her. He just ignored her symptoms and said they would go away.

The worst was when she told me she also had experienced sexual abuse. She suddenly remembered her dad doing things to her. She had gone to the psychiatrist and he told her to go to the Laurel Centre for Sexually Abused Women. I was already in the program and it was helping me a lot. Dr. Stevens never questioned her about anything, which gave me an inkling that he may not have believed her, but I could be very wrong. Because of confidentiality, I could never prove this and it got to a point where I didn't even care.

Our toxic relationship finally ended on the day she started to compare my illness to hers. I didn't think there was a competition going on. She told me that I could just stop praying for six hours a day, whereas she had anxiety and depression which was worse. She called me back in the afternoon she said the exact same thing again. I told her I could not stop praying and I was hospitalized for five months to end it. That was the end of our friendship. She called back many, many times but my husband and I did not answer the phone. Now that I've gone through so much counselling, I think that perhaps I should have verbally told her not to phone me again, but that's not what I did. Our extremely toxic friendship was over and the lies had ended. My family was ecstatic.

Ashley called me hundreds of times, but she finally gave up. One day as I was in the pharmacy I got a call on my cell phone and I just answered it. I did not know who it was until she told me. I was extremely cold to her but softened up after a few minutes. She told me that Dr. Stevens got her on CPP Disability and that she was only getting seven hundred dollars a month. She told me that she would have to go to the food banks for food. She then threw this in my face. She said that I used to complain about the amount of spending money I was getting every month. I had always wanted more. She then tried to compare the money she was getting to the amount I had to spend. This made me angry, considering I spent most of my money on gas and her. Since our friendship was over I have now been able to save several thousands of dollars of my own money for holidays. This was always a surprise for my husband, who worked through the days, evenings, and weekends to earn money for us.

Ashley asked me if I would meet her for coffee one day and all I said was, "Maybe." I got off the phone and felt sorry for her. I then began to gather food and put it into our extra bedroom. I mentioned this to our old friend Cindy and we both decided to give Ashley a food basket. The following day, Cindy and I decided not to do it, given all the things that Ashley had said to me. I immediately put everything away and just did not think of her again until one day I was driving close to home, I got another surprise call from her. I told her I was driving and I could not talk to her. She then asked if I would call her later. My answer was, "Probably not."

The next time I saw her at the Laurel Centre, I was on my iPad, hoping that Ashley wouldn't notice me. She looked so different because she had gained at least seventy pounds. She asked me how I was doing and told me she was there to sign up for a group. I was starting a group and was hoping it was not the same one. Yes, it was. What a trigger! After a couple of groups, my OCD got worse, and my Tourette's and a few added stressors put me right back into the hospital.

Chapter 24

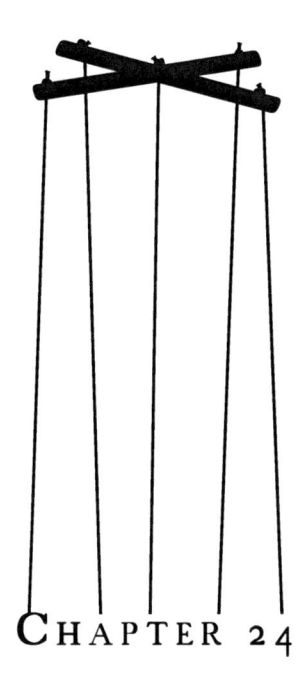

Quite a time had passed since I had stopped hanging out with Ashley. Cindy and I started talking and she told me that Ashley told her she would soon have her children move out and that she would be alone like her, even though she was married. I was shocked at what Cindy was telling me because Ashley had told me the same thing would happen to me if my husband should die. My reply was that I still had children and grandchildren, but she certainly tried to tell me no one would want me around. She was obviously jealous of both of us. Cindy and I compared times and events where Ashley tried to make us feel sorry for her. Cindy was the brave and smart one for leaving our friendship with Ashley at that time. She had known Ashley for many years and knew her better than I did. I was out there to help someone, but I picked a bad seed. We compared dates about when Ashley was calling me in the middle of the night. She was apparently calling Cindy also, but not telling me anything about her contact with Cindy when we were friends.

Cindy and I had so much in common. We had deep dark thoughts and we were able to share them with each other. I had never met someone that felt like me. We started going out for coffee weekly and talked on the phone daily, sometimes for three to four hours. We would laugh at the most ridiculous things, and we got along extremely well. At one point, I remember telling her that I wouldn't have been able to be friends with her when she was overdosing on Gravol. Her personality was completely different then, and she could not even hold a conversation.

There was a time when she was taking oxycodone and hydromorphone together for pain. She was totally out of it. I would ask her how many extras she had taken that day and by 11:30 a.m. she was totally out of it. Also, when I was going for a bladder surgery and they told me I would be getting Tylenol 3 for pain, I had no intentions of taking or filling that prescription. When Cindy found out, she automatically gave me about twenty of them. A few minutes later she took her bottle of pills out of her purse and realized that she had given me twenty hydromorphone pills instead. It was a good thing I had no intentions of taking anything because I would have been high on this medication. I also remembered that after my car accident, morphine had made me feel very sick.

Cindy reached out all the time. She told me several times that she never had a friend before. This saddened me because I found it hard to believe that she lived this long without a friend. There was much more to her life that I will not write about because I respect her, although I know that she was sexually abused when she was younger. I finally convinced her to go to the Laurel Centre for Sexually Abused Women. I had been seeing a therapist there for a very long time, and I was in awe at the changes that have taken place within me. I was convinced this was the place for her to go to talk. You didn't need to talk about the abuse *per se*, but I touched on every topic besides that. When I was comfortable, I was able to speak about the sexual abuse and the abuse from my mother. I was also extremely confused about the fact that no one cared what was happening in my family. They continued to invite this predator into their homes and to their parties. I couldn't understand this.

Cindy was hiding horrible secrets from everyone and desperately needed to talk to a professional about all of the things that had happened in her past. She needed to be guided in the right direction. I knew that the Laurel

Centre was the place where she would get the most help. There were group sessions held several times a year which you could attend, and it was always with women who had suffered from past sexual abuse. I found it to be the safest place I could ever be. The atmosphere was warm and gentle. The staff always got along and all the therapists would pay attention to you whether or not they were working with you. Also, no men were allowed in the building. When I had my appointments no one could come and wait for me. I was to attend alone and no one was allowed to sit in the waiting room. They sometimes had the doors locked, and you would have to buzz yourself in.

These people were women who worked with women. I felt so comfortable there that I would go in early just to be at peace. Others who attended you would meet on a regular basis. You were able to talk freely and everyone that I have talked to who attended the sessions felt the exact same way. I never wanted to leave, but knew that there would come a day that my time there was running out. I was fearful. I would call my therapist whenever I felt that I needed to talk to someone. If she was not there, I would leave a message to have her call me back. She always returned my calls and was always extremely helpful.

I wanted Cindy to feel this security. I wanted her to feel better about herself because she had no self-esteem. She would tell me how her own family thought she was stupid and would laugh at her. They complained about her memory and she never felt she had control of her own home. We both attended psychotherapy with Karen, our social worker, the therapist, and others in our group. There were times when not many women attended. Karen was a wonderful person and treated all of us with respect. She gave everyone time to talk and we would try to help each other. There were many tears in that room. We were all empathetic towards each other. We were solid and tried to help each and every person. I knew Cindy looked forward going to groups. I would pick her up and we would go to her apartment with another member of the group named Andrea. We would sit and have our own sessions together but with lots of laughter. I could always get Cindy to laugh under any circumstance. She had a husband, a daughter who was becoming a doctor, and an older son who had been going to university for years and never knew what he wanted to do with his life. Her husband drank alcohol and did not get along with his daughter until he was diagnosed with cancer.

Cindy wanted everything for her children but felt controlled by them. The two bedrooms in their apartment were given to each child, while she and her husband slept on the floor in the living room. Everyone in our group was so against this but I always understood why she had these arrangements. Every day when we talked, we would say "I love you" before we would go. At one point, Cindy felt that I helped her more than her own psychiatrist. This is when she started calling me her anti-depressant. She would phone or meet her anti-depressant whenever she needed to talk.

I always took the time to listen to or go see Cindy if she was extremely depressed. By the time I left, she always told me how much better she felt. I seemed to be able to change her thoughts in a more positive way. After all, she was my best friend and very sincere. She was such a gentle, kind person and I felt that I also needed her in my life. She was always understanding, kind, compassionate and easy to talk to. I even started calling her my anti-depressant. We were friends that could never be split up under any circumstances. We had promised each other that we would not commit suicide because it would be too painful for one another. I truly loved her from the bottom of my heart.

At the beginning, we would go to psychotherapy from 10:00 a.m. to 11:45 a.m. and then we would go to the cafeteria where I would have a coffee and she would have her Coke. She never left home without Coke. She was addicted to it. We would then have another group session at 1:00 p.m. till 2:00 p.m. I had attended this group for several years and felt that I had learned so much. We once had two facilitators and then Jeff found employment in another hospital. He was someone I could go talk to whenever things weren't going right. He listened and was always kind and did not have an attitude like some other workers in psychiatry. He was patient, always smiled, and would always give you good advice. I missed him dearly when he left. The centre had lost someone very important in psychiatry.

After our sessions, Cindy and I would then go to Tim Horton's for coffee and talk about our day. We were intrigued by the same things. In our afternoon group we often would watch movies and Jeff, the therapist, would make popcorn. The movies were always about addictions. Some were quite educational and interesting. They definitely were an eye-opener. Many sessions were about all the different drugs people were addicted to. I had never done drugs and was quite amazed at what some of them did to you. Some were about illegal drugs and others about prescription drugs. Since I was on benzodiazepines, I always found it interesting to learn how addictive they were.

Cindy was addicted to several medications and abused them. Later, because of her addictions, her family doctor told her to seek another doctor. The doctor wasn't about to feed this addiction anymore. Cindy found a doctor next to her home, at a walk-in-clinic. He basically took her off of all the medications, and she went through withdrawal, becoming extremely sick and losing a lot of weight. She could only get very little prescribed by him and she had to pick it up every couple of days so that she wouldn't take the whole supply at once. She lived through hell.

Once she started feeling better, Cindy tried so hard to get some of my medications and asked for them constantly. I would go to Superstore with her and buy two hundred Gravol pills. She was also hooked on them, and these pills made her shake uncontrollably. I bought these for her twice, at her expense, but talked to Dr. Stevens about it. He highly recommended that I never do that again and to tell her so in advance. She agreed with me but still got the pills on her own. One time, she had come to our condo for just a few minutes and she was in the bathroom the whole time. Our bathroom is right next to the entrance, and I went to the door when I was ready to leave. As I waited, I could hear the pills being poured into her hand. She took twenty-four of my clonazepams and swallowed them all at once. She then became very quiet and I ended up taking her home by 5:50 p.m. because she wanted to go to bed. I only let her in my home two more times after that, but I hid Rite's and my medications in another room. This was not going to happen again, not if I could control it.

She had a hard time getting extra benzodiazepines from anyone and had told me several times that if she would ever overdose to end her life, she would take two hundred Gravol. She was unable to access any other kinds of medications. She would call and leave me messages saying that she didn't know what she was going to do. I would listen to these messages and contact her each and every time. She had always overdosed and slept it off. She did not return to Emergency for any care. We both thought it was a useless place to go to because of the impatient, unprofessional care. The staff would hook you up to an I.V. and close the curtain so they didn't have to pay any attention to you. One nurse told me she was too busy at one point because there were other patients in emergency who wanted to live. They were unsympathetic and did not tolerate anyone who had tried to commit suicide. We were a waste of their time and we were ignored completely. Once we had seen the psychiatrist, we were discharged to go home, yet there were times we would have security guards sit with us so we could not escape. What a waste of time! One time, I was told to go home without having had any psychiatric care. I felt worse than before I overdosed the day before.

I remember the following week when I had absolutely lost it and talked to Karen about it after group. Through group I was crying uncontrollably and she did not want me to leave. She brought me to Emergency even though I told her they would do nothing to help me because I had overdosed twice the weekend before and was told to go home. I was extremely troubled and did not have anyone to talk to or help me. I was devastated. Cindy sat with me the whole time and tried to comfort me but I felt far too overwhelmed.

At that time, I was taking lithium and it affected my thyroid gland quite severely. My family doctor could not understand why my body was not absorbing the medication for my thyroid. Every time she would check it, it needed to be adjusted to a higher dose. This was making me very sick mentally. I felt crazy and was looking for help from anyone. The psychiatric nurse who came to talk to me was laughing at me, degraded me, and most definitely made up stories that she said were written in my file by Dr. Stevens. Some of the things she told me were all fabricated and not something he would have written down. What horrible care! She even told me that Rite and I should go for counselling, because she had made up in her mind what was wrong with me just from seeing me twice in one week.

Whatever the nurse was reading from that chart was definitely not something Dr. Stevens had written because he was very honest and truthful with me. This was by far not an issue at this point. While I was talking with the nurse, Cindy sat with me the whole time and listened to everything the nurse said to me. I was apparently a very aggressive, rude and mouthy person according to her, and I needed to change. I just kept quiet because I knew she had perceived me the wrong way. These were all her comments and not things that were ever written in my file. I eventually talked to Dr. Stevens about all of this and his comment was that they really didn't know what they were doing in Emergency. It was not the place to go get psychiatric help.

That day, Cindy was laughing because I had to go to the washroom but decided not to because the psychiatrist on call would probably think that Cindy was the patient if I was not in the room. Every other psychiatrist knew me by name but this particular psychiatrist looked like a mad scientist. Even my daughter, who visited me once, asked me who that patient was when she saw this doctor. He was dressed horribly and the hair that was left on his head was in complete disarray. When he came into the room he was quite confused by the sight of us both sitting together. He didn't have a clue which patient he was supposed to talk to. It was exactly like we had talked about a few minutes earlier. We were both laughing in our heads because he should have known who the patient was, considering that I had overdosed twice in the past week and had been discharged by him. It was terrible care and a total waste of time on everyone's part to go to the hospital in these situations. I had told Cindy my predictions way ahead of time, and I was right the entire time. If I was going to commit suicide there really was no one I could talk to at the time. I felt like I was in crisis. We went to see Karen and she was very surprised about the kind of care I was given. She eventually talked to Dr. Stevens twice about me, considering they worked as a team.

My feelings had been ignored once again, but I was finally admitted once I saw Dr. Stevens. He was the only person to talk to if I needed immediate care. Through my hospitalizations Cindy would not come to the hospital to visit me. I knew how she felt about coming into the One North hospital. It wasn't exactly a very caring environment, but we did meet up on Tuesdays to go to psychotherapy together.

When I was hospitalized for a few months, Cindy was convinced she had lost her best friend. She would tell this to her family, but they always encouraged her by saying I would be back once I was discharged. In fact, immediately after discharge we would be back together again and know that nothing had changed between us in those few months. I just needed time to get better. She would constantly tell me how she thought she had lost her best friend. I would reassure her that was not going to ever happen, because we had a serious bond through our friendship.

Life with Cindy was always a pleasant time. She had in fact asked me to hold her hand when her husband died, she trusted me so much. She felt she needed me close to her at all times. I promised from the bottom of my heart that I would always be there to comfort her and stand by her. We talked about the mountains and the ocean often. I had always told her I would bring her with me to see the mountains again. She had been in Banff once, and was so impressed by the mountains there that she always wanted to go back. She had never seen an ocean and I promised her that I would take her someday to see both of them and we would have a great time together. We dreamt about this all the time together and talked about it on many occasions. One day she called me, crying, because she wanted me to listen to a song that was made for the two of us. The song was "You've Got a Friend" by Carole King, and it applied to both of us. The lyrics speak about the value of a friend who is always available, no matter what. True friends always remain faithful. I often think of Cindy when I listen to that song. Her friendship meant everything to me.

There were many times that Cindy would call me in times of need and I would drive over to the other end of the city to help her and cheer her up. There wasn't one time that that she told me she did not feel better. She appreciated my visits and thanked me every time, because she always felt better by the time I left and would tell me so. After all, I was considered her anti-depressant.

Meanwhile, my family was having its own struggles. By that time, Monique and Pierre had divorced and he had remarried. Monique mentioned Pierre's name several times when we were together. Her daughter even called him an asshole. Monique kept telling me about the accidents he was having. She felt sorry for him. He and his new wife had gone to celebrate his sister's anniversary in Montreal with them. He called Monique long distance and told her that he cried when he spoke in front of the crowd. All she kept on saying was that he had deep regrets and would have probably wanted her there instead of his wife because Monique spoke French. She never understood why he loved his second wife.

I did not feel sorry for either of them in any way. Monique had never helped me at all through the years. My sister Monique was very sympathetic about what had happened to Pierre and always felt sorry for him. My oldest brother and his wife were devastated about Pierre's misfortunes.

No one seemed to care what I had gone through with him. I was not able to understand this and asked my therapists about it many times. Pierre was important to my family, whereas it didn't matter what had happened to me. I grew a great wall to put up between me and some of my family. They were wondering why I never called. If they only had thought this over, would they not understand? Monique and I became very distant, whereas my sister Angel finally saw the light in this whole situation and could make sense of it. She visited me at the hospital the most out of all my siblings. Some never came, and my mother and father showed up once. I became bitter towards them all because I knew they didn't care, and were probably making fun of me.

There came a time when George had cancer of the bladder. Years later, he had cancer of the prostate, and then kidney. Shortly after that, he had several mini strokes, where he didn't recognize people and would do the strangest things. His wife needed to be with him constantly to take care of him. She is a very caring person and takes such good care of my brother, and also looks after a couple of her grandchildren on weekdays.

Chapter 25

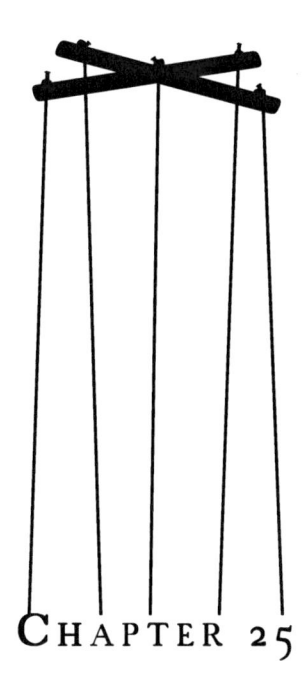

Eventually, Pierre's cancer spread to the lymph nodes, and the doctors gave him six months to live without treatment, or eighteen months if he had chemotherapy done. The choice was not very good but he picked treatment. I felt nothing towards him, and was actually happy to see him suffer before he died. Not that this is very nice, but my past memories kept on coming up and the unsupportive feelings from my family made me not care at all about him. Through the last few years, I had written several letters to him. I actually wanted to put them in his coffin, but thought I probably wouldn't be lucky enough to do so. He more than likely would be cremated.

On March 12, 2013 at my aunt's funeral, I finally confronted Pierre about the sexual abuse. I was seated between my brother and sister, because my sister did not want to sit beside my brother Emile so she slid in first. She was sitting with two of my granddaughters, aged four and six. In front of me sat my abuser. In the middle of the service, I looked over, noticing the girls were so well behaved while their mother Myla sat at the back of the church with her youngest son, Eric, because he moved so much. I kept looking at the four-year-old and remembering my past, and thinking that this was the age I was when Pierre started abusing me. I looked at her arms, legs, and tiny little body, and then looked up at my brother-in-law several times.

I knew his cancer had spread because I was told the day before, and I thought this might be my only chance to confront him before he died. Before I spoke to him, I reached out to a priest whom I had known for years and asked if I could speak to him sometime. He told me that this was not the right time, and he would give me his telephone number to set up a meeting. I felt foolish because I had no intentions of talking to him on that particular day. I had questions that no one can answer; therefore I did not believe in God. My belief is that when you die all that is left are your remains. Nothing else. I was making another attempt to seek answers to the question, "Is there a God?" After mentioning this to the priest, I knew in my heart that he would not give me his number. I was right.

I looked for Pierre in the funeral home and told Myla to take pictures of him. She would have made a great detective. Finally, the crowd scattered away from him and my daughter and sister were so nervous, knowing what I had planned. I had no idea what I was going to say to him, but knew that this was the right moment. He was speaking to one of my cousins when I tapped him on the shoulder to get his attention, and asked my cousin if I could speak to him alone.

I called him a pedophile three times, and he kept saying, "Pardon me" and then said, "No." Within seconds he admitted it because there was nothing he could say against it. He said he was sorry and asked what he could do for me. I told him that he and my mother both had ruined my whole life. They were both to blame. I explained to him that because my own home life was so terrible, I'd had nowhere to go, and my sister Monique felt like more of a mother to me than my own. She always treated me kindly. I mentioned how she took me out and bought me things, so that I wasn't sure which was better of the two evils; being raped or being abused. I chose the rape. My mother was vicious. All my siblings had been abused by her and all hated and resented her; some more than others. Those who had my dad's personality were more understanding, not to say they thought it was right that she was doing these horrible acts.

I told Pierre how I self-harmed at eight, and performed this behaviour in his apartment on Provencher after an incident. I told him how I had cut myself with a blade then, and continued to self-harm my whole entire life. I then told him about all my suicide attempts and how they were related to him. He told me he didn't know how much damage he had done. He kept on saying, "I'm sorry" and asked what he could do for me. I looked at him with a blank stare and said nothing.

He said he did not do this to anyone else, but I challenged him with names of all of the people I knew about. He just became very quiet. He never argued about the others. At one point into our conversation, his son came to interrupt and wanted to know what we were talking about. I was verbally aggressive when I told him I wanted to talk to his dad alone. Myla said people from my immediate family were all staring and wondering. I did not make a scene and spoke quietly. Monique pretended she never noticed anything. She still lived in denial and certainly still loved him. Myla took pictures of us talking and I was very grateful to her. She has always believed me and has been on my side.

I told Pierre how I struggled with the possibility of charging him, but decided there was no use. I also explained to him the process of not being believed and how that hurt. I told him that he knew how conniving he really was when he would run after me in my own home or his, and that he would do this on purpose because he knew I had nowhere to go and no one to turn to. He was well aware of how serious this situation was because I had never mentioned it to anyone. He always felt safe and confident with his threats. Although he would catch me every single time he didn't always attempt to harm me. It was a game to him and he always snickered and laughed about it. He just liked being the dominator and for me to be the submissive. This thrilled him in his own sick mind. He knew my mother would not have cared and my father was so religious he wouldn't want me to jeopardize Pierre and Monique's marriage. I was to stay quiet and not make trouble.

I told him that I had not come to the funeral specifically to tell him anything, but I found the circumstances were timed perfectly. I mentioned his cancer and said that I finally got the courage to talk to him before one of us died. I repeated this once before I spoke and then again when I was done. I really didn't want him to think that I wished he should suffer. Despite, deep inside, feeling that I could care less.

I told Pierre about the many letters I wrote to him but never sent out. He then asked if he could hug me and with total disgust on my face I simply and clearly said, "No." He did tell me that there were times he would stay up at night and think about this and the other things he had done. He was telling me he was remorseful. Before our conversation was over he said that this would bother him for the next three nights, and he wouldn't be able to sleep. I just thought how uncaring he was, saying this. He had ruined my life, and he would be remorseful for just the next three nights? In my mind, I thought it obviously didn't affect him too much. As I walked away, he put his hand on my shoulder. When we left the funeral home, he once again put his hand on my shoulder. I could only feel disgust, guilt, and shame. In the meantime, I was shocked that I had absolutely hadn't forgotten anything I wanted to say. All I could think of at the time was Monique talking and interacting with people. Funerals were entertaining to her. Even when my parents died, she had to have the best of everything, with meals served and bottles of wine on the tables. It always had to be so extravagant for her.

We had taken two cars and I was with Angel. Myla could hardly wait to hear what I had said and made me promise not to say anything until we got to MacDonald's. This way her three children could play while we spoke. I went through the story but had just come to realize that I had depersonalized as a way of protecting myself all day long.

I got back to the hospital and told my nurse what I had done. I'm not sure why I shared such an intimate experience with her because she didn't look like she cared, anyway. She was more worried about her coffee break than about listening to me, and she wanted to end this conversation. I never shared this intimate experience with anyone again until my doctor got back from holidays. I then realized how no one really cared in psychiatry. They were there just to make money and not to help. I'm not even sure she wrote anything in my file because nothing was mentioned by the psychiatric nurses ever again. I once again felt betrayed, and not believed. When I told Rite what had happened, he was very proud of me and told me not to talk about it to anyone else.

I stayed in bed at the hospital for a few days and there were times I didn't even know who my nurse was until the end of their shifts, and then only because she was bringing me my medication. It gave me a lot of time to think. I must have dwelled on this conversation thousands of times. However, I tried to sleep as much as I could. I felt that the more I slept, the less I would have to think about it.

Chapter 26

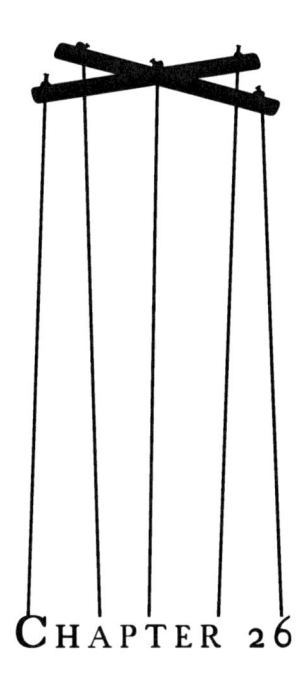

One time, a few months prior to the confrontation, I was waiting to go to my psychotherapy group as an outpatient. Another patient who I had seen for months at the hospital came behind me and put his hands down my shirt and cupped my breasts. I could not speak or move. I just froze. Karen, my therapist, had walked by a couple of times and noticed he was in the area. One other patient going to therapy walked by me and said, "Hello." When I finally got up to go with her to go to therapy, the male patient asked me where I was going. I don't know what he was thinking at the time, but he must have thought I enjoyed it because I just sat there paralyzed and did not scream or say anything.

I went to psychotherapy and never talked about what had happened or mentioned it to anyone. I was trying to put it behind me just like I had done in the past. A couple of weeks passed and I finally mentioned to my therapist and the group. Her advice was to go talk to my doctor. I was later re-admitted but discovered that Dr. Stevens had gone on holidays. I thought about who I should mention the incident to and then thought I should speak to the Head Nurse. I walked into her office and told her that I had an important report to make about something that had happened to me in the hospital. All she said was that she would be busy for the next ten minutes and only then she would come and talk to me. I knew deep down inside of me that she did not want to be bothered and would not come back to seek me. Having been in the hospital so many times I knew I meant nothing to the staff.

I went to group that day with a different therapist who runs a different program, and I didn't want to talk about it in front of others. Once group was over we had a conversation about it and he seemed concerned by what had happened. However, he never got back to me and I felt ridiculous for having spoken out. Once again, no one cared whatsoever. Within a couple of days I mentioned it to Harmony, who works on the other unit, and I felt I could trust her since she was horrified as I stood there crying. She got a psychiatric nurse and brought me into a little room to report the incident. They were both horrified at what had happened and said that as soon as Dr. Stevens came back, he would get the report. They both told me to charge the patient. When Dr. Stevens returned he had already read the report and asked me to repeat what had actually happened. I explained it to him and he suggested that I not lay charges. This patient was also under his care.

I left feeling empty, as if I was talking to deaf ears. Everyone seemed to be concerned about their reputations and the scandal that it might cause if the incident became known. I liked my doctor very much and just let it go. The psychiatric nurse and the worker who took my report came to me on several occasions and told me to lay charges. I was very apprehensive because I felt I would no longer have a good psychiatrist anymore if I did this.

When this event occurred I was an outpatient and my psychotherapist mentioned to me that during his recovery, the man was to attend the same group I had been going to for years. I spoke up and said that he always missed the group and had probably attended only three times in the past five months. Because he was inpatient he was told to attend. It was my choice if I wanted to continue.

I was deeply hurt and have had a hard time talking to that psychotherapist at times. The man's needs came first and I was secondary. I never attended the program again and absolutely not one staff member came to talk to me about it, ever. Now that's what I call betrayal. I'd lost most of my respect for staff members after this, and tried not to talk unless I absolutely had to. Even my therapist, Karen, who was someone whom I had thought was very special and caring, seemed somewhat abrupt; I was heartbroken. However, to this day I wonder if it was my Borderline Personality Disorder making me feel this way. I finally met with her and explained how I felt, because she had always been there for me. I apologized, and we went on from there; but still with some slight resentment.

I had Cheryl to speak to at the Laurel Centre. She was the only one who talked to me about it for several weeks. Even after a couple of years under her care, we still touch upon the subject now and then. The therapists at the Laurel Centre are very kind, and well trained to listen and help both young and older women who have been sexually abused.

At one of my appointments, Cheryl and I were talking about all the letters I had written to Pierre. Even though I had confronted him, I still felt a need to place them in his coffin. My big concern was that I might never be able to do this in my lifetime. She proposed to me the idea that I burn my letters outside at the Centre. This would give me power and I would be set free. I felt like I gave it up to the universe. It was quite a beautiful ceremony. She was my true angel. It felt like a weight had been lifted off of my shoulders, and I no longer felt like it belonged to me. I had returned it all back to him, forever. I told my husband and knew to be quiet about this conversation forever.

Cheryl has always been there for me and is so very kind. She is one of my true angels, but I'm worried I won't be able to talk to her again in a short while. Clients have three years with their therapists and I have reached my three years. It was now extended another year and for this I was grateful. I truly feel accepted, helped, not judged, and I don't have the feeling of being such a stupid person. The people at the Centre build your confidence. This Centre pays attention to each individual, and I would recommend it to anyone with a history of sexual abuse. When I leave I will make sure that Cheryl is recognized for all her hard work.

Cheryl is truly an angel. I have not believed in the existence of angels until I met her. She was born for the purpose of helping others who are destitute like me. She is awesome and I do have a love for her that would be hard to explain. I keep it hidden deep into my heart, and it will be with me forever.

Chapter 27

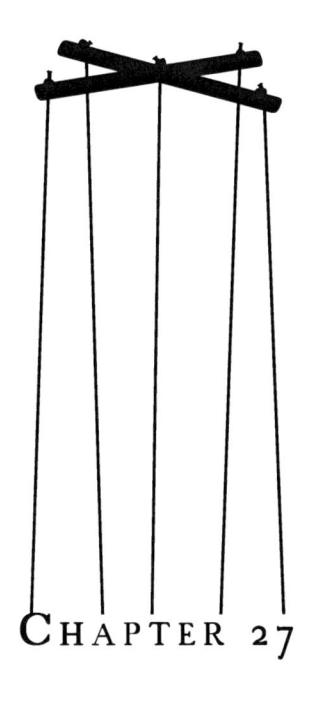

While all of this was going on, I felt like nothing could make me happy except drinking with my husband. We talked a lot and got along very well. This was fun. I enjoyed going out for supper and having two or three wines with dinner. We would talk about everything; our three children, our deaths, where to scatter my remains, where he wanted to be buried, holidays, retirement, and many other things.

I really wasn't supposed to drink alcohol with all my medications because they counteracted each other. When I started drinking I was already living in a condo with Rite, and our children were all married. They never really saw me drunk, except maybe Myla. I would see her the most, and her three children were very attached to me. I would never drink if I was looking after them and just played with them instead. We had so much fun. I was Grandma the Big Bad Wolf, and they would constantly laugh and giggle at everything I would say or do. I would never put them in harm's way.

I was an adult with responsibilities that I always met, and drinking alcohol with Rite was done in our private time. We did not drink and drive and would usually take a taxi or find a ride home. Our condo was near many restaurants and we would usually walk. I went to AA with Rite, but the only thing that I had trouble following was the twelve steps. I found them hard to do because they had the word God in some steps. I no longer believed in God and I had asked so many individuals to prove God's existence to me. No one could, therefore how could I believe?

We both got our one-year birthday cake and owner of Rite's company flew in from Vancouver to celebrate it with us. He once drank and knew how hard it was to stop. After fourteen months of being dry we started drinking again because life was simply boring and we did not have these long conversations any longer without some alcohol to help. We wanted it back. I drank for a few months and told Rite I was quitting once again. I finally convinced him that he could drink and I just wouldn't. I no longer wanted to go out anymore and made supper at home every night. Rite would ask me to go out on his way home from work, but I would already be undressed for the night. I isolated myself from the world since I had no friends and felt so betrayed by my family.

Myla would sometimes call me to do something and I always made up excuses so I didn't have to go out. I rarely heard from my other two children and I really didn't know anything about them or my grandchildren. When I did see them it was awkward because these six grandchildren would not come near me, because they didn't know who I was. I let them live their own lives and never intruded. Some Mother's Days and birthdays they would call and wish me a happy Mother's Day and that would be it. There were some years they would drop by and give me a present, but would not stay. They always had something else to do. Ben always bought me something but I would never receive it on the day of. Perhaps he wanted to spend that special day with Sally. He always would buy something for me but never came over. I would receive it sometimes months later. On Mother's Day, I wanted to be with my children, not just receive presents. Mandy was probably doing the same thing except I'm sure her mother-in-law was involved. Myla was always involved on these special days and would always treat me well and never missed an important occasion. She was my only one.

Many times I would sit and wonder what I had done wrong in my children's lives. Ben and Mandy were always interacting with their in-laws. Mandy loved her mother-in-law and father-in-law. Mandy would tell her mother-in-law how tired she was after her third child. She rarely called me, but there was always a time she needed to talk to someone; and that's the only time she would call me. Her mother-in-law told her that she was tired but still went to work with two children. Mandy had given birth to her third baby three weeks prior to that and was still doing hair in her salon at home. She was up feeding the baby every couple of hours and hadn't fully recovered. I knew where Mandy was coming from because she was my third baby and when she was born, I had a daycare that I had to maintain and I would be back at it after three weeks. If you didn't own your own business you would always get a few months off to recover. This was much better.

Ben wanted us to go to Hawaii one year with them and their three children, but this would never have been affordable for us at the time. Ben was going to Hawaii every winter, sometimes for a month. His oldest son, who was four at this point, had already been to Hawaii four times and they travelled year-round to many places as a family. I was happy for Ben because he had worked so hard at getting an education and it had paid off. As a principal auditor for the government, he was sent to Montreal and Vancouver to correct exams of other students who were becoming chartered accountants. He was a professor at the University of Manitoba, and got paid much more than a regular professor because he was on a contract. He taught students how to do the last three accounting exams in order to graduate. If you took Ben's course, you were more likely to graduate. Ben worked thirty out of fifty weekends a year, and when he travelled to other places to correct exams he was able to bring the entire family with him each time.

This year while in Hawaii, he called to tell me that they had booked the tickets for the family to go to Boston to run the Boston Marathon. Last year, before he ran in New York, he ran the Minneapolis Marathon. Not at the same time, of course, this was months apart. This year he did very well in Boston and came in 240th out of 36,000 people. He also completed the Manitoba Marathon in June 2014 and came in second. He was happy with that because he had been third for the last three consecutive years, although his time was better in Boston.

I truly thought I was a great mother but I guess I failed at that somewhere along the way because Mandy had no interest in spending time with us for twelve years. I was to blame because of all the self-harm I inflicted. I'm very happy that Mandy's mother-in-law was very good to her, because I wasn't the same person I used to be, and needed much therapy. I let her go and knew Keith didn't like anyone in our family because I had hurt the love of his life; his wife, Mandy. She distanced herself from me because of all my attempts at self-harm. I understood her feelings but nevertheless, I was hurt. It has been my fault and now that I feel like I have recovered, I totally understand what I actually did to them. I can only say I'm sorry, but cannot change the past.

Another thing that I learned was that I definitely needed to stay away from toxic people. This was one of my main problems. Never make friends in psychiatry. You can listen and give others advice but no phone numbers. This took me a very long time to finally come to that conclusion. Only after I deleted every single phone number that had an attachment to the hospital did I feel like myself again. I feel whole, but I do still battle with OCD.

Darkness has been a large part of my life. I would feel like the darkness is death where I can speak but not be heard. I can scream but everyone turns their backs. I can run but I can never catch them. It is a nightmare where my arms and legs don't work like they should, and the air is too thick to breathe. Loved ones walk a mile ahead, forgetting to stop as I fall behind. This is the reality of darkness. I feel buried alive inside myself.

One night I knew Rite had just left and was in a hurry to get to work. Suddenly, minutes after his departure, I felt his arm around my throat and fell semi-conscious, whimpering to ask if that was actually him, playing a joke. I suddenly touched his side of the bed and felt no one there. I've been absolutely terrified by these horrible nightmares. The night before I dreamt my mother was making me drink a concoction of poison and I was simply letting her pour it into my mouth. She then took a pair of scissors and cut both sides of my mouth; I was horrified but not allowed to show any emotions. She had done this so she could pour it into my mouth faster. My father was a witness to this and never said anything, and in my dream I believed he was in on it. I'd wake up wondering if he ever really cared but knew that he really did.

The last hospitalization before I felt this way was quite different. Perhaps this was an awakening for me, because I am so much happier now.

Before this happened, I felt that I was falling apart for a couple of weeks, and nothing was going right. My husband came home one day and I told him I was simply losing my mind and could not listen to anything negative from anyone, and I especially did not want to hear anyone who was angry. I felt like I wanted to put myself into total isolation on an island somewhere. I couldn't handle any noise or others talking about each other. I finally had come to the point of exhaustion.

Dr. Stevens put me back in the hospital, and many nights I was scared to fall asleep. There were times you could hear someone screaming in the night as the nurses all scrambled with security to lock the patient in a room behind the nurses' station. They had cameras on all the time and would watch as the patient pounded on the door to be released. They would be screaming out and swearing obscenities and you could see it felt so terrifying to be locked up like this. They were sedated but this did not seem to be effective with some. Others became more subdued and remorseful.

While in hospital, I walked into One North and saw another patient that had just gotten admitted five minutes prior to me. We knew each other from other hospitalizations and as I looked around there were others that I knew, which made me feel more comfortable. I tried to stay in my room so as not to make any more friends who were mentally ill, given my past experiences. I always felt sorry for them and felt I needed to help them.

A couple of days had passed when I realized there was one patient that I seemed to know from somewhere else. We talked and immediately knew where we had met. While I was taking my course to become a Mental Health Support Worker, my first practicum was at Mood Disorders and she was the person in charge of training me. We hit it off and talked together all the time. Her name was Helen. She was severely depressed, but never told me why. I felt she needed support and was told that she had been accepted to live in a brand new apartment within three months. The building still didn't have the balconies installed, but should be ready then.

Helen was so excited at the prospect of having found a new home, and I promised her all my old furniture that I had kept stored for a year. I had everything to fill up her apartment. All this even came with a fridge, stove, and dishwasher. She was thrilled. While we were in hospital we went out with Cindy for coffee and I had mentioned that Helen should move closer to where I lived. I had suggested moving in as a boarder in my area. It wasn't because I intended being extremely good friends with her, but Cindy was very hurt by this and thought that Helen was going to take her place as my best friend. That would never happen, but Cindy was still insecure.

On the day of her release I drove Helen to a hotel off Portage and Main and couldn't believe how awful a place this was for someone to live in. She had a tiny little area with a twin bed, no closets, and a television that didn't work. It was a bad part of the city, and in the hotel everyone was drunk and laughing and making noise 24 hours a day. It smelled of cigarette smoke and alcohol. There was also an area for garbage on the second floor. The garbage bags were all thrown together in a pile. What a dump! They all shared a common kitchen and bathrooms. I personally would never have been able to shower in such a dirty place. Her rent was $500.00 a month. My mouth dropped when she told me this. She had had to spray for bed bugs four times, and had huge scars from bites on her body. It was totally disgusting.

Once again, my heart was broken to see someone live under these conditions. She had told me it was far worse at the Salvation Army than this. This is where the homeless lived and sometimes it was full and they would let people sleep in at the entrance in the extreme cold days. Some slept in bus shelters, under bridges, and many other places that I would probably find extremely horrifying. In this day and age it didn't seem possible to have people live under these conditions in such a rich country. Something was really wrong.

Many of these people were addicted to drugs, and some were prostitutes. My therapist once told me that 100 percent of prostitutes came from abusive homes. How sad and terrible life had turned out for them! If I could have helped anyone in these situations my goal in life would be to get them off the streets, into counselling, and able to go back to school so they could work for a living. Their self- esteem would be much greater when they had succeeded in all of this, since they would be able to afford housing of their own.

That evening I spoke to my husband about Helen living in our extra bedroom for three months. We discussed this and thought we would charge her $300.00 a month, and she wanted to give us $25.00 each week for groceries. Rite and I discussed this, and decided that she would have to give us at least $30.00 a week. This was not going to cover her food costs as it was. Rite liked the idea and so I called her and gave her the night to think about it. She called me back and took my offer, knowing she would be able to use my brand new car and have someone to talk to at the same time.

The next day, there was a problem. When I had called her the night before, Rite and I had a few drinks and now having thought about it, Rite changed his mind and did not want her in our home. I was too embarrassed to tell her we changed our minds. I wanted her to move in but he didn't. I had true feelings to help her for a short time and felt that this was my calling in life, and that was why I never died trying to commit suicide so many times. I was here for a purpose. Rite and I argued about her moving in, but she had already told her landlords she was moving out. He didn't care and just wanted me to tell her she was not welcome. I felt I couldn't turn my back on her now. It was already marked in stone.

Myla was so upset about my invitation to Helen that she did not talk to me for three weeks. She commented that her dad had always said that if anything had gone wrong in her marriage, no one was allowed back. He would say this on my behalf, knowing how much complaining I would have to listen to if this had ever happened. I wouldn't have been able to cope with this after everything I had been through. However, having a stranger was different because I didn't have to listen to these kinds of things. Besides, it was only for a short time, and we knew there was an end to it. There came a time that Rite told me he was going to move out. I was stuck. I didn't want to cause trouble in my marriage but I felt that I couldn't turn my back on Helen. He was very unhappy and would say so, but he put up with it anyway. I never would have believed he would have left me because of these circumstances. I knew he loved me and he knew I loved him but had made a mistake because we were arguing. I wished I had never mentioned any of this to him.

On the day that Helen moved in, I took all my grandchildren's car seats out of the car the night before so that I could put Helen's belongings in the back seat ,and told her I would be at her place early in the morning. We brought down several boxes and a few things to my car. She did not own that many things. While I parked on the street, I saw a sign that said no parking after 12:00 p.m., because of the Santa Claus parade. I kept on telling her to hurry, but she still needed to sweep the floor.

We brought a load down and I ended up getting a parking ticket because it was slightly after 12:00 p.m. Helen said to leave the ticket there because she knew I would not get another ticket and we went up for the last time to pick up a coffee maker she had bought. She was tired and sat for a while as I kept on coaxing her to leave. We walked out and my new car had been towed; I had left everything in the car, including our purses. We certainly did not know what to do. We went to the bar downstairs and asked for a telephone book to look up the number of the closest towing company. They did not have a telephone book. Helen did not have Internet on her cell phone, and we sat with a few drunks that were suggesting ways for me to get my car back.

After forty-five minutes, the worker sitting with us told me there were phone booths about ten feet away. I was then able to call to find out where to pick up my car, but we had absolutely no cash because we had left our purses in the car. We called a taxi and went to the towing company and asked how much it would cost to have the car back. We then proceeded to go by taxi with the same driver, who drove me to the bank where I had been putting money away for holidays for Rite and me. It was in a different account and I couldn't use my debit card to get my car out of impound. I took out the money for towing, ticket, and taxi. I was devastated by the fact that it cost me hundreds of dollars for helping someone. Helen kept on telling me she would give me money back but that never happened. I put it in the back of my mind and simply tried to forget about it, and was happy Rite did not find out.

Helen now had moved in, but there were problems. For instance, when we went grocery shopping, she never wanted to come with us, but gave me a list of things she liked. It definitely exceeded the amount she was giving us for gtoceries, and that wasn't even including making her supper. She needed a gallon of skim milk, cheese, muffins, a huge can of coffee, sweetener, granola bars, chips, dip, ice cream, and many, many other things.

She became totally obsessed with my iPad. I could never use it. She was beginning to get on my nerves because I needed it at times for appointments, grocery shopping, and many other things. If I said I needed it, she just ignored me until I got to the point that I would ask several times before she would let me use it. Even at night when I wanted to use it in bed, she was watching a movie. One night she told me that Rite and she had discussed that she could take the queen size bed with her also. Rite told her that I might not like that, so she asked me the following day and I told her that it was there for my grandchildren; I was not giving it away. The next day we went to IKEA and while we were shopping, she was calculating how much money she would get from her income tax return. She said she would buy an iPad and dresser to match her bedroom. Did she not understand I was not giving her the bed, which had a five-year-old mattress? The only reason why it was in the other room was because we felt we needed a king-sized bed.

Every morning, I would get up extremely early and do the odd things of my OCD. Helen would sleep in and I was able to do many things. I was getting very tired because I would work for hours, then when she got up we would talk for a while. I would then proceed to do more "normal" things in front of her. I would shower and clean the bathroom and she would shower every few days after it was cleaned. This irritated me but I kept on thinking it wasn't forever, and I would not dare complain to Rite about it.

I would go out with Helen in the afternoon every day. Cindy and I would meet every Tuesday for psychotherapy. Helen would drive us to the Grace Hospital and go to her appointment at Seven Oaks Hospital. It was quite a distance from the Grace Hospital. Cindy was absolutely outraged by the fact she had to sit in the back seat, and felt she was no longer my best friend. After psychotherapy she did not take a ride home with us but instead took the bus. I felt really bad because I really wanted her to sit up front with me but the only reason why she sat at the back was because Helen was dropping us off and going to her appointment.

On the day I told Cindy that Helen was moving in with us for three months, her face dropped and she seemed extremely sad. That particular group day I stayed out and thought how awful I felt for telling her this. I had hurt her to the core. She walked out of group and came to talk to me, and she said she was sorry. I kept on telling her no one could replace her. We walked back in and I felt horrible. My intentions were not to hurt her, but to help someone in need.

Helen and I would go to our psychiatrist appointments together and had many coffees at IKEA. She had moved in the middle of November and told Rite she was waiting for her damage deposit from the hotel to pay him for the last two weeks of November. The hotel people did not want to give it to her because they said it belonged to her husband. They told her she needed a letter in writing from him in order for her to get the money. She forged a letter, but they knew it was not real and told her to have him call them. She had no idea where he was. We never got paid for those last two weeks. What a surprise!

During those two weeks, Cindy called me several times a day, crying and saying that I was no longer her best friend. Helen was getting upset about all of this and thought that Cindy was being ridiculous. I knew Cindy had no self-esteem and Helen was angry with her, but I defended Cindy anyway. Helen seemed very heartless and didn't seem to care about anyone. She was very loud while I was talking to Cindy and saying very inappropriate things that Cindy could hear. I was appalled by all of this. She had anger issues and I hadn't been aware of this. If her phone wouldn't work she would start swearing and get very loud. I kept on telling her we lived in a condo and we did not raise our voices at any time.

I did not like people yelling or getting mad and had been in the hospital because I needed a break from all of this. My mother had yelled and screamed her entire life at us, and I just wasn't able to cope with anyone raising his or her voice. She replied to me that she could not live in this kind of environment. Every time she raised her voice I would tell her to stop. She kept on calling me Little Miss Perfect. No, I was not perfect but got completely agitated at the prospect of her yelling all the time. Every single day Cindy would call and cry and I felt upset that I had hurt her. One day she and left a message saying she wasn't sure what she was going to do, but I only heard this message several hours later. I called a few times and she finally answered the phone and told me she had overdosed but did not go to the hospital. We planned a date to go out together but she wasn't home when I was going to pick her up. She called the next day and told me that if I liked Helen then she must be a nice person and she wanted to go out with us together.

On Sunday, December 1, 2013 at approximately 10:30 a.m., Cindy's son called to tell me that she had passed away. I was in shock and did not want to believe it. Her husband had gotten up to make coffee and then went to the store for the newspaper and a large Slurpee for her. This was his routine every single weekend. When he got back at 8:00 a.m. she was not awake and he found it strange so he went to wake her and she was already very cold. Her daughter tried CPR on her but it was way too late. She had died and I felt extremely guilty for her death. I felt like I had poisoned her myself.

The doctors performed an autopsy and all her organs were fine and they checked her brain for anything else, but nothing showed up. The toxicology lab had still not filed their reports. It would take months before they would get the report back. It was my belief only that she had committed suicide. The family was unaware of all the crying that she had done, nor were they aware that she wrote on her upper legs about how bad, stupid, unworthy, and crazy she was. She did this for a purpose, so she could be reminded daily when she went to the washroom of what a horrible person she was. There were only two people who had seen this; her psychiatrist, who found it silly to do such a thing, and me. The psychiatrist's response was to write it on paper instead, but this defeated the purpose. Could she not see that Cindy was in trouble?

I was in shock at the idea that her doctor did not do anything about it. Cindy was just another number to the doctors and really had a hard time seeking help after all of those years. This turned me off of psychiatry and I was unable to see any good in it. They did their work and were immediately gone after a day's work or even a partial day. Dr. Stevens was on holidays throughout the winter and there was no one to talk to except my therapist at the Laurel Centre for Sexually Abused Women. She treated with me with such respect and kindness. I wasn't sure where I would get help at the time my term was ending. Who would I talk to and who could I display my feelings to if she wasn't going to be there the following Christmas?

There were not very many people who showed up for Cindy's funeral; only one healthcare aid and no one else from the hospital. This was proof that no one gave a damn. I guess a psychiatrist who enjoyed their work was very rare. The money seemed to attract them the most. They were just practicing medicine and only practicing on all their patients.

I attended Cindy's funeral with Helen and we were going to meet Andrea. It was held on Portage Avenue near Assiniboine Downs. The music was not your regular kind of funeral music. They played Aerosmith, The Beatles, and songs that she was very fond of. It was a little strange!

After the funeral, I often thought back to my friendship with Cindy. There were so many good memories.

In 2013, on Mother's Day, Cindy's children had bought her two tickets to see Paul McCartney at the new stadium. She had asked me to attend it with her and I was thrilled. We had dinner at my home and a few drinks because they were supposed to be so expensive at the stadium. We walked there because I lived very close and parking was being charged everywhere around our condo. We had a blast, singing and dancing, but upon my return I remembered I had forgotten my Lulu Lemon sweater. It was on my seat but it was a very warm day and I didn't need it. I called the stadium lost and found but of course no one had it. Someone must have taken it, since these sweaters were worth close to $200.00, and I had worn it just a couple of times. Myla came to pick us up to drive Cindy home but we had to walk quite a way before we could get to her. Myla never said anything negative about even one of my friends with mental health issues, and I appreciated it.

Cindy, Andrea, and I spent most Tuesday afternoons together. We considered ourselves our own psychotherapy group. We talked and enjoyed each other's company tremendously. One time they both came over and we sat and had drinks on the balcony. We had gone to the Safeway next to my condo and bought alcohol, chips, dip, tacos, and sauce. We had a great time, although I did take the precaution of hiding all my pills in another room. I wish to have those days back.

Once summer was over, Cindy's family did not want anyone in the house. They were not brought up to be social with others. They did not want anyone in the apartment because I made them feel uncomfortable. This was her home but she could never defend herself. I knew where she was coming from because I was just like her.

The day she had shown me the injuries on her legs was the day before I was going to be admitted to the hospital. I had called her and asked her to go for a drink next to her home. There was a bar located there and we each had two drinks. We had an absolutely great time and I was telling her I was being admitted the following day, but you would never have known it. It seemed so strange, considering that all I had done that week was cry. Cindy always made me feel happy.

She made me happy and our friendship was awesome. Through the week I was unable to put up with anyone screaming, or hear complaining by anyone. I was also tired of my husband complaining about his job and things seemed so hopeless. We were in our mid-fifties and we actually had put too much money away in R.R.S.P 's. Traveling was not something we did often and Rite worked some days for eighteen hours. I was lonely and really had no friends, except those who I had chosen, who turned out to be toxic. We had done much of our traveling with our children and their spouses when we were slightly younger. Cindy and I had a great friendship, and I looked forward to our days together.

Helen was different. Even though I often lent her my car, Helen gave me money for gas only once. She was driving to Seven Oaks Hospital, which was very far from my condo. I really couldn't afford all of this. She definitely was saving money. Before she got paid she asked to borrow money from me to buy her daughter Christmas presents. I felt skeptical but I always seemed to give in. She said she would pay me when she got her CPP cheque. I lent her a few hundred dollars and my thoughts were that I had spent $700.00 on her that month; which included most of my savings, but I thought I would start all over again once she left. She had many anger issues that I didn't know about. Once she had moved in with me, she told me she had been in hospital for homicidal and suicidal feelings. I dared not tell Rite.

Helen had a four-year-old daughter, and seven brothers and sisters. None of them knew she had a child because they would have all been against it. She had gone through severe post-partum depression for a very long time and family services decided to take her daughter away, and now her best friend looked after the child. There came a time that her best friend did not want to have the little girl with her anymore. The child was put up for adoption and she went to court for two weeks, but the judge refused to give her daughter back to her. This had all originated in January 2013, and it took her months of thinking to make a list of who she wanted killed. Her best friend was first and then there were workers at Child and Family Services. She actually told me their names. She also knew where the child lived and this was not something she was to have known. Her daughter lived in Transcona, but Helen did not want to be seen near her because her two supervised visitation rights would have ended. The adoptive mother had actually given her four visitations per year. She was very excited to see her daughter the day before Christmas Eve.

She even had the nerve to ask me to write her post-dated cheques so that she could get her teeth fixed. She once used someone else's welfare card to see a dentist. This was against the law. There was a program at Siloam Mission where she could get free dental work, but it was on a first come/first served basis. If I recall correctly, there was another place you could get free dental work and she told me she waited all day and never got in. I was thinking if I had a toothache that bad I would have waited day after day to get it fixed. Her intentions were to borrow money from us instead. I told her that this was not my account and that Rite paid our bills with it. She flatly told me that it was mine also so that should not be a problem. I told her she would have to talk to Rite about it first, knowing he never would have helped her in this way. She was stepping way over her boundaries.

She also mentioned to me that the police once closed the Osborne Bridge down because she was going to jump over the railing. She had already thrown her purse and coat into the water and stepped over the other side. Two policemen grabbed her and pulled her back over and handcuffed her. The bridge was closed down for all the paramedics, firemen, and police, but she never noticed any of this until she was saved. Psychotic and delusional? She must have been.

On the Tuesday before Christmas Eve, we had gone to Seven Oaks to see her psychologist. I told her to drive back because I wasn't familiar with that area. I suggested she drive southbound on Main and told her when to get into the bus lane to turn right on River Avenue. I must have told her several times that there was a great big green sign right in front of her with River Avenue marked on it. I then told her to turn right at the next big street, but it was a little street that was a one-way. She went to turn there and I said to her not to turn on a one-way street but the one with the big green sign. She literally lost it and screamed and got extremely angry. I kept telling her to keep her voice down and to relax.

Within two weeks of my driving with her, I realized she definitely had road rage. There was a time when she noticed a lady following too close to her on a slippery day. She got out of the car and screamed at her not to follow so closely. She had said to me this was going to be the way she would die. Someone would take a gun and shoot her when she got out of the car to yell at someone. She was so frustrating. After the wrong turn incident, I told her to get out of the car and I was going to drive from now on; she never spoke to me for the rest of the day and all the next day until late afternoon. She was hibernating.

The night before, Rite and I had gone to a Christmas Party and we had to change our plans about who would pick us up and drive us home. Myla was always very considerate, but Helen complained about driving us onto Portage Avenue from the first time we asked her. At the party Rite said we should kick her out the following day or that night. I felt panicky throwing somebody on the streets and this was not something I would ever do without warning. I knew she had an appointment with her psychiatrist at 5:00 p.m., and at 3:30 p.m. she came out of her room to ask if she could borrow the car. I then told her that she could use it today but she would have to take the bus from now on.

This is when she became violent and went ballistic. She slammed her bedroom door and swore at me like there was no tomorrow. I immediately entered the room and told her that she was never to slam a door in my home like that ever again. She said she would do what she damn well felt like. I then told her to leave and that Rite and I had discussed telling her to move out today. She didn't believe that Rite wanted her gone but I told her she was going to be told by him later today. She said she was going to call the police because she had paid her rent for December and it was only the middle of the month. I told her to go ahead and call immediately, considering she never paid for November.

Helen grabbed her purse and put her shoes on and said she would be spending the night where she had lived before. I then told her that everything would be packed for her to pick up the next day. She made it very clear that she did not want me touching her things and then hit me. She slammed the door once again and I could tell she was packing, but I was worried for my wellbeing. I called my therapist and she told me to call the police, my daughter who lived near me, and my husband, who was now on his way home because Myla had called him. I did not call 911 but spoke to a police officer and told her what was going on. I then called my therapist to tell her that I was in the hallway and I could hear something being broken inside the condo.

Karen then proceeded to tell me to call the police again. I did, and explained to the officer that this was the second call and I did not feel safe. The officer told me if Helen was not gone at a certain time to call 911. I eventually called 911.

I knew not to leave my keys in my purse so I hid them in my bedroom. As I walked into my bedroom to get my keys, I noticed a sweater that I had never seen before and threw it back at her, telling her this was not mine. She threw it back saying that it was. I then told her I would just be throwing everything out, including a figurine I had bought her of a mom and little girl. She then lost it and told me she was going to kill me and that she had many friends that would do it for her. While she lived here she would tell me about these people who would kill her old friend who testified against her in court and some CFS Workers. I even knew the names in order of who she wanted dead first. She then proceeded to hit me again and threw me down on the floor, where I landed on my vacuum. I was bruised across my stomach and legs. I still had not retrieved my keys.

I then asked her to return my key to the building because she wanted her things in storage. She told me that she had lost it. Now, this was the second pair of keys we had bought for her. The key to the building cost us twenty dollars to make. When we bought the second building key, I didn't have the chance to get a key made for our apartment. She then told me that she had lost it, but I knew that was not true because when I was showering in the morning I heard her leave to go for a cigarette. She would have needed them to come back in.

Two of my neighbours said she looked extremely miserable and was smoking by the doors. This was not where she usually smoked. She always went further from the entrance. I heard her come back up to hibernate. By the time I asked her to give me my key back she took a sketch board she had bought for her daughter and kept on slamming it on the floor. I asked her to stop, but obviously she wasn't going to do that because she knew how annoyed that made me feel. I went into the bedroom to get my keys and I went to the storage room to give her all her things.

I then told her that she had really lost out on everything. She no longer would have furniture for her apartment and I told her that I had bought her an iPad for Christmas. All she said was that we were all about money. She was angry at the fact that I bought Dr. Stevens and his secretary presents at Christmas, because I truly wanted to make sure that they knew they were outstanding of all the hard work they did for me, and I wanted to show my appreciation to them.

Helen had once asked how much I spent on them and was horrified when I told her. She then got me to go down in the amount of money I would spend. Nevertheless, I spent what I usually do and just never showed her the gifts. I guess she was extremely jealous. Could she not see how much money we spent on her? If we were to be all about money why would I have lent her hundreds of dollars? She then started crying and was talking to her psychiatrist. I returned to my condo and locked the door. I immediately called the landlord for them to recommend a locksmith to come and change our locks. By that time, Myla could see Helen in the lobby in the front of the building but did not want to confront her because she was scared of her. She got in through the side door. Rite showed up and said the police had arrived but they did not come up for at least a half hour. I started taking all the bedding off to wash and I miraculously found Helen's first set of keys under the mattress cover. We then called our landlord to cancel the locksmith, but it was already too late and we were charged $40.00 anyway.

One of the police officers finally showed up at our door while the other stayed with her. I told him my story and he asked me if I wanted to charge her, but he said that if I didn't she would be out of my life. If I charged Helen, it would take a couple of years before we were able to put it behind us. This also meant paperwork on their behalf. We agreed not to press charges and the police officer left.

Within five minutes, the officer called me back to tell me to charge Helen on the assaults and for threatening to kill me. She apparently had assaulted the other police officer, and they arrested her and brought her to the Remand Centre. They called me back to find out the landlord's number, because her things needed to be locked away. There were pools of blood everywhere, on the floor and saturating the carpet. The landlord was only able to clean so much but had to have someone come and clean the carpets that night, and several other times. The trail of blood was smeared all the way to the police car. It was an absolute mess. At the next condominium meeting, Rite, who is the President, told me Karma Properties ended up with a $500.00 bill to clean it all up.

I mentioned the key to the officer, but Helen lied and said it was in her bedroom. More officers came and saw that she had put a hole in the wall, thrown a full glass of Coke, and smashed the glass. She threw things around and everything was in disarray. The officer said that I was very lucky she just didn't kill me then and there or smash the whole place up. He said that by the time they would have gotten there I would have been dead, or at least our condo would have been a total mess with Helen's rage.

The following day, Helen was sent to the Women's Jail in Headingley, and I called Victim Services to see how long she would be in there. She had already gone to court in the morning and now her next date was January 20, 2014. The person I was talking to made it very clear to me that Helen would be in there until then and he highly doubted that the judge would release her even then, because she had assaulted a police officer. I called a few days before her court date and Victim Services told me she had been released on Christmas Eve. One day too late to see her daughter. I was horrified at the idea that they never told me about it. Victim Services told me to leave my home for a while, but where was I to go? They also said that she had done her time and there were no more court dates. I immediately called the courts and they told me she was to appear in front of a judge on January 22, 2014 at 3:00 p.m. I kept telling the person on the phone that Victim Services were telling me there was no more court dates. She reassured me that she was working for the courts and she should know better than them, considering it came up on her computer.

I received papers of a Recognizance Order and all her conditions and restrictions were written on it. She was told to live at the Salvation Army until her sentence. I guess she never did get that new apartment. In her conditions, she was not to contact me, even threw a third party. A third party would have to pick up her belongings from our landlord. I am quite relieved that I didn't know anything about this sooner because I certainly would have been worried she was going to come back and kill me. I have no idea if she still has visitation rights with her daughter, but I would highly doubt so. She had told me she wasn't to break any laws or those would be the consequences. Her next court date was June 4, 2014 and was then changed to August. We shall see what happens then. Hopefully jail time, but I'm not keeping my hopes up too much, because she is mentally ill and will likely get off with that.

The most horrific thought through all of this is that if Cindy hadn't committed suicide on December 1st and had struggled for a couple of more weeks, she would now still be alive and my best friend, and would still be here by my side. Do I feel guilty? Somewhat. It's just like I put a bullet in her head, although everyone is responsible for their own well-being. No one can be there for someone 24/7. In the end it was in her hands and her responsibility, not mine. She chose that path and it was sad that she did so. I am so very lucky I never died when I overdosed, but I definitely know is was because God gave me a purpose in life and I was not finished.

Chapter 28

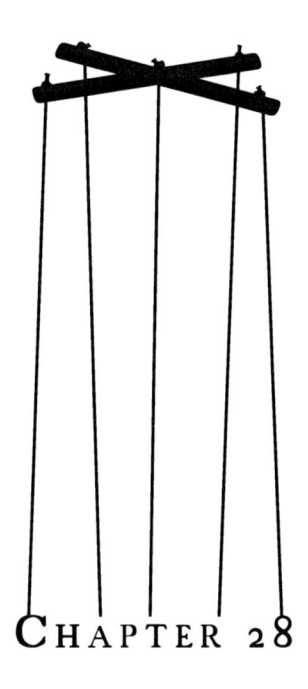

Rite and I had Christmas in the common room at our condo with all our children and grandchildren attending. We had a great time all together. Mandy thought she would have had her baby by then but no, she was still pregnant and waiting. She was trying to be patient. By now we had eight grandchildren, all under the age of six, and they enjoyed playing together. The room was big enough for them to run around in. Mandy was going to have our ninth grandchild. Wow! Who would have thought Rite and I would have so many grandchildren, and there still were more to come. I was a grateful grandmother and blessed with so many wonderful little grandchildren. No one could be as lucky as I am. Mandy delivered a little boy in January and we were all ecstatic. We had been texting each other several times a day for a few weeks. I would constantly check to see if she was in labour. She had me convinced she would have her baby before Christmas and we could celebrate the new baby with all of them. Every day, I would call or she would call me, telling me she was experiencing some symptoms of labour. This was all false labour and she was very late in her pregnancy before she had her baby. I imagine she was getting really tired of waiting.

She finally went into labour later in January. The following day I went to see her son. He was so cute and had blond hair and blue eyes like his sisters have. He resembled his father very much. I have been wondering if Mandy's boy would be as comical as his dad, who was always up to old tricks. For instance, on Christmas Day Keith went to our condo and took several things out of our drawers, putting them all over the counter to annoy me. He would twist my light bulbs, so I would think they were burned out. Since he was an electrician he would turn the power off at times, and he never left without having done something. I would tell Rite to check because whenever our son-in-law was there, something would always be turned around and he was sneaky. He even put his name on our computer, saying that he was the best when we would turn it on. Rite's phone would ring in the middle of the night because he had programmed it that way. This guy was extremely comical and never stopped moving. He needed something to do at all times. He was mischievous. Yes, that was Keith.

Everything went well with the birth and Mandy gave her baby to Rite to hold. Rite passed me the baby and he was so beautiful. He eventually cried in my arms and I gave him back to Mandy. Her children were brought up distant from us and we did not bother them in their everyday life. We just minded our own business, never judging any parenting skills. We knew none of our children were alike and that was fine by us.

A few weeks later, Mandy called me because she needed to vent; those were her exact words. She was upset with her mother-in-law and complained about different situations on an ongoing basis. I could never really say anything because I knew no one was perfect. Whatever happened between them, they would resolve it like all the other times. I could never understand why she would tell me all of this negative information about her mother-in-law, because Rite and I were the ones that felt unwanted.

A couple of weeks later we all had attended Myla's oldest daughter's seventh birthday. She was married to a Filipino and they always celebrated their seventh birthdays with all the importance of a wedding. Myla had put out so much of her time and money for this occasion, but many Filipinos did not even bring anything for my granddaughter's birthday. It was from the white people that they made some money, but they lost a lot because the others were too cheap to buy anything. They all received free dinners and alcohol, but did not bring a gift. Myla ended up spending way too much for this birthday. Next year, it will be her other daughter's turn, but she will do it with fewer people and maybe no alcohol. Cash bar only.

My sister Angel would do a lot of travelling because her youngest son lived in Orange County, California. He would take her to visit many different places. He travelled very often, everywhere around the world, because of his employment. He was the CEO of the company which was owned by a couple in Korea. They treated him extremely well.

Eventually, Sam was not able to travel again because he had an extremely bad heart, diabetes, and was also going for kidney dialysis three times a week. While Angel was away he got sick with the flu. His other two children lived nearby and always checked up on him. Angel would call him every day at the same time to make sure he was all right. She was due to come home from her son's when Sam was hospitalized because he was so sick. He then developed pneumonia and got even more ill. Within a few days his pneumonia was getting better and he was able to play cards with Angel. He was much more coherent and vibrant, and everyone thought he was getting better.

The following morning the nurse from the Gimli Hospital had called around 6:00 a.m. and wanted Angel to come down and see Sam because he had taken a turn for the worse. She got to the hospital and was told he probably wouldn't make it through the day. She immediately called her three children early enough so that her daughter wouldn't leave for work, for which she travelled most of the time. She was due to leave that morning and Angel got hold of her before she left for work. Her son from California was called immediately so he could make travel arrangements to get there a.s.a.p. He did get to talk to his dad before he left, which we were all so happy about. Her family contacted the rest of our side of the family to inform us so we could get to the hospital quickly.

I left with Myla and her oldest daughter, but not her other two children. Her daughter would text Sam all the time and he would always respond. He was so good with all children. We picked up Rite on the way and got there around 2:00 p.m. Sam wasn't really responding very much by the time we got there. I talked to him privately and I knew he could hear me because if I asked him a question he was able to move his head to answer. Within a couple of hours, he didn't look very well and his daughter was getting up to go get some clothes for her mom. I told her to get a nurse to check on Sam because his breathing was so labored. The nurse told Angel to stay because it didn't look like Sam had much time left. He then passed away around 4:00 on February 18, 2014.

The family took it very hard and waited for their youngest son to arrive from California. He got there around 1:00 a.m. and we met him at the hospital. There were more tears and feelings of disbelief that Sam had died at 67. My sister was a widow at age 61. The rest of the family went back home and she asked me to stay with her for a few days. Something had told me to bring extra clothes and the things I would need in case I was to stay. I literally threw everything in a bag before we left.

Because Sam had died that day, everyone went back home except Myla, her daughter, and me. Her daughter was keeping Angel's granddaughter busy for a few days. When Sam died, Angel's granddaughter asked her mom if he was in heaven at this time. We all replied "Yes" and off she went to play. She did lie down with him later and cried at that point, but right then, she was off running and playing. She was eight years old at the time.

Myla freaked out through the night because she couldn't sleep and had a panic attack because she knew she had to get up extremely early to drive into Winnipeg to get to her work. My granddaughter stayed to play with her cousin. I stayed while they made the funeral arrangements and got everything organized. We eventually went home for one night and my granddaughter wanted to see her mom. I had appointments to go to and needed dress clothes for Sam's funeral.

Rite was asked to be an usher, and my family all attended Sam's funeral. We all went to Angel's house after and stayed late into the evening. Her home was about ten miles away further along the highway from Gimli, and at the last second we decided to stay at a hotel for the rest of the weekend. We left early in the morning on Monday to get Rite to work. Too much had happened so fast. My sister Monique's co-worker died a few days later at a very young age, but no one wanted to talk about her death. Everyone in the office believed she had committed suicide. Shortly after that, Pierre fell out of bed and needed to be taken by ambulance to the hospital. He had a blood infection and it looked like he was going to die.

I went to the last night that one of my groups at the Laurel Centre was being held and talked to the two therapists to discuss if I should go and see Pierre before he died. They both told me to do what my heart wanted. I went that evening but did not want to meet up with anyone from the family because they all knew about what had happened, and I hadn't spoken to him since the day I confronted him. The nurse told me no one was visiting so I walked in the room and talked to him. He did cry several times and told me he could not sleep at night many times because of what he had done. He felt guilty, but also expressed that he had blocked many things from his life and I was one of those things. I told him that if he was hanging on because he needed to be forgiven then it was all right to let go. I had gotten so much help in my life that I had moved on but did not condone his actions. I felt if he needed to be told this, he would not need to hang on to life anymore and he could die peacefully. He said that when you're young you do stupid things. In my head, I thought that could be true for many other instances, but not RAPE.

He told me that he wrote something on his computer to be read at his funeral. No one knew, not even his wife. He had shared this with me and only me because it concerned me. He wrote that he was very sorry for hurting the people in his life who didn't deserve it. He told me that this was all geared toward me and not Monique. He promised he would not tell anyone, and said that I was the only one that knew.

We laughed a few times and he was telling me stories of how evil my mother was through all the years he had known her. He said that when he was dating Monique that my mother had taken a pot or pan to hit her in the face with it. He said he was in disbelief that someone could do these things. She was a witch and everyone knew it. He said his second wife was wonderful, but I had never got to know her. Monique was somewhat controlling but did show emotions. I kissed him goodbye and left feeling like I had done the right thing.

The following day I saw my therapist and told her I was feeling depressed that day and yet I had many good things going for me. I finally got a volunteer position at the Osborne House, and it would take seven weeks of training before I would start. My goal was to get in and show them how I could help others but in the end what I really wanted to do was to work on the hotlines. I thought if I had experienced all these things in life, I could relate and use these experiences to help others. This was my purpose in life.

That evening Rite and I went out to dinner, and I began to feel that maybe I had made a mistake in having gone to see Pierre. I had told no one. I stayed up late that night and overdosed on 158 temazepams. Rite had gone to the washroom a couple of times and eventually came to get me to go to bed, when he found out I had overdosed. I usually stayed up late to write. I actually was writing on my iPad and it wasn't unusual for me to work late into the night. I filled a glass with pure whiskey, around nine ounces, and swallowed all the pills within one minute. I was certain that I would not choke on them and I hadn't swallowed them so quickly.

Rite came to talk to me and clearly knew that I had overdosed. He immediately brought me to the Grace Hospital Emergency Department, like he had in the past. I do not recall anything about arriving there. Apparently, I fell out of bed and I would have just stayed sleeping there on the floor if no one had come to check on me. I recall a nurse telling me I had fallen and that they were going to put me back in bed. I don't remember any of this. I had bruising on my face and legs and a sore arm and wrist, but never complained about it. I felt I deserved whatever happened to me because it was my doing. I was treated for three days and sent to the Crisis Response Centre, which had been open for a few months at this time. The hospital called before I got there and this new facility had changed everything in psychiatry. They wanted people to go there with a mental illness instead of emergency because they had promised the intake would only take fifteen minutes. The Grace Emergency and other hospitals would not have to deal with people in this condition because it was time-consuming, and took away the time from patients with physical difficulties.

When I was admitted for suicide attempts, the nurses had absolutely no compassion in their demeanour. There were times they would close my curtain and leave me vomiting all day long without even checking on me. One nurse told me that there were other people admitted there who were fighting for their lives. I was a useless patient because I had tried to end my life. Even the health professionals held a stigma against the mentally ill. What choice did I have at this point except to die? This was my only option. My psychiatrist no longer had privileges to admit anyone in the hospital. In fact, no psychiatrists were able to do that anymore, and psychiatric patients were not allowed into Emergency. This was quite a disappointment for me because my doctor knew everything about me. I didn't want to start my story all over again with a new admitting doctor. Everyone was sent to the Crisis Response Centre where they were to speak to a clinician. It was there that the clinician would decide whether you should see a psychiatrist. I knew one girl that tried overdosing several times in a few weeks, and they still would not admit her.

As I walked in with Rite, I saw that they were expecting me. We were told to sit and wait. There were only three other people in the room. One couple kept on laughing and playing music on their phone and singing. My head could not tolerate this and so I moved as far away from them as I could. The receptionist had seen that I had moved and brought us to a private room and let us each lie down on a reclining chair. It was much more comfortable than the chairs in the waiting room, and I was not listening to anybody being loud. She then offered us coffee or water and brought us several warmed blankets to lie under. It was very soothing.

Eventually a clinician came in and asked me questions that I don't even recall. Rite said she talked to me for two hours and she then needed to go talk to the psychiatrist. She was gone for a couple of hours and a very friendly face walked in, a psychiatrist. He was very gentle with his questions and talked to me for at least another hour. He then told me he had to speak to the psychiatrist who was on call. As it turned out, this psychiatrist that came to see me first was actually the Professor of Psychiatry and Psychology at the University of Manitoba. He had done many studies on suicide, Aboriginals, and so on. I thought I would never get out of there.

Eventually, the psychiatrist and the professor both walked in and the psychiatrist was very kind, wanting to admit me to the hospital. The policies had changed such that if there were an available bed in any hospital in the city, you could be admitted there. I told them I only wanted to go to the Grace Hospital because that was where my psychiatrist was. He was unable to find me an available bed in the city. They were all occupied. He did not want to release me because of the seriousness of the overdose I had taken. He eventually sent me to the Crisis Stabilization Unit.

It took eleven hours at the Crisis Response Centre before I was told where to go. Rite drove me to the Crisis Stabilization Unit. I had been in this place a few times before. They had strict rules, and really didn't have the help that was needed. I walked in later in the evening and they checked everything I had brought in. The person who admitted me asked me where my razor was because I had shaving cream. I simply told him that I had forgotten about it at home. Meanwhile, I had it tucked into the back of my pants because I hated to ask for it each and every time. The staff went through all my belongings and kept everything from me. Everything went into garbage bags; purse and all. They counted my money and put that away also.

I was then instructed to go shower and they gave me a garbage bag with pajamas and robe with shampoo and body wash. I was to take a shower and get undressed and put my clothes in the bag. As soon as I walked out they took my clothes from me and washed it all together with my other clean clothes. The reasoning behind all of this precaution was that they did not want someone bringing in bed bugs. They followed the rules very precisely. I was then shown to my room and they brought back a few of my belongings. Most of it was stored, however. I put my razor in my coat pocket and went to bed.

The following morning I was called in to speak to someone on staff there. She asked me how I was doing and I told her that I wasn't doing any better than before I took the pills. She then told me that one of the staff members had found a razor in my pocket. I couldn't deny this. I got back to my room and my razor was gone, and also my iPad, which I had brought into the room earlier to keep me busy. Everything was found and taken away from me. It was then I had serious thoughts of leaving and getting some different kind of pills in order go into hiding somewhere that no one could find me. I was unable to leave, and my plans were once again delayed.

Once I got to the CSU I did not want to talk to anyone. I did not want to make friends with anyone because I had previously been in far too many toxic relationships. I kept to myself and I was told to sit on one particular chair if I wanted to use my iPad. I did as they requested because they were watching me at all times. It looked like there was a camera in each room, but on the last day before I left I spoke to one of the workers and he had told me that would be an invasion of privacy. I still don't think he was telling me the truth.

I asked for my razor to shave and they had to think about giving it to me. They then called me back into the office and told me that there was blood in the shower. Meanwhile, it was only my body soap that was that colour. They then took my alarm clock away because they said I was going to use it to hang myself. I was getting extremely frustrated and angry at them. I stayed in my room for a couple of days and stayed away from all staff. There was absolutely no one nice to talk to or help me. I was on my own. None of them acted professional except one man. He took his whole shift talking to every client.

I was finally discharged on Friday and that was the day I was to see my psychiatrist. He told me about the changes in Emergency. He was no longer able to admit anyone. He wasn't even allowed in the Emergency department like he had been in the past. I found this ridiculous, considering he was my psychiatrist. Why would I want to talk to another psychiatrist who knew nothing about me? They had got the paramedics to bring me to the Crisis Response Centre. What a waste of time. It probably cost more money to do it this way than it had in the past. I couldn't understand why I would be speaking to another psychiatrist when he knew nothing about me. You were to be seen within 15 minutes and I was there 11 hours.

During my appointment with my psychiatrist I told him several times that I would not permit him to admit me ever again. I never really told him the truth behind it for four months. I had told him I would have to be in a body bag if they were going to admit me. Of course, with his dark humour he said that they don't talk to corpses. My hour-long session with him was nothing but humorous. I did not feel like I required extra help at this point. We had a great talk and I actually left happy. This was different from the past. I knew I was getting better.

Four months later I told my psychiatrist the actual truth about why I would never be admitted. I knew he thought it was because I had made a toxic friend on my last admittance and got scared because she was homicidal. The truth behind all of this was not about that in any way. The doctor left on a Friday to go on holidays for two weeks and his patients were going to be under the care of the last two remaining psychiatrists. When he told me this before he left, I begged him not to put me in the care of Dr. Leech. He said that he wasn't going to look at the names and would assign every patient another psychiatrist by going down the list and ticking one psychiatrist after another.

It so happened that it was a long weekend and I got back on Monday night. The following day I was assessed by the physiotherapists for my balance problem. I had fallen so many times while in hospital. I had bruises everywhere and a deep cut which needed to be stitched, but I had not shown to them. They could have cared less. I took care of my knees with ice packs to get the swelling to go down.

At one point, I had fallen in the shower and made quite the noise as I did so. The nurse came knocking at the door and asked if I was ok. I immediately replied yes because I did not want anyone in the shower with me. It took me a few minutes to try to control the pain I was in. My breasts were bruised entirely. As I fell all my accessories went flying, hitting the door and walls, and that was why I had made so much noise. The blood from my knee poured down my leg continuously. It was deeply cut. As I walked out I told them I was fine but I really hurt everywhere. These nurses were not there for physical issues, but mental; therefore I never bothered them. I was very passive and agreed with everything each one would tell me. I was not a bad patient but minded my own business, and never made them angry.

The Friday when my psychiatrist left was a long weekend and when I returned the following day, I saw the therapists about my falls. They finally found out that I was not able to do certain things and they were going to talk to another therapist who dealt with these types of disorders. As it was, they wasted their time and mine because on that evening at 10:00 p.m. when I got my medications, my nurse told me that Dr. Leech was discharging me in the morning. They gave me no warning like Dr. Stevens had. He would always tell me a couple of weeks in advance to give me a heads up if I was being released. I immediately snapped at the nurse and asked her why she hadn't told me earlier in the evening. She really never said anything and I questioned why Dr. Leech would be discharging me if she had never even talked to me.

The psychiatric nurse told me not to self-harm, but that simply put that idea into my head. I went and got the two things I needed to burn myself with. I was so angry that I burned a big section of my arm before I left, without them knowing. After discharge my burn started getting bigger and bigger. I could not stop. I packed everything up and said I would be out at 9:00 a.m. She called Dr. Leech and told her I was not staying past nine because I had an appointment with an eye surgeon for an operation. I had waited months and wasn't going to miss it. Because she didn't like me, she was not going to help me. The nurse came back and told me to stay because Dr. Leech told her to tell me this. I simply refused and spoke out to say if she is discharging me, then why would I wait for her to come and tell me to leave? It was absolutely ridiculous, and I completely lost all my respect for that unit.

I was definitely mad at Dr. Stevens and finally came to the conclusion that I had only thought he cared, but that he never really did. I do not like to talk to him about any negative things since this realization. I just sit and laugh and keep my true feelings deep inside, like I have in the past. I see him and think he is the greatest psychiatrist, but I need to handle my problems on my own. I've had so much help that it is time to break away from all mental health workers. I need to move on. At one point, I thought that some doctors cared and they would say so, but I have come to realize, why would they? We are all numbers to them, and they keep their distance as professionals so as not to get involved in whether you live or die. It is our own destiny if we choose to kill ourselves. They cannot be there 24/7 to help you. This remains with you, and they do teach you that in therapy. I appreciate everything everyone has done for me but now know that people are only human and have their work and homes to return to. Family is always important and they come first; and a job is a job. Caring in the world is not something that exists. People can care and will say so, but you are forgotten the moment you are not talking to them.

Every name in this book has been changed in order to hide their identities. I do not want anyone to think I am maliciously attacking them.

Whatever I've written comes straight from the heart. This story is told as I know it. Some may say that this is not true, but were they there when I was experiencing all these terrible things? Some may feel guilty and others upset, but I can't tell someone what to think about me. I'm finally in control of my own destiny. Writing this book has helped me to recover, even during those times when I would have to put it down for a month because of deep feelings around the issues I was writing about.

Recovery is hard and can sometimes take years, but there is help out there if you pursue it. I would hope that I can inspire someone to go in the right path. It took me years to finally feel better and I will always work on recovery as my journey continues. I now go to church on Sundays with Mandy and her family, and I feel I have a connection with God. The services are so interesting that I don't feel like they are long enough to me. You're relaxed, given coffee, and able to sing some really meaningful songs. There is a stage with lights everywhere, and the words being sung are all posted in the front in three different areas. I see all the young people with children and feel so lucky to be there. I'm amazed by the changes at this church because when I was Catholic it was always the same boring prayers said in French. Everyone just sat there and their minds would wander in another world because of the boredom. I no longer feel this way at Oasis; the pastor always has something interesting to say because it is what goes on in day to day life. I am so happy that my daughter Mandy has never pressured me but asked me to come with her at times. It is through healing that I feel God was there every step of the way. He connected me with several angels so I could continue my life in a much healthier way.

Chapter 29

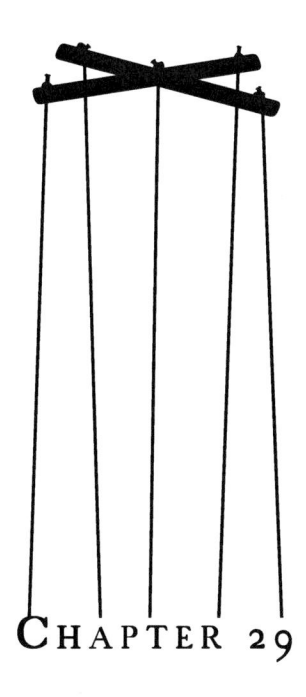

I told my psychiatrist that I forgave him, one day when I confronted him. I still feel hate towards my mother but never did discuss anything with her about violence or abuse. Dr. Stevens told me if I had dealt with it when she was alive, I wouldn't feel so harsh towards her. She was someone who wanted full control of everyone's life. It was my life, but not really mine to control.

My sister Monique never seemed to get over Pierre, although he was sending her mixed messages. He would drop by all the time, have a drink and if she needed anything fixed, he would fix it. His new wife found it very annoying for Monique to be at their home, sitting beside Pierre as he was dying. In fact, I was told if she could have got any closer to him she would be sitting on his lap. His new wife was exhausted and certainly did not need Monique there every day. The only conclusion I have come to was how much she must have loved him, and she couldn't help herself. This was kind of sad. She would be able to end that final chapter with him when he died. As for her daughter, I can see the grief in her and feel very sorry for her. She is a very pleasant person and I love her very much. Life has so much better things in store for her, but I know she can't see them. I will always hope for her life to change, for a time when she can become her own person with someone that will love her and make her happy. She most definitely deserves this more than anyone I know. I will always love her!

Pierre passed away on June 12, 2014 and my three children and husband all attended the hospital in those last days. I was hoping to hear some kind of apology about the sexual abuse but he only briefly wrote that he was sorry if he hurt anyone, but that it was not his intention. He obviously never understood the tortured life I lived because of the things he had done to me. When speaking with him and telling him about all my self-harm and suicidal attempts, he found this hard to believe but did cry on several occasions. I made him aware that I was writing a book and he asked me if he was in it. I told him yes. He also wanted to know if I had put his name down in the book. I was honest and told him I had changed everyone's name in the book. He may have tried to apologize, but I felt the letter at his funeral was never a real apology. Perhaps he was extremely ashamed of all the hurt he has created for many. I had always kept this a secret and through the years I attempted to talk to him alone with no one around. He may think he ended up fooling people, but why would he cry, or why would I make up such a horrible story?

Epilogue

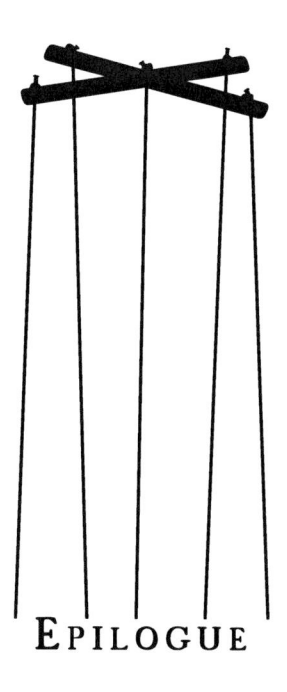

I love all three of my children unconditionally. I am the luckiest person to have such a wonderful husband, children, and nine grandchildren so far. There are always ups and downs in every person's life but you should think of the positives and not dwell on the negatives. I am a completely different person now and I'm not intimidated by people as much as I was in the past, but I will always have to work on this aspect of my life. My OCD and depression will never disappear, and I will always spend many hours daily doing repetitive things.

Next year, I look forward to traveling with Rite, Ben, Sally and family, Myla, Bill and family, and my sister Angel. It is my father-in-law's 95th birthday reunion in Twillingate, Newfoundland, which is a place my children absolutely love. This is very exciting for Rite and me. Rite's best friend for thirty-five years will also be attending, along with his girlfriend. He has been there when we had a lobster party, but is looking forward to going back to meet the wonderful people of Newfoundland. I have also reconnected with a friend that I worked with before I got married. She and her husband have always been there and I am truly blessed to be with Sandy and Myles. My new life has just started and it is very exciting.

I recently have gone through weeks of training to become a volunteer at the Osborne House. I feel connected to the people there and I am always eager to help those in distress. This volunteer position keeps me going and alive. These were the reasons I never died when I attempted suicide. It was not my time, and I have so much to give.

This has been quite a journey, but nevertheless a journey of healing. I will always be in recovery, but my life has completely changed because of my psychiatrist, therapists, and group sessions I attended. Never give up. There is a light at the end of the tunnel even if you can't comprehend that you will ever see it. I have been in darkness so many times that I really didn't think I belonged here in the light. Here I am happy, surviving, and feeling at my best ever. Not to say that I might not have slips now and then, but I will never permit myself to go back down that lonely dark deep tunnel of hell.

Now I am so happy to have worked with my dream psychiatrist, Dr. Stevens, and feel I owe him my happiness. I believe he has been the one who has given me the most hope of all, along with my therapist at the Laurel Centre. I have spent thousands of hours talking to different professionals and I live every single day, one day at a time. The writing of this book has definitely brought me back to the old person I used to be. I have changed it hundreds of times because if I was upset with anyone, that's what I would write about. Rereading it has shown me how wrong I was about many things. I felt unloved in my younger years and now I feel like I am on top of the world when I am with my husband, children, their spouses, and my grandchildren. I am so lucky to be alive and I live for the moment. I also know when I feel like it is my Borderline Personality Disorder that has taken over.

Recovery is a process, a way of life, an attitude, and a way of approaching the day's challenges. It is not a perfect day-to-day greatness. At times our course is erratic and we falter and slide back, but then we pick up the pieces and start over again. I will be in recovery for the rest of my life, but I now have the skills to change.

In memory of my brother-in-law, Robert Anderson, who passed away on February 18, 2014. Peace be with you!

In memory of my best friend, who passed away on December 1, 2013. May God be with you, my Angel. You will be forever missed.

My story is about true events of my past. It may be shocking and it may help others who have gone through the experiences of physical, sexual, and emotional abuse. Anyone could be subjected to this, and may be unable to help themselves. It took me twelve years to recover to where I was feeling whole again. I lived in denial for over forty years until tragedy struck, and the uncontrolled feelings I was stuffing down all those years came back like a raging river. It is about forgiveness, recovery, and about my journey that still continues.